PIONEERS' COUNTRY

GLENVILLE PIKE

PIONEERS' COUNTRY

Published by the Author, Glenville Pike, FRGSA.,
P. O. Box 822, Mareeba, North Queensland
Australia.

Production supervised by Bruwal Limited,
621 Holland House, Hong Kong

Printed by Cosmos Printing Press Ltd.
Hong Kong

ISBN 9598960 7 4

CONTENTS

OTHER BOOKS BY THE SAME AUTHOR

Frontier Territory, 1972, (out of print).
  (Winner, Litchfield Literary Award, 1972.)
An Untamed Land, 1973, (out of print).
Roads of Yesterday, 1977, (out of print).
The Queensland Frontier, 1978.
Voice of the Wilderness (with C.W. Teece), 1978.
Queen of the North, 1979.

––––––––––––––––––––

––––––––––––––––––––

PIONEERS' COUNTRY won the Foxwood Literary Award of $5000 — then the richest literary prize in Australia — presented to mark the Centenary of Cairns and District, 1976.

––––––––––––––––––––

AUTHOR'S NOTE

This could be termed a local history, but as such it is part of the whole stirring story of the exploration, settlement, and development of North Queensland, for the area dealt with is an important sector of the State of Queensland. This is an inspiring story of the pioneers and is no dull record. It is entertaining as well as informative.

This book covers in particular the region included in the Mareeba and Herberton Shires which have a combined area equal to almost the whole of Tasmania, or Ireland, and is twice the area of Belgium.

The beautiful region over the Coastal Range behind Cairns is loosely termed "the Tablelands" but is more accurately, the Hinterland or Highlands. The Mareeba and Herberton Shires are not the real Atherton Tableland, they are, in contrast to the lush wetness of the Tableland, mainly dry and at first glance, rather infertile, more in keeping with Cape York Peninsula and the Gulf Country but with a much better climate, being from 1300 feet to 3000 feet above sea level.

It is mineral country, "open range" grazing and, with water, highly productive. This book deals with the struggles of the miners and settlers during the one hundred years since the Hodgkinson Gold Rush which brought white men to the area and led to the founding of the city of Cairns.

This is not a history of Cairns — that has been well covered in other books — but of a major portion of its Hinterland. There is still scope for another book about the Atherton Tableland proper. The Atherton district is included here only as a link between the Mareeba and Herberton Shires which in the mining and pastoral sphere cannot be separated.

This book is by no means complete, being restricted by economics. I have tried to briefly deal with as many pioneering stories as possible and must be forgiven if some names and incidents have been missed. To adequately cover this area, a much larger volume is needed but it could contain so much minor detail as to be wearisome.

I think sufficient has been told here to pay tribute to the pioneers of this area and to awake strangers to the historical wealth of the "Pioneers' Country". It is rich historically, and an integral part of our heritage, a fact little known in the South. It is prosperous now only because of the tenacity and sacrifice of its settlers, from the early days to modern times, and the pioneering spirit is still needed in this farming region in the tropics.

While I received every assistance from people in the area dealt with, including Government departments, I would, however, like to state that when researching for this book I received no co-operation whatever from the relative Government departments in Brisbane who studiously ignored all letters.

It seems that one has to be in Brisbane to be favoured if one is doing even minor research on North Queensland. All North Queensland records should be preserved and kept in archives in the North where they are at least accessible to those most interested.

The basis of this book is two booklets which I wrote in 1951 and 1952. The first was entitled "Pioneer Pageant" and was produced by the Mareeba Jubilee Committee, and the other was "In the Path of the Pioneers", published by the Herberton Shire Council. Some material in these small books "Pioneers' Country" was first published in June 1976. There were three reprints up to October 1977. This is a new edition, with more material, including photographs added. I am indebted to all those old timers who came forward with additional information for inclusion in this Second Edition. I also wish to thank Ruth and John Kerr for making available the result of their research, and North Queensland artist, Bob Tretheway of Yungaburra for reproductions of his paintings taken from old photographs.

Mareeba,
North Queensland

GLENVILLE PIKE
F.R.G.S.A., F.R. HIST. Q.

ACKNOWLEDGEMENTS

For assistance rendered I would like to acknowledge the following:

The Cairns Historical Society; W. H. Peterson, Innot Hot Springs; Gordon Hay, Dimbulah; Mike O'Callaghan, Cairns; Bill Roberts, Sydney; Mrs. E. Bryant; Ralph Arnold, Mareeba; Mrs. O'Leary, Mareeba; Doug Lawson, Mareeba; John and Ruth Kerr, Brisbane; Department of Primary Industry, Mareeba office; Queensland Irrigation and Water Supply Commission, Mareeba office; Warden's office, Herberton; Herberton Shire Council; W. Pearson, when he was head teacher at Ravenshoe School; and Mareeba Shire Council. Much source material was obtained years ago from friends now deceased such as the late J. W. Collinson, Hugh A. Borland, A. F. Waddell, T. H. Crowe, H. Foulis, J. Stenhouse, J. Newell, and others.

For assistance with photographs, my thanks goes to Ernie Stephens, Mrs. D. Webb, Milton Moore, Hisine Technique Co., Mrs. A. Harriman, Mareeba Shire Council, Mrs. V. Reichardt, John McElhinney, the Queensland Government Tourist Bureau, State Public Relations, and the Department of Mapping and Surveying for allowing use of copies of original maps of Thornborough, Kingsborough, and Mareeba.

MAP OF QUEENSLAND

showing the area covered in
this book (in black)

ENGLAND and
WALES on the
same scale

GULF OF
CARPENTARIA

CAPE YORK PENINSULA

COOKTOWN
PT DOUGLAS
CAIRNS
INNISFAIL
INGHAM
TOWNSVILLE
BOWEN

CROYDON
GEORGETOWN

North Queensland

CHARTERS TOWERS

ROCKHAMPTON

BRISBANE

50 100 200 300

MILES

Cairns Range Railway construction up the Barron Gorge, 1889. —Painting by R. Tretheway.

Herberton late in 1880. —Painting by R. Tretheway, from an old photo.

Cobb and Co. on a steep pinch up the Herberton Range.
—Painting by R. Tretheway, from an old photo.

"With axe and fire they cleared the acres". It was a superhuman task to clear land by hand on the Tablelands before the advent of machines.   —Painting by R. Tretheway, from an old photo.

CHAPTER 1

THEY BUILT FOR THE FUTURE

Early Navigators — Dalrymple — Kennedy — Covered Wagon Pioneers — William Hann — James Venture Mulligan — the Palmer Rush.

What lay beyond the ranges no white man knew.

Captain James Cook of the little "Endeavour", sailing northward along our then unknown eastern coast, passed Magnetic Island and Hinchinbrook, Cape Grafton and Trinity Bay — named for Trinity Sunday, June 10th., 1770.

From his quarterdeck, Cook viewed the rugged coastline of this strange new land with misgiving — the steep, jungle-covered mountains rising tier on tier from a low mangrove-fringed shore.

What lay beyond those forbidding ranges no white man knew . . . .

The "Endeavour's" oaken prow was the first in recorded history to cleave these tropic seas, yet others, phantom-like may have come and gone — Chinese, Portuguese, and Spaniard, leaving nothing but vague legend and one or two unexplained relics to mark their passing.

(1)

Captain Matthew Flinders in the leaky old "Investigator", beating north before the trade winds, passed far out to sea in 1802. Captain King in the survey ship, "Mermaid", sailed by in 1818; he came again in 1821 in the "Bathurst" and sought shelter from a storm in Trinity Bay. The survey ships "Beagle", "Fly", and "Rattlesnake" sailed by in the eighteen-forties.

Not until the magic lure of gold on the Palmer River in 1873 drew settlement northward, was a great deal of interest shown in this savage coast. Then, at the spot where Cook had beached the "Endeavour" for repairs, a lonely river mouth to which he gave the name of his ship, was chosen as a likely port for the goldfield that lay deep in the Northern wilderness, and an expedition set out to explore the coastline in detail.

It was the North-East Coast Expedition in two tiny cutters led by George Elphinstone Dalrymple, explorer, politician, land commissioner, and one of the handful of visionaries who formed the Colony of Queensland out of almost nothing. Coming in contact with true tropical Queensland for the first time, he was impressed and delighted. He likened the dense jungle of the Johnstone River area to that of Ceylon with which he was acquainted.

On 16th. October 1873, Dalrymple and Sub-Inspector R. A. Johnstone of the Native Mounted Police from Cardwell— then the nearest settlement to the south — sailed up Trinity Bay in a whaleboat into what they thought was the mouth of a large river.

Dalrymple named Walsh's Pyramid after a cabinet minister and the nearer Mt. Whitfield after a merchant in Cardwell. A native well providing fresh water was found at what was later the intersection of Abbott and Shields Street in the centre of the city of Cairns.

Dalrymple was disappointed to find Trinity Inlet was not the estuary of a river with fertile soil on its banks, but he was impressed with the inlet as a likely seaport for the interior. Prophetically he wrote: "It may some day serve what may

(2)

prove to be a highly auriferous back country."

The port of Cairns was founded only three years later, in 1876, but that year also marked the death of Dalrymple, one of the great men who made early Queensland but who is little remembered today.

Over the blue-misted ranges behind Trinity Bay where an unknown river, the Barron, cascaded by falls and gorge to the sea, this vast north land slept for a century after Cook first sighted it. Only its dark-skinned children roaming its ranges, rivers, and bushland, knew its mysteries. They would guard them jealously.

To try and discover what lay beyond that wall of coastal ranges was the object of Assistant-Surveyor Edmund B. C. Kennedy — one of Australia's most courageous explorers.

The lion-hearted Kennedy gave his life when within sight of his goal, Cape York, and eight of his gallant party died of hunger and despair. Only the faithful Aboriginal lad, Jacky Galmarra, reached Cape York and the waiting ship, bearing the story of tragedy.

Landing just north of where Cardwell now stands, on 24th. May 1848, Kennedy's party, with dwindling horses and supplies, hacked their way through the terrible scrubs of the Coast Range for three months. Just how ignorant the planners in Sydney were concerning the type of country to be traversed is indicated by the fact that Kennedy had carts and a flock of sheep. After progressing through the dense, sodden jungle, on slippery mountainsides in almost continuous rain for weeks, at the rate of two or three miles per day, Kennedy left the carts behind and packed all the gear on the horses.

Dark jungle creeks were crossed and the roar of waterfalls heard; there was no grass, and the horses were starving. At last, on 9th. August, the expedition came out of the scrub into grassed, forest country. Camped in the vicinity of the later site of Mt. Garnet on 23rd. August, one of the men, Goddard, went out to shoot wallabies and was lost for two days.

(3)

Kennedy and his party camped on the headwaters of Emu Creek, in rough granite ranges south-west of the present site of Irvinebank, on 25th. August. They followed Emu Creek down over tin-bearing country to the Walsh River — a broad bed of sand with fine large teatrees and she-oaks. They passed close to the present site of the township of Petford.

Kennedy thought the Walsh may lead him to Princess Charlotte Bay far to the north, so he and his men followed it in its tortuous course, its bed hundreds of yards wide and full of great boulders and fallen timber, its steep banks almost gorge-like. The weakened horses continually fell on the slippery boulders as they struggled along the river bed. Carron suffered a bad fall and broke Kennedy's barometer.

This country is as wild and rugged now as it was in 1848. Impassable sandstone ranges tower line upon line to the river bank, and southward lie more desolate ranges, known to later pioneers as the "Featherbeds" — because they were the reverse of soft. In places along the river, boiling springs bubble up from between lava rocks. Kennedy spent his thirtieth birthday in this inhospitable gorge.

Ludwig Leichhardt, on his expedition from the Darling Downs to Port Essington, had followed down the Lynd River and discovered the Mitchell, which he named, in June 1845. Kennedy gradually realised the Walsh was a tributary of Leichhardt's Mitchell River and it was taking him too far westward. Near where the present Beef Road from Mungana crosses the Walsh, Kennedy turned northward and reached the Mitchell on 16th. September. Here he had his first serious clash with the warlike Aborigines of Cape York Peninsula. Dr. R. L. Jack, in his reference work, "Northmost Australia", vol. ii. (1922) believed it was the Palmer River that was reached on this date. He also thought Kennedy followed down the Hodgkinson, and not the Walsh, to reach the Mitchell.

When Kennedy was speared by the Aborigines near Cape York, his journal was lost and only a few damaged notes and maps were recovered. For a century, until they were deciphered, Kennedy's route from Cardwell to Cape York was not definitely known. The names he gave physical features are still unknown.

*   *   *   *

The years rolled on. The frontiers of settlement were pushed further northward as the pioneers followed in the tracks of the explorers; sheep and cattle stations were founded, settlements came into being. The establishment of the new Colony of Queensland in December 1859 caused a great impetus to settlement. Exploring parties rode the length and breadth of Queensland from Brisbane to Cape York, from the Cooper to the Gulf. Within five years, Queensland was unknown no longer; Burke and Wills, McKinlay, Landsborough, Walker, McIntyre, and others had explored the Gulf and the inland plains. The Jardine Brothers had reached Cape York; the northmost station had been established six hundred miles northward from the earlier frontier at Rockhampton. The edge of settlement had leaped northward from Rockhampton to Cardwell and to Burketown on the Gulf of Carpentaria; dray tracks had been blazed all through the back country — a truly wonderful achievement in the five years from 1859 to 1864. All the more remarkable because when Queensland began it had only 28,000 settlers and only 50,000 out of its 700,000 square miles was explored, and it had an empty treasury.

But everyone was a pioneer, and men, women, and children were willing to work. They had a vision of the future, and they built for future generations. Compared with today, they built with their bare hands, with flesh and blood, by their sweat, and muscle, and the sinews of their only helpers, faithful horses and bullocks. The pick, the shovel, dynamite, the block-dray, and a woodfired steam engine or two, their only labour saving devices.

As soon as news of the vast pastoral empire the explorers had revealed was made known, land-hungry settlers as far south as Victoria packed their belongings on their drays, and with

(5)

their families and their flocks and herds, they pushed northward to the base of Cape York Peninsula. Neither hundreds of miles of wilderness or hostile Aboriginal tribes cculd stop them.

As the great wheels of their creaking bullock drays slowly turned, the vast untamed land that spread before them lured them on — the same lure that sent the American pioneers westward.

The Firth and Atkinson families were in the forefront of the migration of pioneers northward. James Atkinson joined Ezra Firth and his family on the northward trail and he and Firth were partners on Mt. Surprise Station in early times, James Atkinson established Farnham near Ingham in 1871 and bought Wairuna about ten years later. He founded a dynasty of pastoralists.

Slowly the bullocks in the pole drays of Ezra Firth, travelled onward. Firth, the former stonemason from Yorkshire who was imbued with a spirit of adventure was bound for the northmost frontier at the pace sheep can walk. The Moreton Bay district became the Colony of Queensland, and the outpost of Bowen was established. For two years the Firths lived by a lonely lagoon on the headwaters of the Burdekin River, then moved on over the divide on to Gulf waters and took up Mt. Surprise — so called because of the sound of the drays bumping over the basalt boulders startled a tribe of Aborigines who fled into the scrub on the mountain. It was then 1864.

Ezra Firth and his wife were wonderful pioneers, but they are almost forgotten today. Success was theirs only after long hard years of fighting the blacks, the elements, and the loneliness. Descendents of Ezra Firth reside in Mareeba and Townsville.

Gold was discovered on the Gilbert River in 1869, followed the next year by a big discovery on the Etheridge; the frontier town of Georgetown was established. The country north-east of Georgetown was still quite unknown as the Eighteen-seventies dawned and the gold rush-fever increased.

William Hann, pioneer of Maryvale and Bluff Downs, was

the one chosen by the Government to explore this mysterious region. He was a fine example of the bearded bushmen of his day — 6 ft. 6 ins. tall and built in proportion; he was fearless, a born explorer and leader of men.

He and his party of five men set out from Firth's out-station, Fossilbrook, in June 1872 with a team of packhorses carrying supplies for five months. Hann named the Walsh, Tate, Palmer, Normanby, Kennedy, Stewart, Hearn (Laura), Bloomfield, and other rivers.

At the same time, other white men were out riding the trackless bush. Late in 1870, a party comprising Tom Leslie, Jack Edwards, Harry Edwards, William Baird, Charlie Ross, Tom Hackett, and John Duff, set out from Glendhu Station on the Upper Burdekin, and were out in the wilds for months. Because their search for gold was in vain, their expedition has been forgotten.

Hann named the Tate River after the party's botanist and the Walsh after the Minister for Mines. A Walsh tributary was named the Elizabeth, and with a pastoralist's eye Hann noted the fine blacksoil downs-type country in the area. Wrotham Park cattle station was to be established here.

Hann and two of his men, Taylor and Tate, rode up the Mitchell River from their camp, over very rough country. Away to the south amid blue-hazed hills and peaks they saw a conspicious flat-topped mountain which Hann called Mt. Lilley. It was probably Mt. Mulligan.

He named the Palmer River after the Premier, Sir Arthur Palmer. The surveyor, Frederick Warner, discovered gold in a gully nearby, thus winning a reward of half a pound of tobacco that Hann sportingly offered.

It was left to James Venture Mulligan from the Etheridge to report, the following year — September 3, 1873 — of the existence of a new payable goldfield on the Palmer. It was the greatest alluvial goldfield in Australia since the Turon and Ballarat. He received the Government reward of £1000, a

(7)

reward that could easily have been Hann's.   Incidentally, Hann and Daintree discovered the first copper lode in North-east Queensland, on the Einasleigh River, in 1866.

A few old timers remain who still remember J. V. Mulligan —the quiet, kindly Irishman whose name was once a household word in the North.   He did more than any other man to open up the vast mineral areas of the Peninsula and the hinterland of Cairns.

Though Mulligan made many other discoveries, his crowning achievement was the discovery of the Palmer Goldfield, closely followed by the Hodgkinson.   Though he was still searching thirty years later and less than two years before his death, he could not find another Palmer as he always hoped. There could never be another goldfield as fabulous as that. In four years it yielded forty tons of alluvial.   Its discovery galvanized the whole of Queensland into activity, and soon all Australia was affected.   The news spread to New Zealand, Great Britain, the United States, and China.

Mulligan led the first party of a hundred diggers with three hundred horses and bullocks from Georgetown to the new field across 200 miles of wilderness.   Behind the armed mounted men the teams streamed past the Firths' once lonely homestead; they followed Mulligan's roughly blazed tree-line, the bullocks groaning and straining under the greenhide whips to haul the heavily-laden wagons through loose sand, over precipitous ridges, and across dry rivers with banks of moving silt.   Behind them came men on foot with swags; they would be the first to succumb to sickness, starvation, and Aboriginal spears.

In May 1954, a memorial was unveiled on the Kennedy Highway just east of Mareeba to honour J. V. Mulligan and his explorations.   Present at the ceremony was an old lady who had known the explorer and who was then the only surviving member of the party he had led from Georgetown to the Palmer.   She was probably the last survivor of the Palmer Rush. She was Mrs. Mary Ann Finn, who was then a child with her parents, the Peters.

It was Mulligan who suggested that a seaport for the Palmer be opened at the Endeavour River. Dalrymple's expedition reached there by sea only one day before the "Leichardt" steamed in and landed diggers, Government officials, horses, drays, stores, and building materials to establish the new port of Cooktown, soon to be the third busiest seaport in Queensland. At its zenith there were at least 25,000 white men and Chinese on the Palmer and probably 10,000 in Cooktown.

But Mulligan went on searching for new goldfields. He and his mates fought the blacks at the Battle of Round Mountain, and after recovering from their spearwounds set out from Maytown, "capital" of the Palmer, after the wet season of 1874 to prospect the rivers to the south-eastward.

Where Hann turned back at the Mitchell, Mulligan pressed on over the rough ridges and discovered the Hodgkinson River which he named after William Oswald Hodgkinson, M.L.A., founder of the "Mackay Mercury" newspaper, crushing mill proprietor on Charters Towers, and erstwhile despatch rider for Burke and Wills and McKinlay.

Mulligan and his mates rode up the Hodgkinson, over very rough country, and the great rugged flat-topped mountain Hann had seen from afar, came nearer. Mulligan's companions insisted it be named "Mt. Mulligan", much to the chagrin of the man himself who seems to have shunned publicity of that sort. But in this imposing rocky rampart, he has a fitting natural monument. On this expedition, he failed to find the gold-bearing reefs east of the Hodgkinson River.

The Government had noticed Mulligan's ability as an explorer, and when he set out from Cooktown on a fifth expedition on 29th. April 1875, he was financed by the Government. He had an outfit of 23 horses and was accompanied by Surveyor Frederick Warner, and four of Mulligan's old mates — James Dowdell, William Harvey, Peter Abelsen, Jack Moran, and also a blackboy, Charlie.

The expedition followed up the eastern branch of the Hodgkinson, crossed the Granite Range — that prominent landmark northwest of Mareeba — and came down on to low country bordering a fine north-flowing river.

Mulligan believed it was the Mitchell, for he knew it came from the south before turning west below the McLeod River which he had discovered. Actually, he had passed over the source of the Mitchell without being aware of it. He had now come upon a new beautiful river — the Barron. Mulligan was near the later site of Biboohra which is the Aboriginal name for the Barron at that point.

On May 26th. 1875, the explorers rode up the Barron's eastern bank. Mulligan passed the junctions of Emerald and Granite Creeks and the site of Mareeba on the opposite bank, camping near Rocky Creek. He traversed the present tobacco lands along the river. The stone cairn on the Kennedy Highway with its appropriately worded plaque was erected by the Mareeba Shire Council in 1954 to commemorate Mulligan's discovery of the area. He was the first white man to officially see the future site of Mareeba. The pastoralist, John Fraser, may have been there the same year.

Near the present site of Tolga, the explorers came face to face with the dense primeval jungle that then clothed the Atherton Tableland. Mulligan marvelled at the great cedar trees and kauri pines; he was forced to skirt the scrub and follow Aboriginal paths from pocket to pocket. He remarked on the "villages" of well built thatched huts that he saw. Dr. R. L. Jack, the historian, believed Mulligan's camp of June 4th. 1875 was between Prior Creek and Scrubby Creek and about two miles south-west of the present town of Atherton.

When the horsemen got clear of the scrub they climbed a rough granite range. Camped on a swift-flowing clear mountain stream that ran in a general southerly direction and which Mulligan called the Wild River because of its turbulence, a day was spent shoeing horses. Mulligan spent the time prospecting.

He brought back "a fine sample of tin ore."

Mulligan wrote in his journal: "There may be any quantity of it here, but of what use is it at present, considering the price of carriage? Yet it is well for the future of the Colony to know that there is tin in this locality . . . . "

The nearest seaports, Cardwell and Cooktown, were from 150 to 200 miles away, and inaccessible. But the discovery of tin on the Wild River was to eventually have more influence on the development of Far North Queensland than the opening of the Palmer, but Mulligan was not to benefit personally. It is, however, another of the debts we owe this great prospector-explorer who has been overlooked by Southern-produced history books.

Mulligan's expedition rode over the future site of Herberton about June 7th. 1875, and followed the Wild River down to the Herbert River.

They sighted a blazed tree line "running fifteen degrees west of north." This marked a vain attempt by the people of Cardwell to capture some of the Palmer trade, and an extremely fine piece of bushmanship on the part of the men who blazed the line — Scott and Thorne.

Mulligan then headed south-west for Firth's outpost, Mt. Surprise, and arrived back in Cooktown on September 23, 1875. He and his men had ridden 1100 miles in five months and some of the previously unknown country hidden by the coast ranges behind Trinity Bay had been revealed for the first time. Mulligan was convinced that somewhere in the wild tangle of mountains in that dry bushland, probably on the Hodgkinson, a new goldfield lay waiting.

CHAPTER 2

GOLD ON THE HODGKINSON

The Hodgkinson Rush — When Life was Wild and Rough — Bill Smith, Douglas, and Doyle — Christie Palmerston — John Fraser — the Port Douglas Road.

Within four weeks Mulligan, Warner, and Abelsen started out again from Cooktown, without Government assistance, and with the wet season imminent. They left on 23rd. October 1875 and headed straight for the Hodgkinson. The reward that the Government was offering for the discovery of a payable goldfield urged them on. The reward was £1000 ($2000), a large sum of money in those days.

They struck gold on 17th. January 1876 at a spot "due east of Mulligan's Range (Mt. Mulligan) where a large creek comes in, having Mt. Megan (McGann) on our north side." The gold was in alluvial and in outcropping reefs.

Unknown to Mulligan, another veteran prospector, William McLeod, with two mates, Nat Williams (some records say Robert Sefton), and Hugh Kennedy, were out prospecting the Hodgkinson hills at the same time.

The first that Mulligan's party knew of them was when they heard their horsebells. Peter Abelsen approached the newcomers' camp at dusk. In those days on the frontier when wild blacks and lawless whites were abroad, it was customary to shoot first and enquire afterwards. A bullet whizzed past Abelsen's ear. Seeing a figure looming up in the half light, Hugh Kennedy had grabbed his Snider rifle and fired. Soon the two parties of explorers were shaking hands and joking over Abelsen's narrow escape.

By February 7th., Mulligan had found several good quartz reefs and some patchy alluvial. McLeod's party prospected many miles to the east and south. The McLeod Hills were named after this great bushman and prospector. He died of fever on the MacArthur River in the Northern Territory in 1885.

(12)

McLeod was a typical contemporary of James Venture Mulligan. It was fitting that when the roaring goldfields capital of Thornborough sprang up, the two principal streets should be named in their honour.

On March 16th. 1876, Mulligan reported a new goldfield on the Hodgkinson to Warden Coward at Byerstown on the Palmer. Mulligan and McLeod shared the Government reward. Thus did Mulligan open the door to the development of one of Australia's wealthiest districts — Cairns and its hinterland.

The first coach service to Maytown was apparently by way of Byerstown. The Brisbane "Courier" reported in March 1876 that a service had been started from Cooktown. What a rough journey it must have been, especially over the mountain spurs running into the Palmer River between Byerstown and Maytown. Emanuel Borghero is listed in Pugh's Directory for 1878 as the "coach proprietor" in Cooktown "for Cobb & Co." — probably the same "Manny" Borghero well known around Irvinebank and Herberton some years later as a packer and handler of horses.

Byerstown was a transient town that existed only while the gold lasted; a settlement of bark huts, tents, of primitive grog shanties, stores that were only a few sheets of iron nailed to sapling frames with canvas walls. They were the supermarkets of their day, being crammed with crates of "bouilli" beef in seven-pound tins, bags of flour ("twenty-fives" and "fifties") a few tins of jam, bottles of Worcestershire sauce, and tins of baking powder, all mixed up with prospecting dishes, miners' picks, horse-shoes, "American felt" hats, boxes of flannel shirts, and Blucher boots hanging from the rafters like strings of sausages. Somewhere there might be found cases of dynamite and boxes of Snider cartridges, American axes, and a few bolts of check gingham and turkey twill cloth to excite the ladies.

All this would have come from Cooktown by bullock wagon to supply the needs of the miners at this new rush where the last of the alluvial on the Palmer's headwaters was being feverishly panned. When all that was considered payable had

(13)

been garnered and only enough left to provide a few Chinese with a pittance, Byerstown would, along with the thousands of goldseekers, vanish so that today it is difficult to find where it was.

But the pickmarks and the cuttings, and washouts that are the eroded ruts left by ironshod wagon wheels, remain.

Byerstown was a town of Yesterday. A town that never had a future; a town typical of many others which, ghostlike, may still be found on some maps of North Queensland.

*　　*　　*　　*

James Venture Mulligan, accompanied by Frederick Warner and Peter Abelsen, ragged and half starved after losing their supplies in a fire and held up for a week by the flooded Mitchell River, rode into Byerstown on jaded horses. They came in from the mountains to the south and had been out prospecting and exploring for ten weeks during the wet season.

They were near exhaustion but they were elated. Back in among those blue-hazed ranges there was gold — not another Palmer, Mulligan cautioned, but it was a new goldfield.

Warden Coward of Byerstown was excited. Mulligan was on his way to Cooktown and did not want the news to break until after he arrived. But Warden Coward could not keep a secret. While the tired prospectors slept, he sent a police trooper galloping through the night covering the seventy miles to Cooktown.

Within days the gold rush to the Hodgkinson was on. Excitement in Cooktown was intense; Cooktown little knew it was the foretaste of doom: gold on the Hodgkinson would mean that within a year Cooktown would have two rival ports — Cairns and Port Douglas. With a rich hinterland which Hodgkinson gold was to be the key to its opening, Cairns would completely supersede Cooktown as the major port north of Townsville.

At first, Cooktown was the nearest port to the new Hodgkinson field. As soon as news of the discovery reached the South, diggers arrived in Cooktown by the shipload.

(14)

Hundreds of men and horses gathered at Byerstown until it looked like a depot for an army of cavalry. Miners threw up good claims on the Palmer to do as they had done ever since gold was first found in Australia — and there were some veterans who had been in every rush since the Turon in '51 — to chase the will-o'-the-wisp of fortune at the end of the rainbow.

On 30th. March, Mulligan rode out of Cooktown at the head of a motley throng. At Byerstown, the crowd doubled in size. About four hundred men on horseback, on foot, and some pushing wheelbarrows, followed Mulligan southward. There were about thirty women also, many walking beside their men.

They cut a swathe through bog and slush as the last of the wet season rain — thunderstorms — poured down after hours of steaming heat. On one of the creekbanks scores of human bones and skulls with gaping holes made by Snider bullets, were found years later. Thus the primitive owners left mute testimony of their hopeless struggle. As a miner of the day is said to have cracked: "It takes more than a few niggers to stop a gold rush."

The gold-crazed horde plunged into the flooded Mitchell River and scrambled on over the rough ranges to what they believed was another golden river where Mulligan had made his strike.

At the beginning, Mulligan warned everyone that the Hodgkinson was not a rich alluvial field and that most of the gold would be found in the reefs. But most people refused to listen and when he was proved right, they were bitterly disappointed. At one stage, Mulligan narrowly escaped being lynched.

Life was rough and hard for those staunch men and women — and children, too — who flocked to the Hodgkinson in its early months. The blacks were hostile and tragedies occurred, but few records have survived. Mt. Mulligan, known to them as Woothakata, was the stronghold of the Wahoora tribe with the Muluridji further east.

(15)

Not only were the Aborigines wild, but so were some of the white men. There were robberies, murders, drinking sprees, brawls outside the shanties, and fist-fights without number. As on all the old mining fields, drink was a terrible curse on the Hodgkinson also, and many crimes and most of the rowdyism was committed under the influence of liquor. When the real thing ran out, some shanty keepers made and sold their own vile concoctions.

There was no law at first except one or two Justices of the Peace. One of these was Dr. Jack Hamilton, a particularly colorful character who was not only a doctor but a good boxer, horseman, swimmer, footrunner, swordsman, and revolver shot— qualities that stood him in good stead in the Wild North of a century ago. In his shack hospital on the Palmer, he saved many lives.

Sub-Inspector Alexander Douglas with a Native Mounted Police detachment arrived in July 1876 and formed a camp about four miles down the river from Thornborough, "capital" of the Hodgkinson field. In 1877 he moved the camp to a beautiful spot on a hilltop overlooking a lagoon, and called Baan Bero. It was about four miles north-west from the later site of Biboohra. It could command the track to the coast opened at that time.

Mulligan opened a store and hotel, built of bush timber and bark at first, on the corner of Mulligan and McLeod Streets in Thornborough, named after the Premier of Queensland. Soon the place had twenty hotels and shanties and at least a dozen stores of all kinds. There may have been 10,000 people* on the Hodgkinson at its peak, but as with Cooktown and the Palmer, the number has probably been exaggerated. The Government erected handsome brick buildings in Thornborough.

Four miles eastward, tucked away amongst precipitous hills, on the slope of a spur around which curled Caledonia Creek,

---

* According to a report in the "Hodgkinson Mining News" on 30 June 1877, the population was then 7500 — 4500 Europeans and 3000 Chinese.

the town of Kingsborough boomed and faded and like Thornborough, eventually died. In their day, a century ago, they were the two largest and most important towns inland from Cairns.

Though prospectors found the barren gullies and creeks scanty in alluvial, very rich reefs were discovered, and in the late 'Seventies and early 'Eighties the hills echoed to the thud of pounding stampers. Spain's mill at Glen Mowbray was the first to crush, followed by Martin's mill at Thornborough. These and other early plants were dismantled on the Palmer and transported over an incredibly rough track by bullock teams.

Of the 4,415 known lines of reef that were discovered, the most famous were the Tyrconnell, the Kingsborough (which briefly yielded 17 ounces to the ton), General Grant, Hero, Columbia, Waverley, Tichborne, Caledonia, Bismarck, Great Britain, Mark Twain, Black Ball, Homeward Bound, Monarch, and the Flying Pig on top of Pig Hill overlookng Thornborough; it returned 748 ounces from 84 tons of stone, and there were other rich crushings in 1877. The Explorer, one of Mulligan's claims, returned six and a half ounces to the ton for a brief period.

Up to early this century when the field had faded into insignificance, its yield was 300,000 ounces — small compared with the mighty Palmer's yield of three and a half million ounces, but nevertheless the Hodgkinson was one of the North's richest reefing fields after Charters Towers. The gold-bearing stone was easy to get at first. The eyes were picked out and when water level was reached the shafts were abandoned. In this way, the old timers said, the riches of the old Hodgkinson were plundered   In its first year the yield was 33,887 ozs.

Townships mushroomed around the principal reefs. Few people now remember or have heard of the townships of Wellesley, Waterford, Watsonville (not the town near Herberton), Stewart Town, Union Town, Beaconsfield, New Northcote and Old Northcote which once flourished and died as the gold ran out.

*   *   *   *

Back in those days of horse transport, the Hodgkinson, hemmed in by high rough mountains, with impenetrable jungle between it and the coast, was very isolated. Thornborough received its first overland mail from Cooktown. In the early days of the rush, the Government engaged a Chinese to ride with the mail, at a cost of ninepence per pound for letters and parcels. What a long arduous ride every week from Cooktown to Thornborough! But Chinese as well as Europeans, played their part in opening this Pioneers' Country.

The nearest telegraph office was at Maytown, seventy miles away. The only way official and other urgent messages could be got to the outside world was for a horseman to ride to Maytown. In the wet season when the Mitchell was in flood, even this was not possible. A telegraph line was opened to Thornborough on November 10th. 1877; it was constructed over the mountains from the Tate River on the line to Cooktown. It was extended eastward to Cairns in 1878, and opened on August 30th. A branch line was erected in 1882 from Northcote to Herberton.

A meeting was held in Thornborough on Saturday afternoon, July 8th. 1876, outside J. V. Mulligan's store. The warden and Police Magistrate, Howard St. George (a popular official) presided. The object was to form an expedition to find a wagon road to a convenient point on the coast. Five hundred miners rolled up. Bill Smith, a packer and miner, and a former beche-de-mer fisherman who knew the coast, described the advantages of Trinity Bay as a likely seaport for the Hodgkinson. Quickly £200 was subscribed as a reward to be offered for the discovery of a road.

John Doyle, an expert bushman and horseman who had been in the Palmer Rush, accompanied Smith and a man named Cardnow to try to penetrate the ranges to the coast. When Doyle came upon the majestic spectacle of the Barron Falls tumbling into a jungle-filled gorge amid clouds of spray, he was amazed. The Aboriginals' name for the falls was Dinden.

(18)

Map of Thornborough 1877

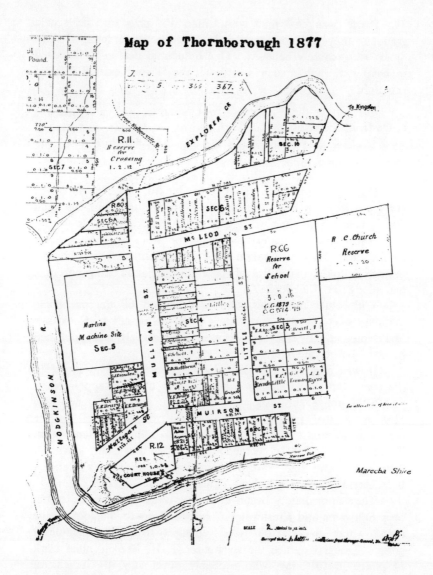

Doyle was the first white man to gaze on the scenic grandeur they then presented. In Thornborough later, Doyle's report was scarcely believed. One influential person is supposed to have said that if such a river as the Barron existed it must run uphill.

Bill Smith then returned to Cooktown and attacked the range from the seaward side with two mates, Stewart and Lipton. They arrived in Thornborough on September 17, 1876, having covered seventy miles on foot.

*   *   *   *

On September 20th., 1876, Mr. Jenkin, the Thornborough correspondent for the "Townsville Herald", took up his quill and in neat copperplate wrote a despatch containing these words: "Bill Smith and his mates have been the 'lions' of the place for awhile, and the consumption of 'James Hennessy' has notably increased in the two cities of Thornborough and Kingsborough, and along the Caledonia."

With other mail, this news was carried by the packhorse mailman over the dry dusty track over the ranges to Cooktown and sent south by the regular mail steamer. It was published in the "Townsville Herald" on October 10th.

It was now believed that a good road had been found to the coast, but the Hodgkinson people were to be disappointed.

Two police sub-inspectors, Johnstone and Townsend, with nine Aboriginal troopers, sailed north from Cardwell in the police whaleboat, powered by oars and sail, and landing at Trinity Bay met Sub-Inspector Douglas, Fred and Charles Warner (surveyors who had also been exploring the ranges), and a detachment of Native Police. This was on September 23rd.

They immediately began cutting a track through the scrub, over Saltwater and Freshwater Creeks and on to the foot of the range where the Barron River emerges from its magnificent gorge. Douglas named the river after T. H. Barron, chief clerk of police in Brisbane, who probably never saw it. Tracks of Bill Smith's hobnailed boots were sighted. A path was cut

(20)

through the scrub up the incredibly steep range between Glacier Rock and Red Bluff.   In the scrub, the wild blacks were like flitting shadows dogging every movement of these intruders. A trooper had to guard the scrub-cutters and be ever watchful.

Meanwhile, Bill Smith had started back from Thornborough leading 160 men on foot, carrying swags and mining tools. Their hobnail boots cut a broad path through the dry speargrass in the forest country and churned up the banks of Leadingham and other creeks as they slogged eastward.   They waded the swift flowing Barron River near the later site of Biboohra.   They thought the Barron was the Mitchell.

Warden Mowbray's mounted party which left Thornborough a day later, caught up with the footmen.   With Mowbray were J. V. Mulligan, Johnny Byers, E. M. Geary, Williams, Sharpe, and a dozen others including the intrepid "Townsville Herald" correspondent, Jenkin.

He noted the mineralised country in the area that was to become the short-lived Clohesy Goldfield in 1893.   Jenkin, his mind attuned to the surest means of transport of his day, believed that if a gold discovery was made here it would cause a rush "to Trinity Bay from which *swagmen* can easily reach the locality in two days."

Following the newly cut tunnel-like path through the jungle in single file, the correspondent came to a pinch that winded both the men and the horses but they were "gratified by the sight of the sea and a large river at the base of the spur on which we were standing," Jenkin wrote.

"From this we descended sheer down about half a mile and after considerable swearing, slipping, and blowing, we emerged suddenly on a splendid flowing stream [the Barron where it receives Stoney Creek] with both sides covered in mountain scrub . . . . We came to the conclusion that if this was the dray track of Douglas' and Bill Smith's was no better, Trinity Bay would remain in the possession of its dusky inhabitants for all time . . . . "

The correspondent caught sight of a fine tidal reach in the new river and prophesised that a town would be built there. It was to be the site chosen for Smithfield — unwisely, as the floodmarks were ignored.

Mowbray's party reached Douglas' camp on the future site of Cairns on 30th. September. The correspondent added:

"I am of opinion the Government would not be justified in spending money on either of the present tracks . . . . A party headed by John Doyle are about to start out for the ranges again, hoping to find a better road . . . . "

John Doyle led a party comprising Edward M. Geary, Harry Evans and William McCord from Trinity Bay on 6th. October. After searching fruitlessly for "leading spurs" up the range from the Mulgrave River to the Barron River, they finally found a route up a spur on the northern side of the Barron. They crossed the river above the falls at what became known as Middle Crossing (later Kuranda) and linked up with Douglas' track at Grove Creek which would lead to Thornborough. This time a passable wagon road had been found.

Edward Geary, who kept a diary, definitely states that John Doyle was the discoverer of the famous Barron Falls, whether — this expedition or earlier, is not very clear.

Frederick Warner and Sub-Inspector Douglas traversed the route Doyle had discovered and reported favourably to A. C. Macmillan, Engineer for Roads, and work was immediately begun by the Government with overseer McDonald in charge.

But although almost £10,000 was eventually spent on it, the road proved too steep for loaded teams; they managed to struggle up by double-banking all the way to the top. Part of the route is now followed by the power line from the Barron Falls where hydro-electric power has been generated since 1935. That year the poles for the line were placed in position by Rod Veivers' bullock team — the last time bullocks trod the "Smithfield Track".

When Christie Palmerston found a better road to Port

(22)

Douglas in 1877 it was abandoned by teamsters; packers still used it for a while. Early in 1877 the first gold escort from the Hodgkinson came down to Trinity Bay by this road. On its first trip it was bailed up by a bushranger.

Packers camped at Kamerunga roistered in nearby Smithfield and used Douglas' Track at first, but soon it, too, was abandoned in favour of the road to Port Douglas.

Situated possibly within a stone's throw of where the hold-up took place, is a nine-foot memorial cairn, now a landmark on the Kennedy Highway. At the suggestion of the writer it was erected by the Mulgrave Shire Council, and the plaque, unveiled on June 9th. 1958, by Mrs. Daisy Hine, a daughter of John Doyle, states that the monument is in memory of "The Men Who Blazed the Track — 1876 — Those Pathfinders who, between June and October 1876, discovered the Barron River, the Falls, and a route to Trinity Bay as an outlet for the Hodgkinson Goldfield." It carries the names of William Smith, John Doyle, Sub-Inspector Alexander Douglas, Frederick Horatio Warner, Edwin Crossland, "and the other pioneers of Smithfield."

The old bridge over the Barron River at Mareeba was fittingly named the Doyle Bridge, but the new bridge has been named the Edmund Kennedy Bridge and the Cairns-Tablelands road is the Kennedy Highway. Yet the explorer Kennedy was never in this locality. The name of the real discoverer, John Doyle, should be transferred to the new bridge. A street in Mareeba is named after him. This fine old pioneer died in Mareeba in 1932 when ninety years of age.

Cairns, founded in October 1876, soon had its Hodgkinson trade strangled first by Smithfield then by Port Douglas, and with a seemingly impassable mountain barrier at its back, it withered and almost died. Only John Robson's pack track to Herberton in 1882 and construction of the railway over the range from 1886, was to save it from extinction by Port Douglas.

When the wet season set in in January 1877, the Hodgkinson

towns and mining camps found they were as isolated as ever, as the much vaunted "roads" to the coast at Trinity Bay were found to be useless.

In heavy monsoon rain, teams could not negotiate the Smithfield (or Doyle's) Track and only packhorses could struggle up and down the sheer mountainside on Douglas' Track, and it too became impassable. For long periods the flooded Barron River and Freshwater Creek inundated the flats.

As for Cairns, it was a row of huts and wooden buildings on a low sandridge surrounded by foetid mangroves, all but under water at high tide or in flood rains; a foot of rain overnight was not unusual in the January to April period. Only clearing, drainage, and filling over many years was to raise Cairns out of the swamps to make it the beautiful tropical city it is today, a Mecca for a quarter of a million tourists a year seeking the winter sun. Few cities in Australia had such an unpromising start. It speaks volumes for the tenacity, hard work, and stubborn faith of the pioneers.

On March 8th. 1878, a cyclone threatened to wipe off its tenuous grip on the map, but somehow the place survived. Smithfield, already practically deserted, suffered severe flooding in 1878 and 1879. That was the end of what had started as a roaring goldfields port, notorious for its sinfulness according to some writers, but it was probably no worse than other similar settlements.

The story has been told several times in print how Bill Smith, the pathfinder, had his horse shod with shoes of Hodgkinson gold by Edwin Crossland, the blacksmith from the Palmer; and of how, as his fortune waned, he shot the storekeeper Craig and then turned the gun on himself. This has become part of the folklore of Cairns and as such it has become difficult to separate fact from fiction. It provided heady stuff for the background to the Cairns Centenary of 1976.

The Aborigines on the mountains and on the coast waylaid the pack teams as they threaded their way up to the Hodgkinson.

A packer known as George the Greek was attacked in the scrub near Middle Crossing (Kuranda). He arrived at Groves' shanty seven miles away with three broken-off spears in his legs. He lost all his packhorses with their loads of stores needed in Thornborough. Most of the packers rode heavily armed and were able to beat off the natives. Pat Downey was another packer who was wounded in an attack at Middle Crossing; in another attack he lost nearly all his horses.

There were wild white men as well. A man wanted for horse stealing on the Hodgkinson murdered a packer on the road known as Frank the Austrian.

*   *   *   *

James Atkinson's nephew, John Fraser, came north in 1874 to seek pastoral land. Equipped by his uncle, Fraser and a companion named Arthur Temple Clark, set out from Farnham on the Lower Herbert, for the North. They avoided the jungle on the western edge of the Atherton Tableland and followed down Granite Creek to the Barron. They could have been twelve months ahead of Mulligan, but the latter's journey was official and Fraser's was not. On the headwaters of the Mitchell, Fraser decided to take up several hundred square miles of country. It was well grassed and watered. It was probably late in 1875 when he returned with 400 head of Lower Burdekin cattle to stock it.

Fraser called his run Mitchellvale. In the Eighteen-eighties it was divided to form part of Brooklyn, Font Hill, and Southedge. The Mary River where the Maryfarms tobacco community is now situated, was named by Fraser after his sister, the mother of the later Harry and Eric Baker. The former resided most of his life in the historic old homestead near Mt. Molloy, recently demolished by a new owner. Eric died in Mareeba in June 1979, aged 91. Born at Font Hill in 1888, his life was spent among cattle and horses, on stations and on long droving trips. He was one of the North's fine old pioneers.

The Kokokulunggur tribesmen speared Fraser's cattle and

(25)

horses, but he tried to treat them with sympathy. He also befriended a white man who was an outcast for a time.

This was the mysterious Christie Palmerston.

Fraser was in his mustering camp one day when a bearded fierce-eyed man in red shirt, moleskin trousers, and worn top-boots, suddenly appeared out of the scrub. He carried a Snider rifle, a Colt revolver, and a Bowie knife. He said he was Christie Palmerston, was wanted on the Palmer for the murder of a Chinaman of which he was innocent, and vowed he would never be taken alive. He told Fraser he had found a route over the mountains to Island Point (Port Douglas) and that his mate was now at Thornborough to claim the reward that was offered for finding such a track.

Years later, John Fraser wrote: "He eventually got a reward and a pardon but he still remained in the bush. He was a brave man who would face anything." Today, Christie Palmerston — the son of Madame Carandini, a famed opera singer of the times — is an almost legendary figure, but all accounts agree on his superb bushmanship in the dense rain forests of the country behind Cairns.

Several old timers have said, however, he was utterly ruthless with the Aborigines. On one occasion he had a horse speared at Mt. Pompo (near Mt. Molloy of later years) and a dozen black men, women, and children were shot in consequence. In those days a horse was considered of greater value.

Palmerston's friends on the Hodgkinson were evidently working on his behalf, for on 11th. June 1877, an official report on the new route was issued, giving Christie Palmerston full credit for the discovery.

The "Hodgkinson Mining News" of Thornborough reported on 16th. June that at a hastily summoned meeting in front of the Royal Hotel, Mr. Byers proposed that a subscription be opened to pay a reward to "Christie Palmerston and his mate, Leighton." Later, the newspaper referred to the latter as Lakeland. He has also been variously called Layton and Little.

Whoever he was, this mystery man reported at the open air meeting that after weeks in the jungle in the wet season, he and Palmerston had found a route for a road down a main spur of the Coast Range onto the coast plain near Island Point. They had carved their initials, CP/WL on a tree on the bank of the Mowbray River, first sighted by John Doyle in 1876. This historic marked tree stood until modern times.

After an abortive attempt at establishing a settlement called, of all things, New Jerusalem, at the mouth of the Mowbray, the inlet sheltered by Island Point was decided upon. Captain Daniel Owen of the coastal steamer, Corea, recommended it as a proper site for a new port.

Callaghan Walsh, a leading Cooktown merchant, chartered the Corea, loaded her with building materials and stores and arrived at the new harbour on 30th. June, 1877. They found Mr. Jenkin and two friends, Pintcke and Ohlran, already in residence, having come up from the Mowbray, and that they had christened the new port, Port Salisbury "after the great statesman who lately represented England at the congress of the Great Powers at Constantinople."

Mr. Jenkin had neither quill, ink, nor paper, but he still sent his despatch to his paper, this time the "Hodgkinson Mining News". He wrote in pencil on a sheet of bark to describe the birth of the new seaport!

In Thornborough, a committee of five were elected — Mulligan, Martin, Cosgrove, Swan, Cooper, and Booth — to draw up a petition to the Government to open the road and make it trafficable. The sum of £143/3/6 was quickly collected. The "Palmerston Reward Fund" reached £201/12/-.

The "Hodgkinson Mining News" reported on 21st. July that "Mr. Moss of Kingsborough brought the first packteam through from Port Salisbury. He departed from Port Salisbury on Wednesday and arrived at Kingsborough on Saturday . . . . "

At a public meeting in Port Salisbury on July 26th., six hundred people rolled up, indicating the rapid growth of a

(27)

goldfields port.

Correspondent Jenkin reported that the area near the jetties was piled high with iron bedsteads, sewing machines, handsome cedar tables, billiard tables, feather mattresses, kerosene lamps, thousands of feet of timber, "an acre or two" of corrugated iron, tarpaulins, and canvas for "instant hotels and stores", and also smiths' anvils, bellows, carpenters' and miners' tools, and mountainous stacks of barrels containing beer and spirits. Most of these goods were intended for the Hodgkinson.

The public meeting was held to raise money for a party to go out and clear the scrub to allow wagons to get up the range. Axemen from the settlement had already cleared about four miles of road and were half way to the foot of the range. Later swampy sections were corduroyed with logs cut and placed by hand.

By August, horse and bullock teams were waiting impatiently at the top of the range for the scrub to be cleared and cuttings made to ease the grade on the terribly steep "Bump" section.

Early in September, 1877, a convoy of thirty teams came down the road and camped at Craiglie, the best grass and water nearest to Port Douglas.

Mackie's six-horse dray was the first to ascend the range, loaded with stores for John Fraser's Mitchellvale Station. Mackie settled near the headwaters of Leadingham and Cattle Creeks.

A week or two later, thirteen wagons left Port Douglas for the Hodgkinson, carrying over a hundred tons of stores. Eighteen days later, the leading teams crawled over the last rough ridge and the ponderous wagons, high swaying loads under dusty tarpaulins, wheels turning ever so slowly, pulled by tired bullocks, plodded down McLeod Street, Thornborough.

The street was crowded on both sides with timber and iron buildings, the sidewalks thronged with cheering people, mostly men in the rough garb of working miners who called greetings to the sun-browned flannel-shirted drivers trudging in the dust beside their teams, long greenhide whips trailing over their

(28)

shoulders.

There were shouts and handclaps, excited barking of dogs, frightened horses pulling away from crowded hitching rails, and round-eyed children clinging to their mother's skirts, awed by this momentous happening — the arrival of thirteen bullock teams all at once, and from a new port on the coast, at that. An occasion as unusual and as important to these folk as would be the arrival of some giant new plane ushering in a new era in transport in this modern age.

It was an occasion for celebration. Thornborough's twenty hotels roared late into the night as round after round of drinks passed between several thousand men, some singing, some laughing, some arguing, congregated in the dim light of swaying kerosene lanterns and smoking slush lamps to celebrate and to fight.

McLeod Street from Mulligan's store to the brow of the hill where a school and a church were to be built, and from the corner up Mulligan Street to Wooster's Hotel was a seething mass of humanity. Over the babel of voices and the blare of music from squeaky concertinas and overworked pianos coming from the hotels and saloons as the proprietors made the most of this unusually exciting Saturday night with the huge crowd in festive mood, there came a call over a loud hailer: "Roll up! Roll up, to a monster meeting at Jim Mulligan's! "

The crowd that had been wavering back and forth uncertain of direction, now converged to hear what was happening at popular J. V. Mulligan's hotel and store in the centre of town.

A man of medium height, brown bearded, Mulligan addressed the crowd in his soft Irish brogue. It was a vastly different crowd now, he no doubt reflected, to the hostile miners he had confronted, rifle in hand on horseback, at Glen Mowbray only a little over a year before. They had been carrying ropes ready to lynch him because they believed he had led them to a duffer goldfield.

But all that was past. The Hodgkinson's rich reefs had

(29)

fully vindicated his reports. The rumble of stampers that was a constant background noise was music to his ears for it meant continued prosperity for the field.

Resolutions passed at the meeting included that of Mr. McPherson : "That the meeting regards the arrival of the first teams from Salisbury with the greatest satisfaction." Jem Cosgrove proposed "that this meeting regards the arrival of the teams from Salisbury within eighteen days as sure proof of the practicability of the road and is of the opinion that the Government should be called upon to expend £1000 in forming it for dray traffic during the ensuing wet season." Johnny Byers seconded it and it was carried unanimously.

A few days later the newspaper reported that another nineteen teams were coming up the range on their way to the Hodgkinson. A bridge had just been built over Rifle Creek but the "Bump" section was so steep it took 36 horses to pull a wagon loaded with four tons up the incline.

The more direct road that was blazed over the Granite Range from the present vicinity of Mt. Molloy township, westward to Dora Creek, the Eastern Hodgkinson, and so to Kingsborough, was unusable in the dry season owing to absence of grass and water. The longer route was necessary — southward to the Big Mitchell, then the Mud Springs, Flat Rock, and westward along the earlier road to Cairns through Northcote and so to Thornborough. It was twenty miles longer but with plenty of feed and water for the teams and no very steep grades.

The road was what the Hodgkinson had been waiting for, but it was a terrible track by modern standards. One can imagine how the iron-shod wagon wheels churned out a deeply rutted track across granite hills and gullies of knife-edged slate, sandy creek crossings, up rock-strewn hillsides, and across teatree flats where the wagons sank to their axle-beds in the wet season. Yet to the Hodgkinson pioneers it was a highway. In places it is still plainly visible, but it looks more like a creek-bed than a road.   The Government spent about £2000 on it, mainly on cuttings in the "Bump" section and on Granite Range just west of Mareeba.   Between Sorensen's Mud Springs and Flat Rock the pickmarks of the roadmakers can be seen today.

At a meeting in Thornborough, reported in the "Hodgkinson Mining News", on 12th. January 1878, Stenhouse and Martin asked that Engineer MacMillan be requested to make the road directly over the Granite Range fit for wheel traffic as it was 25 miles shorter.   Owing to its roughness and lack of grass and water, this short cut remained useful only as a pack track. Most horsemen travelled down to Port Douglas that way. These were the first roads in the Mareeba Shire.

In 1879 it was reported that the road at the Port Douglas end was in a deplorable state "since the rains".   The gold escort could not proceed on that occasion, past Rifle Creek and packhorses had to be used.   The Coast Range section was always a bugbear..

The gold escort was diverted from Smithfield to Port Douglas in 1878.   A former coach driver on the Palmer, Johnny Hogsflisch, took the first mail by packhorse from Port Douglas to Thornborough on 12th. December, 1877.

The freight from Cooktown to Thornborough had been £100 per ton, but it was much less from Port Douglas. A carrier named Bill Clark is said to have taken the first wagon load of machinery up "The Bump" — a six ton boiler for the Hodgkinson.   In his first attempt the wagon capsized and most of the bullocks were killed.   It is recorded that the first load of machinery reached the Monarch Mine at Beaconsfield late in October 1877.

Ted Troughton took a record load over this range some time in 1878.   It was a boiler weighing nine tons eighteen hundredweight for Jackson and Plant's mill at Kingsborough. He used two teams of bullocks yoked four abreast and the journey took two weeks.

Ted Troughton died in Mareeba at the age of 103. He was born in Parramatta, N.S.W., in 1839 and arrived in what was later to become Queensland in 1857. He was a resident of Mareeba from the late 'Nineties, and spent most of his active life on the roads carrying.

The old Port Douglas Road was a lifeline to the pioneers. As they pushed further out, the road followed. The slowly turning wheels of the heavy bullock wagons, and later the swifter wheels of the Cobb and Co. coaches, overcame the mountains and linked the Coral Sea with the Gulf of Carpentaria.

CHAPTER 3

OUR HARDY PIONEERS

John Atherton — Wrotham Park Station — Alexander — Settlers of Leadingham Creek — Along the Walsh River.

Gold had been the magic key that opened the door to the development of the Far North. To the pastoralist pioneers gold had no attraction — it was the news of the wider grasslands, the rivers, and the waterholes, discovered by the gold-seekers and the track-blazers that made these men's thoughts turn towards the unstocked North.

Over the ranges from Cashmere on the Burdekin headwaters, with 1500 head of cattle, a hundred horses, and two bullock wagons, came John Atherton to found a station in the Northern wilderness. With him was his brave wife, Kate, and their two eldest sons, eleven and thirteen years of age respectively.

Skirting the impenetrable scrubs near where a town would rise bearing his name, John Atherton rode northward on the tracks of Mulligan, and perhaps of John Fraser, by a swiftly flowing river, over basalt ridges, and finally fertile flats, towards a sugarloaf-shaped hill where a scrub-born creek with banks of emerald green joined the river.

There, on the rise above the junction overlooking the turbulent Barron, the Athertons built their homestead of slabs and shingles, erected yards and post-and-rail fences. Atherton called his home Emerald End and the nearby hill — a district landmark — Kate's Sugarloaf.

Thus, a century ago, came Mareeba's first settlers. There was not to be a town for years, and neither was there a road. Miles to the north, the Port Douglas Road veered westward to Thornborough, but the track to Cairns, used mostly by packers, crossed the Barron four miles downstream and the telegraph line was to go that way also. At first, Emerald End was the only homestead between the headwaters of the Burdekin River and the Mitchell.

Emerald End was the end of a long pilgrimage for the Athertons.

It had begun back in 1858 when their covered drays had rolled northward from New England and they had settled near Rockhampton, then the most northerly settlement.

In 1875, John Atherton formed Basalt Downs on the old telegraph line from Cardwell to the Gulf. His brothers had settled in the Bowen district, but in 1873 John had driven a mob of cattle to the Palmer diggings and had explored some of the country.

When the Hodgkinson gold rush broke out in March 1876, John Atherton became more restless. Mulligan had reported good country on what he thought was the Upper Mitchell, and then John Fraser had disappeared into the wild lands to the north with a mob of cattle to found a station. On an exploring journey, Atherton took up all the country between Fraser's run south to the jungle-covered Tablelands, east to the Coast Range jungle, and west beyond the Barron River.

He then sold Basalt Downs to McDowall of Kangaroo Hills, and with his family and wagons set out for Emerald End.

Where Mareeba now stands, Atherton's cattle once grazed. Old-timers say the seasons have changed. So, too, has the vegetation. Where John Atherton saw sweeping parklands, lush grass, and wildflowers, are now the undergrowth and inferior grasses of drier country.

The Atherton homestead stood for ninety years until destroyed by fire. It was substantially built; the pioneers did not do their work by halves. The bush-built home withstood the cyclone of 1878 which almost destroyed Cairns.

The Aborigines were hostile. This was the territory of the Barbaram tribe and they were not to be dispossessed easily. Scores of Atherton's cattle were speared, and seeking them far and wide over the Barron and Clohesy valleys, he carried his life in his hands. A tomahawk thrown from ambush almost killed him; he carried the scar for the rest of his life.

A hill called Bones Knob near Tolga township is a grim reminder of the revenge taken on the Barbaram, for these were ruthless days on the frontier, the pioneers believing as they did in the "civilising" effects of the Snider rifle.

From Baan Bero Native Mounted Police camp, Sub-Inspector Douglas and his black troopers frequently rode out to "disperse" the tribesmen. Snider bullets — they made a hole in a human body as large as a twenty-cent piece — and European diseases did it so effectively that the natives were not only dispersed, they were practically annihilated.

John Atherton, the expert bushman, noted landmarks with an explorer's eye, and his namings have endured — Shanty Creek, Granite Creek, Mt. Twiddler, Kate's Sugarloaf, Tichum Creek, Cobra (Cobbera) Creek, Tinaroo, etc. Chinaman Creek has become Atherton Creek in his honor.

John Atherton, though a cattleman, recognised minerals when he saw them. One day in 1879 he and James Robson, prospecting in the ranges south-east of Emerald End, discovered alluvial tin. As his dish came out of the creek, heavy with black tin, Atherton is said to have shouted to Robson — "Tin—hurroo! " Thus was a name given to a creek, a scrub-covered range, and a tinfield. Later came other namings — Tinaroo Falls, Tinaroo Shire, and Tinaroo Dam — the latter the key to the modern development of what was once real Pioneers' Country.

Atherton blazed another new pack-track to Cairns, through dense jungle and high mountains by way of the Little Mulgrave to Redbank at the head of Trinity Inlet, and grateful businessmen gave him a reward of forty pounds, no less.

A small rush set in, and late in 1879, two men named John Newell and Willie Jack arrived from the Hodgkinson. They obtained beef from John Atherton and camped at Emerald End. They were carrying their swags, as all miners did as they moved from field to field. Atherton told them he had seen great slabs of tin-bearing ore up in the ranges on Herbert

River headwaters. It was what Mulligan had seen over four years before.

Atherton led Newell and Jack to the spot, and returned to his cattle, but swiftly now the ways would change . . . .

Long after the mines and the mining towns and their restless crowds of humanity had passed away, the work of the pastoral pioneers endured, in most cases to the present day. And but for the pastoralists, the gold seekers would have starved; for a few pounds of beef they willingly paid out their gold.

William Hann reported excellent grazing country on the Lower Walsh River and Elizabeth Creek, and early in 1874 the first pioneer arrived — a hardy Scot named A. C. Grant, a former commanding officer in the Queensland Rifles. He selected the country for Henderson and Skene of Havilah Station, inland from Bowen, and entering into partnership with them, Grant returned late the same year with 700 head of cattle and occupied the country.

The first Wrotham Park homestead was on the Mitchell River not far from Mt. Mulgrave, taken up by Patrick Callaghan as a depot for cattle supplying his partners, Edwards, Leslie, and Duff, the main butchers on the Palmer Goldfield. After the Palmer faded, Callaghan lived at Mt. Mulgrave for many years. In 1911, it was still necessary to carry firearms because of the hostility of the blacks. Unrolling his swag one day, Callaghan's revolver fell out, discharged, and killed him. The monument over his grave is one of the finest in the Outback.

Wrotham Park, comprising about four thousand square miles, was named after Skene's home town in Kent, England. It was a beautiful virgin wilderness such as the pioneers had found in the South a decade or more earlier. Ellen E. Arnold compiled an interesting booklet in 1973 on the history of this station to mark its centenary. It was published by the station's present owners, the Australian Agricultural Company.

Grant moved his homestead and his cattle to Elizabeth

Creek in 1875 after a travelling mob infected some with pleuro on the Mitchell, so the present homestead site — and an old buggy shed — dates from that period. Grant withdrew from the partnership in 1878 and eventually went to the United States with his family. He died at Long Beach, California, in 1930, aged 89 years. Henderson and Skene owned Wrotham Park until 1906.

In 1879, Edward Palmer and Walter Reid established Gamboola, thirty miles to the west. Highbury, forty miles further down the Mitchell was taken up by Edward Bostock in 1878. Gamboola, Highbury, and Drumduff have for long been part of Wrotham Park, making it one of the largest cattle stations in Queensland, running 45,000 head. The late Walter Lawrence, part owner for many years, was probably one of the best known graziers in the Far North in recent times. Bulimba, and Torwood on the Lynd were Lawrence-owned properties at one time, also Bolworra on the Tate, pioneered by the Dicksons (See Chap. 9). The Stewarts originally took up Rookwood near Mungana, but the Fergusons have owned it for many long years.

John Atherton's son, William, formed Chillagoe Station in the 'nineties. He was evidently a Gilbert and Sullivan fan, for many of his namings are derived from songs and catch-phrases of that era — Chillagoe, Ruddigore, Wallabadory, etc.

*   *   *   *

Many of the teamsters settled down on cattle and farming properties near the old roads, their maize and vegetables being sold in the nearby mining towns. Few of these old homes have withstood the test of progress, but these families were the first European farmers — as distinct from the Chinese market gardeners on the goldfields — in what became the Mareeba Shire, a district whose wealth now lies in agriculture. Usually only a grove of gnarled mango trees and a few adzed posts and beams, and parts of post-and-rail fences that bushfires have left, with sometimes a lonely grave or two, remain to mark brave pioneering efforts of a hundred years ago.

On the edge of the Hodgkinson Goldfield particularly can these be found, and few people now remember their history.

John Alexander was one of the first of these. At the close of the Eighteen-seventies, he settled on Pinnacle Creek about three miles west of Northcote and within sight of the busy carrying road. The name of another settler, Loudon, has been mentioned as the first here. However, there seems little doubt that it was Alexander who cleared the enormous box and river gums from the fertile creek flat, hitched his bullocks to a heavy single-furrow plough and prepared the ground for corn. On the Palmer in early times, corn fetched a sovereign for a sugarbagful. Passing carriers would have been Alexander's customers, and one can imagine that many a team rested in the shade of the big box trees near the crossing. Alexander enclosed his farmland and a large paddock with a stout fence of forks and logs, portions of which can probably still be seen.

This pioneer died in the early 'eighties — from appendicitis, it has been said; it was then known only as "inflammation of the stomach" and caused many deaths. Around 1885, the Mackenzies are said to have been in possession of the property, breeding draught horses in demand by the carriers. Years later, about 1912, when the Murphy family acquired the place, some fine police and cavalry horses were bred on Pinnacle Creek. Many a cavalry horse in Palestine during the 1914-18 War was bred around Pinnacle, Leadingham Creek, or the Hodgkinson. From these, the brumbies that used to roam the area thirty years ago were descended. There are still a few wild mobs in the ranges of the Eastern Hodgkinson.

A fine old time tradesman, Bob MacFarlane, built a large six-roomed homestead with wide verandahs and an imposingly steep roof, at Pinnacle Creek for Joe Murphy in 1912. While it was being built, Joe used to ride regularly across country from Wolfram Camp where he had mining interests. Gordon Hay of Dimbulah remembers that Joe paid an old friend of Gordon's, named Andy Coyle, five pounds to blaze a direct track as Joe Murphy was a poor bushman and was frightened of getting lost. He did not live long to enjoy the comforts of his new home.

Mrs. Murphy then married an ex-policeman and a clever horse trainer named Jack Robinson. He had served in the Boer War and had been wounded at the Battle of Elands River (August 1900). He was killed at the Cairns Show in July, 1946, while putting his favourite grey mare, Amy Johnson, over the jumps. Jack was a wonderful horseman and in his younger days it was said he never opened a gate but always jumped his horse over it. At the close of World War II., "Robbie" as he was known, entertained thousands of troops camped on the Tablelands with exhibitions of his trick horses which were very intelligent animals and a credit to his prowess as a trainer.

In 1921, Jack Hay, a well known horse teamster, and Gordon, then a young man, were engaged by Mrs. Robinson to move the Pinnacle homestead, dismantled, to the railway at Dimbulah for re-erection in Constance Street, Mareeba. While loading the house sections, Gordon remembers hearing the boom and echo of a distant explosion. Later he knew what it was: the terrible disaster at the Mt. Mulligan colliery that took 75 lives on September 19, 1921.

Over on Leadingham Creek, a Walsh River tributary which runs an almost parallel course with Pinnacle Creek, were the townships of Old Northcote and New Northcote, the former dating from the rush of 1876. There were several settlers along Leadingham Creek.

The creek was named after Jack Liedingham, a German-born carrier on the Hodgkinson road — probably one of the first to bring in stores from Trinity Bay by the Smithfield track up the range. The story is that he saw a plain turkey near the creek, pulled his rifle off the wagon to have a shot at it and accidentally shot himself. Other carriers found him later and he was buried at the foot of a box tree. The blazed tree still stands.

(39)

The Jackson family came to Leadingham in 1878. The Miner's Homestead Lease they took up dates from August 1879, and the family owned it until recent times though the property had been abandoned for many years. It was the home of the Jacksons for forty years. One son, George, was killed in 1938 when his horse ran into a one-wire fence, and Joe died in March 1946, in Mareeba.

Good old Joe Jackson spoke of the years of unrelenting toil that he and his parents and sisters spent on Leadingham. As well as cattle, they raised horses, goats, and poultry. The fine draught horses they bred — many of them were an attractive iron-grey color — are still remembered by old timers. They were in demand by the teamsters. George Jackson, the father of the family, was a carrier and also supplied cypress pine timber for the mines and buildings in Thornborough and Kingsborough. It was the job of his daughters, the late Emma and Lizzie, to have a wagon load of timber cut ready for him each trip. They were typical pioneer women. In 1908, they erected a post-and-rail fence five miles long almost single-handed.

The girls also handled a heavy "swing" plough to break up twenty acres of creek flat for corn growing. The land yielded thirty hundredweight of corn to the acre year after year; lucerne, potatoes, and even wheat flourished in the moist sandy soil. As the old timers say, the seasons have changed and the land has become poorer and water scarce. Where the Jacksons swam in Leadingham Creek there is only dry sand today, erosion having caused silting.

Gordon Hay of Dimbulah remembers: "Those people lived very hard, all right. Goats, pumpkins, sweet potatoes, and corn were their mainstays in food. They used to grind their own corn for flour, you know. The late Bill Hambling showed me the corn grinder that they used to grind corn for porridge.

"All these people made butter by setting the milk in big shallow dishes and skimming the cream off. They put the cream in a big jar and then all hands took turns at shaking the jar. Quite a lot of butter was taken to Kingsborough and Thornborough on packhorses or in a splitbag on a saddle horse and sold there."

Another old timer recalls that the Jackson girls had a fine trotting stallion which they harnessed in a light buggy and by this means delivered milk, butter, and eggs to Thornborough regularly. In the wet season, no doubt, packhorses were used.

The 1902 drought was but one of the many setbacks suffered by these undaunted battlers. With great labor, a seventy-foot well was dug, and during drought periods hundreds of head of cattle were watered daily by windlass and bucket. In 1911, there was a tremendous flood, and water was a foot deep in the homestead and most of the poultry were drowned.

George Jackson snr. had the reputation of being a very hard man; in 1912, when seventy years of age, he was killed in a fall from a horse. In March 1919 he was followed by his brave wife. They were laid to rest on the site of their labors, in a picturesque glade of giant boxtrees. The mangoes, tamarinds, and other trees they planted over a century ago still flourish, as if guarding this quiet spot. The daughters who married Jerry Healy and Pat Murphy respectively, abandoned the old home in 1923, and the work of half a lifetime was left to the mercy of bushfires and floods. The gates were opened and the mobs of fine thoroughbred horses were turned loose. A nearby creek has been named Jackson Creek in honor of these grand pioneers.

John Hambling also lies buried on the site of his long abandoned home on Leadingham Creek, only a mile or two upstream from the Jacksons. Two sons, Bill and Bob, were prominent residents of Dimbulah for many years. As well as being interested in cattle and tobacco growing near the township, Bill was the mailman to Wolfram Camp for thirty-odd years.

On Leadingham above New Northcote, Harry Fryer had a homestead in the early days, and so did the O'Briens. Further down the creek below Jackson's were the Quills near where the late Wally Reichardt established a tobacco farm in 1930 and he and his wife did pioneering work equal to that of other Leadingham settlers of earlier times. Lower down the creek were the Malcolms, and where Ernie de Lacey, for many years a leading figure in tobacco growing and marketing, had a farm, there was a big Chinese garden in early times owned by Ah Tye. Over on Pinnacle Creek, Ah Chuck had a garden.

At the junction of Pinnacle Creek and the Walsh River, Chris Cummings established a station in the 'eighties which still exists — Cranbe Station, owned by Gordon Morrow. The late Jim Cummings, and his nephew, Tom Volkman, were well known district graziers until recent years.

After the old Murphy homestead was moved from Pinnacle, the country lay abandoned until taken up again in 1945 by the writer and his mother. Considerable development work was done by the present owner, Ted Marshall, who has made Pinnacle Station into a valuable property covering over fifty square miles. Relics of Alexander's occupation have been found — a Gaelic Whisky bottle, a rusted pistol, and a horsebell inscribed, "Good luck to horse teams."

Lower down the Walsh, Byrnes Bros. had a station in early times, and up above Dimbulah, the Petersons settled on a small tributary, Prices Creek. Nearby, Marsterson Bros., packers on the Port Douglas Road, established a farm and station at Mutchilba.

The first of the family, Joe Marsterson, was born in Whitby, Yorkshire, England, from whence came Captain Cook's little ship, the Endeavour, originally a Whitby collier. It was probably natural that he should decide upon a naval career. An accident, however, injured his eyesight and he was discharged, so he set out to try his luck in Australia. He landed in Townsville in 1870, just when the gold rush to the Etheridge began. He was successful at prospecting and when the Palmer broke out, he did well with a packteam. This also brought him to the Hodgkinson. When tin was found at Herberton, followed by silver at Montalbion in 1883, a track was blazed turning off the Port Douglas-Hodgkinson road and traversing the Cattle Creek flats to the Walsh River, then southward over the mountains. Joe Marsterson decided to settle near the Walsh Crossing and built a slab homestead. The Petersens were at a spot called Price's Bend, also on the Port Douglas-Montalbion road where the teamsters camped before climbing the range towards Stannary Hills.

Joe got his younger brother Ben out from England, and the two of them ran cattle and horses on the property. Their horses, of the 3KA and BM7 brands, were soon in keen demand. The remains of some of the post and rail fences they built can still be seen. Before long, Joe met his English bride at Port Douglas and took her on horseback to his little home on the Walsh, a home typical of those pioneering days. He died there forty years later. His son, also named Joe, was at World War I at the time. A well known citizen of the Mareeba district, as his family still are, he passed away in 1948. The old homestead was in the way of progress. It had to be demolished to make way for the new highway to Dimbulah and beyond.

Among the early settlers of the fertile Mowbray Valley inland from Port Douglas, were the Reynolds family. James Reynolds hailed from County Fermanagh, Ireland, and back in the Eighteen-sixties, was a teamster assisting pioneers such as Kellett and Spry from Natal Downs, and later overlanding to the Cape Goldfield and Charters Towers. When the Palmer rush began, he began carrying to and from Cooktown. In 1876 he opened an hotel in Kingsborough and in 1877 a roadside hotel where the road to Port Douglas crossed Cattle Creek. His third son, Charles Edward, was born there in 1879. The family moved to Port Douglas about 1883, and Denis Horan took over the hotel and coach change at Cattle Creek. When I saw it years ago, only a mango tree, a dogleg fence, two rusted dray tyres, and the grave of Horan marked the spot.

(43)

A battle is supposed to have taken place between the Aborigines and the Native Mounted Police on Cattle Creek about 1881. Most of the tribe was wiped out; it may have been in retaliation for an attack upon the Jacksons on Leadingham. Mrs. Jackson and her children took refuge in the cool room of the dairy which was a tunnel in the creek bank. Signs of this tunnel are still visible. A survivor of the massacre of the natives was a small girl; known later as Maggie Anderson, she was a popular figure around the Hodgkinson.

The other tribes were not cowed by this massacre; in 1888 it was still dangerous to travel between Thornborough and Kingsborough. The wagon road around the cliffs of Caledonia Creek provided ideal spots for an ambush. In April 1888, the Thornborough school teacher, Mrs. Omerine Carandal, was attacked on two occasions on the Kingsborough road and "only saved herself by an exhibition of firearms" as a contemporary report has it.

Cattle Creek is now on Kimalo Station, first taken up by the writer's family, and now owned by the Mareeba Rodeo Association.

Springmount Station on the head of the Walsh River, was established by the Marnane Bros. — early day packers — in the 'eighties. It has changed hands many times since early in World War II.

The Halpin Bros., butchers in Montalbion and Irvinebank, had a station on Chinaman Creek, an Emu Creek tributary. Two early day bullock teamsters, Keron Glendon and Denny McGrath, took up grazing country on the Barron at Kambul.

The Groves' farm at Mt. Molloy which they called "The Weatherboards" as they had called their earlier roadside hotel at Grove Creek, became Wetherby Station in recent times. The de Tournouers bred prize Zebu cattle on the property, and expanding, owned Southedge for some years. This station, one of the best known in the Mareeba district, is now part of the Peter Dane group of stations which also includes Brooklyn, near Mt. Carbine. Covering over a thousand square miles at one time, Brooklyn was established in 1886 by the Ord family and as previously mentioned was originally part of Mitchellvale. A well known Mareeba personality years ago, the late Jack Meehan, managed Brooklyn when it was one of a chain of State Government owned stations.

Curraghmore, down on the McLeod River, was taken up by the Crowleys and Roberts Bros. had it for years. The Thorntons have owned it for some time. David Thornton's grandfather was, incidentally, one of the earliest pastoralists in North Queensland; he was associated with Philip Somer on Dotswood Station in 1861 and in 1864 discovered a track down Herveys Range to Cleveland Bay before Townsville was founded. Thornton's Gap is named after him.

Southedge was taken up by a man named Williams who was the drover in charge of the mob of cattle with which John Fraser stocked Mitchellvale. The lease Williams acquired also included Northedge. He sold to Charlie McDonald who stocked the place with Herefords from the Hughenden district. When the tick plague came in the 'nineties, he had three thousand head but only a hundred or two survived. McDonald abandoned Northedge.

Two former teamsters, Mick Tyrell and Malachi McGrath opened a butchering business at Mossman when that area was settled for sugar growing in 1897. They needed country to hold bullocks they purchased on the Tableland, so acquired Southedge. McGrath died suddenly at his dinner camp out on the run one day. Tyrell carried on for a time, then sold out to Tom Kilpatrick; in the first two decades of this century he was one of the best known cattle buyers in the North. "Dry or wet, 'Kil' always got through with his mobs, whether it was from the Flinders, Vanrook, the Upper Burdekin, or the Peninsula," an old timer has said. A typical old time cattleman, "Kil" as he was known, was universally popular. He died at Ormond Private Hospital in Mareeba in November, 1934. Up to that time, Southedge Station was controlled by the partnership of Kilpatrick, Buchanan, and Hughes. The latter sold out to Glenville Massey in the 'fifties, and with John Hamilton as manager, the property was used for a time as a depot for cattle overlanded south from Rokeby in the Northern Peninsula. Southedge comprises much country that would be suited to a new district industry — ricegrowing.

CHAPTER 4

ECHOES FROM THE PAST

The Tyrconnell and General Grant Mines — Relics of the Golden Days — Kingsborough, Thornborough, Beaconsfield, Northcote, and other Ghosts of Gold.

Every great mineral field in the North has had its famous mine. Charters Towers, of course, had the Day Dawn and others; Herberton had the Great Northern; Irvinebank had the Vulcan; the Palmer had the Anglo-Saxon, and the Hodgkinson had the Tyrconnell.

The Tyrconnell worked on and off for sixty years. Its poppet-head and chimney stand sentinel on a lonely rocky hill overlooking Glen Mowbray and the deserted Hodgkinson field. There have been moves afoot to preserve it for posterity through the National Trust.

Like the other great mines abovementioned, romance also surrounds the discovery of the Tyrconnell, according to the popular story. In the rush of '76, Redmond pegged out this likely looking outcrop of gold-bearing quartz and named it after an Irish patriot of long ago. Not far away he pegged another reef which he called the Lizzie Redmond.

A couple of miles from the Tyrconnell, a miner from the Palmer named Isaac Fretwell, who became one of the pioneers of Cairns, found a fine-looking reef that he called the Great Britain. When Redmond saw it he offered Fretwell both the Tyrconnell and Lizzie Redmond in exchange for the Great Britain. Fretwell refused the offer, and it was well for Redmond that he did so.

Redmond's first crushing yielded four ounces to the ton and he erected a battery. Throughout the years, crushing from the Tyrconnell were regular and very rich. On the other hand, Fretwell's Great Britain was only a surface show.

Soon Redmond and his partner, McGhie, were employing one hundred men, and Thornborough was kept alive for years

(47)

on Tyrconnell gold. Redmond became one of the leading men on the Hodgkinson. Every month, heavily armed, he rode with his gold to Port Douglas, taking the packers' track through the mountains. On one trip, the packhorse carrying the gold bolted in the rough country, but was recovered. Redmond sold the Tyrconnell to a Charters Towers company in the 'nineties, but its richest days were then over. Records show that in 1878 the Tyrconnell produced 5023 ozs. from 1898 tons of stone. Lack of capital hampered development, as it did most Hodgkinson mines. After closing for a few years it was reopened in 1914 with Oliver Reece as manager. At the end of World War I., a southern company worked it and Thomas Harley was manager. Mrs. E. Volkman remembers Harley coming into Thornborough regularly with a little bar of smelted gold and depositing it in the Bank of New South Wales. Nearly 2000 ounces were produced between July 1918 and April 1919. Up to 1934, the Tyrconnell's production was 52,753 ounces of gold.

The machinery and boilers at the Tyrconnell were all hauled there by horse teams — a tremendous feat in mountainous terrain — the last by Jack Hay's team in 1915. It was a 13½ ton Cornish boiler and it was brought to Thornborough siding on the Mt. Mulligan line (then not long opened) by train. Hay had his old mate, Abe Rolls, with him and between them they had 28 horses, two box wagons and a timber wagon hired from Ward and Petersen of Mareeba.

The wet season was on and the empty wagons went down to their axle beds and the horses to their bellies in the boggy country between Dimbulah and Thornborough, but with the aid of a 300 ft. rope they snigged the wagons through. On the road to the mine the wagon was in danger of capsizing several times, but the load was balanced by twenty men from the mine hanging onto ropes as the 28 horses hauled it around the sidelings in the rocky hills.

The Tyrconnell closed in 1937 and reopened in 1939 with Amos Jones as manager. But for World War II, the Queensland

RUINS OF THE TYRCONNELL MINE — ONCE THE BEST ON THE HODGKINSON

GPIKE

(49)

Gold Development Syndicate would have continued working, but the mine closed for the last time in 1942. Amos Jones lived at the mine as caretaker until just before his death about twenty-five years ago, riding into Mareeba on horseback in the old time fashion. Some of the buildings are still in good repair. There is a magnificent view — Mt. Mulligan on the north-west horizon and a maze of tumbled peaks and rounded rocky bush-covered hills in every other direction. A ribbon-like wheel track can be seen winding upward through a saddle to Kingsborough. From the Tyrconnell it dips steeply to a crossing of Explorer Creek and the little valley of Glen Mowbray where the miners gathered in June 1876 outside Byers' butcher's shop threatening to lynch Mulligan.

The General Grant was a mine once as well known as the Tyrconnell. It was the deepest on the field — 725 ft. — and dates from 1876. Early yields do not seem to be available, but in 1896 the Cecil Syndicate was formed in London with English capital to rehabilitate and develop the old mine, with Charters Towers mining men, Miles and Millican, directors, and a very competent manager, William J. W. Richards, recognised as one of the most experienced miners in Australia.

A three-chambered main shaft was sunk and cut the reef at 300 ft. A level was put in, followed by two more at 500 ft. and 700 ft., each following the reef for about 750 ft. The Kingsborough Battery owned by Knudstrop, treated 18,000 tons of stone, but the yield of just over an ounce of gold to the ton was regarded as poor. Additional gold was obtained from a cyanide plant, however. The company's London shareholders thought they would benefit if they had their own mill, and the Reconstruction battery was built, costing £11,000. A dam on Caledonia Creek held twenty million gallons of water. This was built in 1901, but the wet season of 1902 did not eventuate and it did not fill until 1904, hampering milling operations.

The General Grant reef improved and yielded three ounces to the ton, then decreased so that the rising costs of the twentieth

OLD CRUSHING BATTERY AT KINGSBOROUGH

century made working unprofitable. About 20,700 ounces had then been won by the Cecil Syndicate.

Today, from across Caledonia Creek, the chimney and buildings of the General Grant stand out clearly on the opposite mountainside. They are reached by a very steep track from the long ridge upon which the town of Kingsborough was situated. There are mullock heaps and a series of gaping shafts along the slope of the mountain with more workings and remains of buildings in the gorge below. Buildings and a tramline are teetering on the edge, in danger of falling 200 or 300 feet into Caledonia Creek.

The huge winding gear, boilers, chimney, and some machinery remain, and again one wonders how, as with the Tyrconnell, it was placed there by horse power alone. It has remained silent and deserted since 1924. A faded Mining Regulations notice is still tacked up in one building, dated 10th. January 1920.

Operations of the Cecil Syndicate caused a short lived revival in Kingsborough when its roaring days were well past. The Syndicate bought Patsy Rowan's Reconstruction mine lower down the ridge from the General Grant as the reef seemed to be dipping that way. Rowan was the father of Mrs. E. A. Volkman, Thornborough's last original inhabitant. She also owns the deserted Kingsborough battery that was built by the Danish engineer, Knudstrop; it has not worked since 1916.

The collapsed building with rusting chimney and stout framework of still sound cypress pine tree trunks, is a landmark on the bank of Caledonia Creek, surrounded by gum trees and brown grass-covered hills gashed by rocky gullies rising vertically behind it.

Here at the end of a long ridge encircled on three sides by Caledonia Creek, is the edge of the once large town of Kingsborough — first called Kingston — with its ten hotels. The main street, Jackson Street, ran up the ridge for about a mile with the Roman Catholic church and Dr. Koch's private

Map of Kingsborough 1880

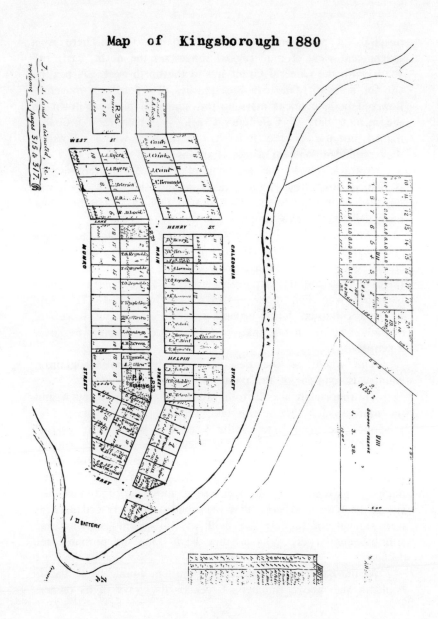

hospital on reasonably flat ground at the top. There is a magnificent view of blue rugged ranges on the north, east, and south, with the General Grant hill to the north-west. A healthy site for a town. One can see splashes of color from magenta-flowered bougainvilleas marking the homes of pioneers down on the meagre flats of Caledonia Creek — which they probably named because of the hills so "stern and wild." Possibly they reminded William McLeod of his native land.

A track follows the big bend of the creek and crossing, it is vaguely discernible running eastward into the ranges — it was once the main road to the coast at Port Douglas. The brumbies have their pads across it today.

On the high hill above Caledonia Creek was the school and nearby a tombstone shows up starkly on the edge of an eroded gully among stunted greybox trees, common to the hard ridges in this country. It is the grave of a blacksmith, William Compton, who died at the age of 47, on July 22, 1877. Close by is a collapsed fence around another grave, and there are mounds where others, unknown, have been sleeping for over a century.

The whole of the deserted, deathly quiet, Hodgkinson country is redolent of the pioneers and their handiwork.

Thornborough is only four miles east of Kingsborough, but the road is such that it can take an hour in a Toyota. This was once the main road to the coast and would have carried much traffic between the two "twin cities" as they were known. There is evidence of much work having been done on it — massive cuttings, sidelings along Caledonia Creek, and stone-pitching. A wall of boulders on a ridge above the road marks the site of an hotel and store that once had a fine terraced garden, now a jungle of rubber vines with several enormous poincianas still blooming every year as they have done for probably ten decades.

At the back of this once lovely garden, among black basalt boulders high above Butcher's Creek, is the grave of its owner,

Carl Alex Egerstrom, "Born in Sweden, 1829. Died in Thornborough, 1900." He is said to have dug his own grave out of the rock and carved his own tombstone from a natural slab. His friend, Knudstrup, made the brass plaque with its inscription, when he died.

This place is known to the old timers as Baker Burns'. Apparently, Jim Burns was the last owner and ran a bakery here to supply both Thornborough and Kingsborough in the latter days of the Hodgkinson field. Gordon Hay remembers he and his father resting their team in the shade of these poinciana trees over sixty years ago.

Just after leaving here the road crosses Caledonia Creek for the third time. It is a wide crossing among the giant teatrees and gums with one of the few waterholes nearby. Here is some impressive evidence of the work of the pioneers. The crossing originally had a causeway, not of concrete, but of huge flat basalt boulders, some as large as dining room tables, extending all the way across, individually placed with great care and stupendous effort in the very early days of the road — probably late in 1877 when improvements were made to the Port Douglas-Thornborough road.

From here, the road ascends the Rob Roy Hill by very steep cuttings and sidelings for about a quarter of a mile, deep ruts and loose boulders testing the climbing powers of even a Toyota. Up grades like this the carriers hauled thirteen-ton boilers with teams of up to thirty-four horses.

Knudstrup of Kingsborough built a steam-driven motor car in the early 1900's, and came to grief with it on this hill, and no wonder. The fact that this engineer was able to build a car — perhaps on the lines of a "Stanley Steamer" — in his workshop in Kingsborough over seventy years ago speaks much for his ingenuity. The story is that he took his wife with him when testing it out, but on the Rob Roy Hill he ran out of steam. The brakes would not hold and the car ran backwards and his wife was thrown out. He did not drive the car again and

(55)

Gordon Hay remembers seeing the vehicle left under a tree. He thinks that someone bought it from Knudstrup's widow. This would be the first, and one of the few, cars built in North Queensland and would be worth a fortune if it still existed.

Gordon Hay believes that Knudstrup's battery, now ruins, at Kingsborough, was built by him in the early 'nineties. Mr. Hay has recorded: "In the early times most of the gold was caught in an ordinary blanket spread over a table at the outlet of the stamper boxes. The blanket was taken off and washed in a tub and the gold collected. Later, a copper plate dressed with quicksilver and cyanide was used with a well at the bottom of the table with quicksilver in it. This was put into a retort pot on the fire and smelted, the quicksilver going out of the retort in a vapour into a tin of water and thus saved for further use".

One of the bank managers in Thornborough long ago, lost the keys to his safe. It was Knudstrup who saved the situation. On his second attempt he made a key that would fit, much to the relief of the banker. Knudstrup was working on an invention when he died. He was building a three-head battery at the Monarch mine that was to be driven by a windmill with 12 ft. blades.

*   *   *   *

Thornborough is a fine site for a town, and judging by the signs that still remain, it was obviously a large one — possibly with two thousand population. The road in from Kingsborough becomes McLeod Street and runs down a long ridge to a flat near the river with the main street, Mulligan Street, crossing it. It was fitting that the two principal streets in this town, once capital of the Hodgkinson Goldfield, should have been named after the two discoverers. The site of J. V. Mulligan's store and hotel, marked by remains of a cellar, stood on the right-hand corner with the river flat in front — the place where 500 miners gathered at the open air meeting on July 8th. 1876 to discuss the need for a wagon road to the coast.

The only building left from the pioneer days is Mrs. Volkman's house, once the Canton Hotel and part of a much larger building. Wah Lee's big store adjoined on the corner of Little Street (named for Billy Little, later M.L.A.), with a few bricks marking the site opposite in McLeod Street, of Horn and Petersen's jeweller's shop. It was a two storey building and in the town's latter period was a cordial factory. Next was Geilis' Commercial Hotel.

A fine view of Mt. Mulligan and a panorama of other ranges is obtained from the hilltop where the Catholic Church once stood, and from the site of the school on a lower level facing McLeod Street. The stone foundations, 40 ft. by 20 ft. remain.

At the top of Mulligan Street was Freeman's Hotel on the corner of Muirson Street, Wooster's Hotel opposite, and lower down was Frank Grainer's store and butchery. At the top of the street was the police station, Court House, Post Office, and the telegraph repeater station; all except Wooster's and Grainer's were built of brick and were functioning up to the early 'twenties.

These brick buildings, including the school, were bought for a total of £100 by the Eureka Farming Syndicate (H. H. Collins, secretary) of Dimbulah in 1932. They were pulled down and the bricks used to build tobacco curing barns at Leafgold. Many of the bricks at Thornborough were made by a builder named Bowcher. He built the school, opened in August 1878 with fifty pupils, for £1050. Badly damaged in a cyclone in 1920, it was repaired, but closed for good on 28th. March 1924, for lack of pupils. The first teacher, in 1878-82, was Patrick Houston, an Irishman.

Across the river is the cemetery. About a quarter of the graves are marked by tombstones dating from 1877. A pathetic headstone is that of the five Murphy children all of whom died within eleven years of one another, from 1899. At that time the Murphys had an hotel in Kingsborough, and this is the same family who were later at Pinnacle Creek.

The surrounding hills, brooding and silent now, where thousands once worked over a century ago to wrest gold from their unyielding rocks, bear but a few faint scars of man's unrest. Dominating the townsite on the north is the Pig Hill, so called from a rich mine, the Flying Pig. Old timer's stories are recalled. One has it that on top of this hill an Aboriginal woman found a nugget of gold as big as, and the same size as, a woman's shoe. She showed it to Fred Geilis, the publican, who generously gave her two shillings for it . . . . James Rolls and Harry Purcell took out a crushing of twenty ounces to the ton from the Pig Hill.

They talk about the time Bill Clark brought his bullock team straight down the face of the Pig Hill with the wheels locked with tie chains so they tore up the ground; the tracks were visible for many years afterwards. It is so steep that a bulldozer could not climb it without a winch rope. Bill Clark and Con Quill ran the two last hotels to function in Kingsborough, in 1913. The school teacher was Ellie Rowan who became the Mrs. Volkman previously mentioned.

Madagascar rubber vines have almost completely covered the site of Thornborough; they are at Kingsborough too, and all along Caledonia Creek and the Hodgkinson, Leadingham Creek, and Pinnacle Creek. They are a curse in these areas and seem to particularly flourish on nearly all the old mining fields.

Back in 1878, before Herberton drew away their population, the Hodgkinson towns were flourishing. Pugh's Almanac listed the towns of Thornborough, Kingsborough, Stewart Town, and Beaconsfield as the principal towns on the goldfield, with Northcote on its eastern edge. That year the field produced 60,000 ounces of gold.

Storekeepers in Thornborough were then J. V. Mulligan, Clifton and Aplin (a large merchant firm with branches all over the North), J. Loldman, O'Donohue and Greenwood, and G. Schott. There were ten hotels in the town itself, five in Kingsborough, three in Beaconsfield, two in Stewart Town, three in Northcote, and probably a dozen others in mining camps and along the carrying roads. In those days the number of hotels

One of the two houses left in Thornborough — Mrs. E. Volkman's home formerly Wah Lee's Canton Hotel, McLeod Street.

in a mining town or on a field were indicators of the importance and prosperity of the area. A business directory for 1877, lists 22 hotels and nine general stores in Thornborough.

In Thornborough in 1878 there was the Albion (D. McPherson); All Nations (German Charlie); Commercial (J. Little); Crown (W. Freeman); Lindsay's; London (C. Crisp); Queen's (G. O'Loughlan); Royal (J. Byers); Thornborough (J. Dowdell — one of Mulligan's old mates); and Thornborough Arms (J. Middlemiss). Martin Bros.' Hercules crushing mill of sixteen stampers was at work on the river bank on the edge of town. W. J. Cosgrove was a mining agent and auctioneer, G. H. Boughtman an engineer, and Parker and Vautin, assayers.

The weekly newspaper was the "Hodgkinson Mining News", published by John S. Reid. As we have seen, it published reports, now historically valuable, of the opening of the roads to the coast. Only a few tattered copies survive in Brisbane archives. I am indebted to Ruth Kerr for delving into these files to provide much interesting information on the Hodgkinson. In the course of her research, she also provided something about this pioneer newspaper and its rivals.

John Reid sold the "Hodgkinson Mining News" plant to William Douglas Reid and William I. Booth in August 1877. Reid became sole owner soon afterwards, and in May 1879 he sold out to J. R. Boyett. The paper ceased publication in July 1880 following a bitter libel case. There was actual physical violence and some of the paper's type was thrown in the Hodgkinson River during a fight.

As a result, Kingsborough briefly had its own newspaper. A Mr. Pilbrow bought the "Hodgkinson Mining News" plant for 152 pounds and proposed to issue the "Hodgkinson Independent" at Kingsborough. It lasted until September 1881 when the boom town of Herberton looked more inviting. The plant was loaded on a bullock wagon and transported thereto, with M. C. Greene as editor.

Meanwhile, the Thornborough people were not to be outdone by their rival, Kingsborough. They subscribed 200 pounds and purchased a new plant to produce a new paper, "The Hodgkinson Miner". It lasted until October 1881.

The two banks were the Bank of New South Wales and the Queensland National. Later there was a branch of the Bank of North Queensland also. The town supported two solicitors, F. A. Cooper and P. F. O'Reilly, and two chemists, J. Hopkinson and W. R. Irwin. The doctor was then Dr. E. Mohs. In 1880, Dr. J. E. Fonsworth of the Hodgkinson District Hospital was killed when thrown from his horse on the road to Kingsborough.

In those days of the horse, the blacksmith and saddler were important people: D. McPherson and B. Smith were blacksmiths and G. Badkin was a saddler. The lucky miners who wanted to dress for special occasions could get handmade suits from Mr. Halkier the tailor for three guineas. The ladies were catered for by Mary Smith, widow of the pathfinder, Bill Smith. On March 1st., 1880, she married again — a miner named Robert M. Shaw. Thornborough people were also readers, for there were two bookshops — T. Willmett & Co. (a branch of a Townsville firm that still exists), and D. Roberts. Bakers were G. Wason and C. Crisp, and Johnny Byers and Little Bros. were butchers.

The official name for Kingsborough was "Kingston" but popular usage of the former eventually prevailed. It honored Mr. H. E. King, Minister of Works. (From 1874 to 1876 there was a town of the same name on the Palmer Goldfield).

The hotels in 1878 were Bindon's; Royal (kept by R. Mc-Kelvey); McManus' Hotel; Golden Cannon (Miss Muldoon); Reynolds'; King Christian (Petersen); and the Welcome, (W. B. Stenhouse). The three stores were kept by Kiley, Henry and Templeton. G. Frankfort was a blacksmith, and A. McNutt and Carlton Bros. were butchers. Plant and Jackson who were early on the field from the Palmer, had the Vulcan Mill of sixteen stampers. Out along the Port Douglas Road was Rolls' roadside hotel and farm where, like the Jacksons and other early day settlers, they bred fine draught horses for the carriers.

Some ten miles east of Kingsborough, on the headwaters of the Hodgkinson, was the town of Beaconsfield. Practically nothing remains there now, yet a century ago this town, named after the celebrated British Prime Minister, Disraeli, Earl of Beaconsfield, had two stores, three hotels, and a good dam in the river, now long sanded up.

The hotels were the Monarch, kept by J. Weitzel who also had a store; the Exchange, (Norman James), and the Beaconsfield, run by D. N. Rice who was evidently a leading citizen for he had a store and a butchery as well. It was the Monarch mine and its mill of ten stampers that provided most of the employment, and there were other good mines nearby, such as the Just-in-Time which worked off and on until the 'thirties.

W. M. Thompson discovered the Monarch in 1876. He and his mates raised enough rich stone to warrant the erection of a crushing mill and this was done with the assistance of J. Weitzel and H. C. W. Buls. The latter became a leading mining man on the Hodgkinson. His tombstone in the Thornborough cemetery is dated September 27th., 1894. His widow, Fannie Maria, married J. V. Mulligan in 1905. A rocky hill near the Monarch mine was named Bul's Pinnacle after him, though on modern maps it is mispelled as "Bull's".

Henry Buls led a party of diggers to the Palmer rush from the Etheridge and fought off attacks by Aborigines along the way. When the Hodgkinson broke out, he brought mining machinery from the Etheridge, cutting his own track across very rough country so that his bullock wagons could get through. This may have been the plant used for the battery at the Monarch mine. He bought out Thompson's interest in 1878. Thompson, who later became a railway contractor, is credited with making the first sluicebox and wheelbarrow on the Palmer Goldfield, thus being able to work more ground than with the old tin dish and cradle.

(62)

Northcote existed for no more than ten years — 1877-87. It was prettily situated in a big bend of Leadingham Creek where the Port Douglas Road crossed it. Several rich reefs were found in this area and two crushing batteries were at work in 1880. The Princess of Wales of twenty stampers was at Northcote itself and the other was on Slatey Creek.

The town was a coach change and had a telegraph station, and at its peak boasted three hotels — the Northcote, run by Thomas Nathanael Cartwright who died in 1883 and whose ornate tombstone, recently collapsed, is in the little graveyard that marks the site of the town today — the Overlander, kept by R. Gummow, and the Dominion, run by McLean.

Another tombstone marks the grave of Margaret Mary Johnston whose husband William had an hotel in New Northcote in 1897. By that year, most of the town's population had moved to the antimony mines at the new town higher up Leadingham Creek. Mrs. Johnston was burned to death on November 30, 1897 when her clothes caught alight when cooking Christmas puddings, probably over an open fire. Her coffin was carried at night, by the light of hurricane lanterns over the rough track to the graveyard at Old Northcote.

The Bimrose family had an hotel near the battery on the opposite side of Leadingham Creek to Old Northcote. When they heard of the new rush to Herberton, they hurriedly dismantled the timber and iron building, packed it on a bullock wagon, and set out. The route they followed down Leadingham Creek and across the Walsh River would have brought them on to a blazed tree line which ran from Cardwell to the Palmer. This was never more than a pack track and had been a vain attempt by the Cardwell pioneers to capture some of the trade from the Palmer Goldfield. It was a stupendous feat of pathfinding. Both Fraser and Atherton probably brought their cattle this way.

With the rush to Herberton, it was to provide a link with the Hodgkinson towns. Following this old road on horseback,

(63)

I found it barely discernible now, but there are a few cuttings and piles of rock on the "pinches" where some attempt at roadmaking was made. From 1880 to 1893 it probably carried a good deal of traffic. A telegraph line was erected along it to give Herberton telegraphic communication in 1882, the line joining the Cairns-Thornborough wire at Northcote.

An imposing natural gap between enormous granite boulders as big as two-storey houses on this road was known to the pioneers as "Little Hell's Gates", doubtlessly so named after a notorious mountain pass on one of the tracks from Cooktown to the Palmer, where the Aborigines lay in ambush and killed scores of white men and Chinese.

The township of New Northcote, three miles up Leadingham Creek from Old Northcote, was reached by rough tracks from either the latter or Beaconsfield through gaps in the Northcote Hills.

Antimony was worked at New Northcote in the early 'Eighties and a smelter was erected, managed by John Mundey. The brick chimney, sixty feet high, was a landmark until 1942 when someone dynamited it for the sake of the bricks, but most of them still lie there in a heap.

New Northcote had four hotels and a school at the beginning of this century. The Winfield family were some of its citizens. The Irvinebank Mining Company owned the antimony smelters at that time, but because of low prices and the wind up of the company in 1919, operations ceased and the town disappeared. Just after World War II, when antimony was ninety pounds per ton, Dan Molloy had a profitable mine and battery there. Up to 1941, Northcote had produced 1500 tons of antimony; the mines included the Emily, Ethel, and Black Bess.

At Old Northcote, Harry Thompson of Mareeba had a large gold mine and a battery in the early years of World War II. It was called the Great Australian.

The Minnie Moxham gold mine is further up Leadingham

(64)

and was opened in 1912, having been missed by the early Hodgkinson miners. Connected with it were Charlie Jenkinson, Fred Baines, Tom Kelly, F. Gregory, and Bob Muhldorff of Mareeba. This mine worked off and on until the beginning of World War II.

The gold reefs extended for many miles down the Hodgkinson River below Thornborough. Opposite the northern end of the great bulk of Mt. Mulligan, was the township of Stewart Town. There were three hotels and two stores here in 1878, and the principal reefs in the area were the Union, Geraldine, and Result. Blair and Co. had the Loadstone Battery of ten stamps. The storekeepers were Barry Bros., Brophy Bros., and G. Miall. W. Moore and J. Crowley were butchers. Another flourishing township was Woodville, first called Watsonville, at the Dagworth mine.

Nearly a hundred years ago the Union was a rich mine. The machinery for the mill was brought by Crowley's bullock team over the fearful track from the Palmer and erected by a man known as "Darky" Green. Members of this mining syndicate were shadowy men of the past — Lyons, Grogan, Murphy, Hohenhouse, Johnson, Hughes, McManus, and Rank. Some of their descendents are still with us. From the Hodgkinson came many of North Queensland's citizens who helped mould other towns and districts to prosperity.

There were men like George Jonathan Evenden from Rochester, England, who made bricks and built some of the brick buildings in Thornborough.

He arrived carrying his swag up the packers' track from Port Douglas, but the bricklayer's trowel he possessed was to prove more useful, and lucrative, than his miner's pick and shovel. He stayed for thirty years until his death in August, 1907. He and J. V. Mulligan were firm friends, and they both died within days of one another.

Evenden is distinguished as being the first chairman of the Woothakata Divisional Board at Thornborough in November,

1879. He was chairman for many terms, totalling 22 years out of the 27 he served the Local Authority. He was appointed a Justice of the Peace in 1883 and in the 'nineties, when a magistrate, he caused the bush Aborigines to be brought close to town to prevent them from being shot down like kangaroos.

Evenden brought his family up from Brisbane in 1878. They rode on William Louden's bullock wagon from Port Douglas. Their home in Thornborough was noted for its beautiful garden. Mrs. Evenden died on 16 July, 1888. Grandchildren live in Mareeba and Cairns.

The Woothakata Divisional Board comprised most of the present Mareeba Shire and the name is reputed to be an Aboriginal word meaning "mountain of strange shape" referring to Mt. Mulligan. This early day shire covered 27,380 square miles. In 1885 the population was 1,800; there were 360 rateable properties and the revenue was a mere £643 per annum! The first members, in 1879, were Hodgkinson pioneers — W. A. Martin, battery owner; W. B. Stenhouse, publican of Kingsborough; W. C. Little, butcher; T. Jackson, battery owner; B. Smith, W. B. Redmond, W. Blackmore, and R. Jones, miners.

In 1885, with G. J. Evenden still chairman, the members were H. C. W. Buls, Thomas Templeton, J. J. Denny, R. C. Eagle, G. M. Towner, and W. Blisner. Secretary was Arthur Arnold Mayou. The board (shire council) met in its hall in McLeod Street, Thornborough, on the first Tuesday of each month. In 1919, with Thornborough a ghost town and Mareeba in the ascendent, the headquarters were moved to Mareeba. John Rank the shire clerk, moved with it. The building was also shifted to Mareeba where it served for years until the present concrete premises were erected in Walsh Street. Additions have been added in more recent times. Incidentally, G. J. Evenden was John Rank's father-in-law and his nephew is J. Arthur Rank, the film magnate,.

Thornborough's last burst of activity was probably in 1914 when the railway from Dimbulah to Mt. Mulligan was under construction and a sale of the first town lots at the latter place was held at the Court House, Thornborough, on August 15th. W. Williams was then the official in charge and the last warden at Thornborough. The Cummings family who lived in what had been Wooster's Hotel, were among the last inhabitants.

Gordon Hay recalls that Chinese New Year was celebrated in Thornborough right up 1923 for Wah Lee's store was possibly the last business place to close. He also remembers that in 1913 he saw squads of Chinese disinterring the bones of their countrymen, buried thirty or forty years before and despite the absence of any markers they apparently knew just where to dig. The remains, which after such a lapse of time, had to be recovered by sifting the ground, were to be taken back to China. Gordon says the Chinese must have been buried with their boots on as the sieving brought up hobnails and steel heel and toe-plates, eyelets, etc. Before the graves were filled in again, strips of white paper were thrown in "to pay the devil." There was still a Chinese josshouse in Thornborough at that time.

KINGSBOROUGH STATE SCHOOL, 1902-06.

Mrs. A. Carmichael (nee Winfield), now of Cairns, remembers that Mr. Plunkett was head teacher at Kingsborough for many years and was transferred to Marmor near Rockhampton. Following him was Mr. Kilby, then Sam Favell, Mr. Orr, and Miss Boyns. Mrs. Carmichael also recalls that Kingsborough had a lady doctor, Dr. Rosalind Taylor, at the hospital.

Pupils at Kingsborough School in 1902-06 were: Dickenson, Crittenden, Westbury, Joseph Murphy, Jack Whittle, Harry Hatfield, Dick Collins, Henry Gadd, Mark Trevarthen, Edward Listner, Julia Howie, Patrick Winfield, Harry Fryer, Malcolm Swanson, Les Raper, George Robins, Tom Lees, W. Richards-Harris, —Bolton, —Reid, Geraghty, Ellie Rowan, W. Clark, Jack Maund, Jack Manning, Pat Quill, —McElhinney, —Minogue, —Keating, Frank Lawlor, —James, William Fitzgerald, and James Rolls. This is practically a list of the families who lived in Kingsborough or nearby in those days. Many have descendents still living in the Far North of Queensland.

CHAPTER 5

IN THE DAYS OF COBB & CO.

Tin on the Wild River — the Founding of Herberton — the Granite Creek Coach Change — Coaching Days.

In November 1879, a party of fourteen men, led by John Newell and William Jack, and guided by John Atherton, arrived at a spot now known as the One Mile on the Wild River. The party divided, Newell, Jack and some mates going upstream, the others downstream. They were disappointed at the small quantities of alluvial tin in their prospecting dishes so without wasting time, all returned to Tinaroo, some of the men going off to the Woolgar, a Flinders River tributary where a new gold discovery had been made. Newell, Jack, and some of the others returned to the Hodgkinson.

In April, 1880, a Chinaman reported that tin had been found at a place seventy miles from Thornborough, and that a crowd of Chinese were preparing to rush there.

Newell and Jack concluded he was referring to the Wild River locality. Rather than see what may after all be a worthwhile tinfield overrun by Chinese, Newell and Jack decided to return and prospect the area more fully. Accompanied by two mates, Brown and Brandon, they hastened back to the old spot.

This time they found payable tin in Prospector's Gully, also great slabs of cassiterite. This they did not recognise as tin ore, but by working up the gully they discovered the Great Northern lode on April 20, 1880. Camped on the site of the old post office, they smelted tin ore in the stump of a tree, using a felt hat for draught.

John Newell then made a fast ride across country, with wild blacks all the way, to Thornborough by way of the Watsonville Range, the Walsh River at the Planted Tree Crossing, the Mutchilba Crossing, and then straight through the bush. He filed applications for a Reward Claim with Warden Mowbray in Thornborough. The discoverers received a grant of sixty acres at thirty shillings per acre. It was the first official discovery of lode tin in Northern Queensland.

If Mulligan had not had his eyes so blinded by the glitter of gold that he was not interested in other minerals, he could have had that honor. It would have been timely, too, for in 1880, his storekeeping business in Thornborough was bankrupt. He had trusted too many people and been too liberal in helping others.

"Tin on the Wild River!" was the cry that went from camp to camp, from one bark hut homestead to another, yelled by the mailmen as they rode by, as horsemen greeted one another; the only subject discussed in the shanty bars from Port Douglas to Thornborough, from Woodville to Northcote. Within days an excited crowd was turning off the Hodgkinson road at the Big Mitchell and heading for Granite Creek, following it up by Mt. Abbott to the western edge of the scrub and somehow struggling over the rough gullies and up the steep sides of the Herberton Range to the new Eldorado — named Herberton because it was on the headwaters of the Herbert River.

In July 1880, Christie Palmerston, Mullins, and McLean cut a track through the Atherton Scrub, and soon carriers were loading machinery and building materials in Port Douglas for Herberton — ten to sixteen days' slow journey over The Bump, through low country impassable in the wet season, across Granite Creek, across miles of basalt boulders in the open forest, then through dense jungle and up the Herberton Range, double-banking on the pinches. Packers could travel faster, and reaped a rich harvest.

From Emerald End homestead, John Atherton saw the dust of their passing. By the eddying pools and green flats of Granite Creek the carriers and packers lingered awhile, the din of their horse and bullock bells and the flickering lights of a score of campfires cleaving the solitude of the bush.

This spot, half way between Port Douglas and Herberton, was a convenient camping place. Quickly, in the manner of the

(69)

times, came passenger-laden mail coaches — first run by Murphy and Macdonald, but acquired by Cobb and Co. on 18th. September 1882.

For the convenience of the coach travellers and the hundreds who streamed along that dusty road all through the dry season of 1880, John Atherton engaged Chinese carpenters to build a two-storeyed hotel, rest house, and coach change on the high south bank of Granite Creek, right at the crossing. Eccles and Lloyd conducted this business, and so these families became the first citizens of the town of Mareeba. But so far it was known only as the Granite Creek coach change on the lonely road to Herberton. All around was a waste of grey-green bush and heaps of basalt boulders among the tall speargrass.

Joe Eccles had two good horse teams on the Port Douglas-Hodgkinson road, and he was able to cart all the supplies needed for his business at Granite Creek. A creek on the Chillagoe Railway bears his name.

His wife managed the roadside hotel very efficiently and was a popular hostess. Mrs. Eccles gave birth to the first white child born in Mareeba, but a few weeks later the mother died tragically. The pioneer women had no conveniences which today would be considered essential. All the washing for the hotel had to be done down in the bed of Granite Creek, and all water needed for other purposes had to be carried up the steep bank in kerosene tins.

Evidently Mrs. Eccles did not shun hard work even with an infant to nurse, for she collapsed from sunstroke after a big day of washing in the creek.

Joe was on the road with teams, but a messenger was sent to fetch him, and to bring a doctor over forty miles from Port Douglas. Mrs. Eccles died a few days later, and her unmarked grave was probably the first in what is now Mareeba. With several others it is situated right on the creek bank almost in the town street, shaded by a gnarled old frangipanni tree. The one marked grave is that of Henry McCrohan and is dated

March 1888.

A Chinaman built a store on the north side of Granite Creek as soon as the Herberton rush began, but there is a story that it was burned and looted by Aborigines and the Chinaman speared. Freeman, from Thornborough, built a shanty there in 1885 but within a year it was destroyed by fire.

With the opening of Herberton, the Port Douglas Road lengthened. From the early Wild River mines, eager prospectors pushed out over the rugged mountains westward, their discoveries resulting in the founding of Watsonville, Irvinebank, Montalbion, and other centres. Soon the Cobb and Co. coaches were running right through from Port Douglas to Georgetown, and still further to Croydon, pausing at the many mining camps on the way.

Thus, within a decade, the tide of settlement had turned full circle — from the Etheridge to the Palmer and back again via the Hodgkinson and Herberton.

The unknown land beyond the coastal ranges that had lured brave Kennedy to his death and Hann and Mulligan along the paths of fame, was unknown no longer. The hinterland of Cairns had been opened to receive the pioneers, and drawn onward by promise of golden reward they had come, and were conquering.

Few now remember those bearded weather-beaten men — and those courageous women — of long ago who rode down the blazed lines that were the highways of yesterday. They were the brave souls who laid the foundations of our present prosperity.

In fancy we will follow those old roads back, and their routes and stages come echoing to us down the years. In some places they can still be followed by the faint axe-marks and blazes on the ancient trees.

The story of the old roads out of Port Douglas through what is now the Shires of Mareeba, Atherton, and Herberton, reads like a romance, for interwoven with it are tales of the coaching days and the carriers and pioneers who lived along that forgotten highway. It is an essential part of our history, and for some of this information I am indebted to the late Thos. H. Crowe who once lived in Mareeba; he could speak from personal experience of the days of the Granite Creek coach change. His parents ran the change at the Little Mitchell in the 'eighties and early 'nineties.

From old Port Douglas and the carriers' camping ground at Craiglie, in imagination we follow the Bump Road upward — up Slatey Pinch, around The Blackguard, and down to The Landing; through heavy scrub to Running Creek, and across the dreaded Gluepot, then up a long hard pull through more scrub to emerge into forest country at Cobb and Co's first stage, in charge of Jack Allen. The seven-horse team was changed here. All harness was also changed, replaced by fresh sets, oiled and polished. Cobb and Co. had to maintain a big plant of horses on this road. From Allen's, a five horse team took the coach on over the Rocky Mowbray Crossing where Reynolds' hotel was situated from 1885 onwards.

O'Donnells were early settlers on top of the range, then came Mullavey's Hotel with Groves' place next, and Hughes' shanty near where Mt. Molloy later sprang up. There were big Chinese gardens along Spear Creek — so named because a white woman was speared there in the early days of the Hodgkinson. As previously mentioned, the packers' track turned off near here and ran in an almost direct line to Kingsborough.

Travelling southward, leaving the dust of many horse and bullock teams far behind, the coach rattled on to the next stage — Crowe's coach change and carriers' camping ground at the Little Mitchell where good food and accommodation for man and beast could always be found. When the railway reached Mareeba in 1893, Mrs. Crowe shifted to the north bank of Granite Creek and conducted a boarding house.

At the Little Mitchell stage the old time settlers met and parted — the Bakers of Font Hill, McDonalds of Northedge,

A Cobb and Co. horse change or "stage." (From a drawing, artist unknown).

Andersons of Southedge, and the Wades, Wrights, and Spurriers from Dora Creek. It was the junction of bush highways. The Sorensens lived at the Big Mitchell until the 'nineties. They then formed a station at the Mud Springs at the foot of the Granite Range.

At Granite Creek the Port Douglas and Croydon coaches used to meet and stay the night. Leaving Granite Creek at 4 a.m., Rocky Creek was the next stage, a spot much favoured by teamsters going down to Port Douglas with bagged tin from Herberton and smelted ingots from Irvinebank and Montalbion. Barney Hayes had an hotel at Rocky Creek, and also owned a butcher's shop. Coach passengers breakfasted there on fresh juicy steaks; a rest here was welcome after a jarring journey over basalt boulders. The next settler's home was Pat Molloy's Rocky Plains Station, then came the tiny settlement of Martin Town (Tolga) on the edge of the scrub.

By a tunnel-like track through the scrub, knee deep in red mud in the wet, the coach came to Kelly's hotel at Prior Pocket on or near the present site of Atherton, then on to Scrubby Creek where Matt Petersen kept an hotel. He afterwards shifted to Biboohra where his descendents still reside.

Wrote the late Jim McDonald in a letter to me in 1969: "There were fine drivers and fine horses back in the old coaching days, all right. People like myself who can clearly recall the days of Cobb and Co. or who actually rode in the lurching thoroughbrace coaches over the long rough stages of the North, are a vanishing race. Very soon none who actively participated in, or who remember those stirring times, will be left. Such is the march of time and of progress . . . . "

The late Jim McDonald's father built an hotel at Tolga in 1898, opposite Cobb and Co's change.

Through the Chinese settlement of Carrington, then with a fresh seven-horse team, the Herberton Range was tackled.

The rugged Herberton Range rose like a wall. Horses were again changed here for the road ahead — a white ribbon snaking up the spurs and around the mountainside with a long steep "pinch." The male passengers were always asked to walk to save the horses. Lunch would have been very welcome at Finnegan's Hotel in Herberton — a night stage for Cobb's coach on the way back from Croydon.

In the heat of afternoon, a fresh team climbed another steep range westward to Watsonville, then on through more ranges to Orient Camp, and into Montalbion at sundown. Cobb's passengers stayed at the Miners' Arms Hotel in busy Montalbion, its smelters pouring out a stream of silver-lead ingots.

The coach was on the road again at 5 a.m., and at The Pocket change where Sam Luxton was in charge for years, the coach from Croydon was met again. The next change was Denford's hotel at California Creek where hundreds of "stream tinners" once gathered a harvest of alluvial to be bagged and packed down to Port Douglas. Lunch was taken at Emmerson's on the Sandy Tate. They were a family of pioneer cattlemen and teamsters. Charlie Emmerson had bullock teams on the Port Douglas Road, and had also carried to the Palmer.

The hard rough road was on the Gulf watershed now. The third night would be spent at Petty's change at Bullock Creek. Then next day it was on across the sandy bed of the Lynd to the running stream, Fossilbrook, then on past Firth's Mt. Surprise Station, once known as "the back of sundown."

Quartz Hill was the fourth night stage from Port Douglas. Next day the Einasleigh River and the rough Newcastle Range were crossed. A coach and team capsized there over a narrow ledge the old timers say. The passengers, dust-grimed and weary — no luxuries like hot baths available on the trip — arrived at Georgetown on the fifth day after leaving Port Douglas. The two hundred mile journey cost five sovereigns. Another two days would take the travellers on to Croydon, the Gilbert River a major hazard in the Wet. From Croydon it was another two days over level country to Normanton.

If coaching was a trial for horses and drivers it was for

(75)

passengers also, yet as Tom Crowe said, when he was a boy he thought a Cobb's coach the fastest and most exciting thing on earth.

With the opening of the Granite Creek coach change, the Port Douglas-Hodgkinson road was altered. A branch coach service ran direct from Granite Creek to Thornborough via Northcote. In 1885, James Gibbons' Royal Hotel was Cobb and Co's booking office in Thornborough.

In March 1959, Tom Crowe had some of his reminiscences recorded by the Cairns Historical Society, in their Bulletin No. 5.

"The coaches used were of the thoroughbrace type, that is, they were suspended on leather straps called thoroughbraces. They were of eight to sixteen passenger capacity. The latter had a box or driver's seat on top in the front that would accommodate three passengers as well as the driver. A similar seat on top at the back held four passengers. The body of the coach carried eight passengers inside. Under the box seat was a large boot for mailbags, and under the rear seat was a large luggage rack. On the roof was another luggage and mail rack enclosed with an iron rail.

"When a coach arrived at a 'stage', the driver would stay in his seat until the groom came out and unhitched the team and led the horses away. Then he would get down and deliver mails and parcels, and if a meal stage, eat his meal. When departure time came the driver would climb up on to the box and sit down. The groom would lead out the two wheelers from the stables, hand their reins up to the driver, and then hitch them to the coach. He went back and brought out the leaders and, after handing their reins up to the driver, hitched them up also and stood by their heads. The driver called 'All aboard!' and the passengers climbed in. When they were seated he called 'right away!' The groom stepped aside, the horses reared into the air and the coach would get under way."

All the drivers took great pride in their teams. They liked to have a good "scratch puller" in their team.

(76)

What wonderful horses, and what hardy men those Cobb and Co. drivers were! What experts at handling spanking teams through dense bush, over rough mountain ranges and treacherous river crossings, guiding passengers and mails safely to their destinations year after year. They were an integral part of this Pioneer Country. None of those drivers in the days of the Port Douglas Road are still with us. Long ago they drove their last team over the last mountain range into the sunset.

Echoing out of the past come their deeds, and their names — Joe Hirschberg, Bill Millett, Rod McCrae, Jack Allen, Bob Walsh, Jim Hutchinson, Robert Croft, Sam Cousins, Jack Warner, Ted Richards, Joe Greer, Ralph Fairbanks, and Bill Richardson.

Old time drivers who were still living around Mareeba thirty-five years ago and were known to the writer, were Joe Mosch, Jack Swan, and Mick Carr.

The great coaching firm of Cobb and Co. which, at its zenith, was harnessing six thousand horses every day to haul its American-type stage coaches on countless routes throughout Australia, extended its operations to Far Northern Queensland in 1882 when it bought out Murphy and Macdonald on 18th. September and began services from Port Douglas to Herberton and Thornborough. Bill Millett and Tom Crowe came to Port Douglas to inaugurate the service. Rod McCrae was driver-manager. In 1888, Ned Gallagher of Southern coaching fame became general manager, and shortly afterwards Rod McCrae and Bill Millett left Cobb and Co. and started an opposition line out of Port Douglas.

The late Tom Crowe, once of the Little Mitchell change, recalled that Cobb's coaches were "lovely coaches to ride in; they would rock like a cradle on their leather springs. If sitting on the box seat when the vehicle dipped into a gutter you would think you were going over the footboard until you got used to the motion. Then the only inconvenience was the dust which got pretty thick at times as we would be passing packers and travellers every day." He did not say anything about the

(77)

lack of cushioned seats and resultant bruises on rough roads.

Nevertheless, it is significant that when an opposition coach line started on the Port Douglas Road it got most of the passengers even though Cobb and Co. cut their fares to a minimum. Tom Crowe told me how it happened.

"In the wet season of the year 1888, my father took sick and died at the Little Mitchell change — fever and ague was very bad on the road at times. This meant the old trio of McCrae, Crowe, and Millet was broken again. Arthur Lambert came to groom for Cobb and Co. at the Little Mitchell after my father's death.

"Shortly after this, Tom Gallagher became road manager for Cobb and Co. and Rod McCrae was given notice he would be reduced from driver-manager to driver only, and his salary would be reduced from £22 per month to £16 [that is $8.00 per week, not a princely wage considering the skill and responsibility involved]. McCrae and Millet decided then and there to resign and start a coach line of their own from Port Douglas to Herberton.

"They had a good deal of work before them in getting horses together and forming stages; they were soon very unpopular with Cobb's managers. One thing they did not lack was the loyalty of the people on the road and particularly of the travelling public.

"Prior to this, the fare by Cobb and Co. was £5 from Port Douglas to Herberton. McCrae and Millet brought it down to £3/10/-. Cobbs cut it to £3.; McCrae and Millett cut it to £2/10/-. Cobbs came down to £2, so McCrae and Millet cut it to 30 shillings. Cobbs immediately came down to £1, but McCrae and Millet did not go below 30 shillings, and they still got the passengers. Cobb and Co. made another cut to ten shillings. I heard Ned Gallagher (who was now driver-manager) say one day that if they didn't get the passengers for that they would carry them for nothing and 'shout' them a bottle of porter at each stage. It never came to that and Cobbs put their fare up again to £1, and McCrae and Millet were still getting the bulk of the passengers.

"I have seen Cobb and Co's lovely thoroughbrace coach and their team of fine horses drive up to our place with one and two passengers and sometimes only the driver and the mail. What a difference to before the advent of the opposition! Then they nearly always had ten or twelve passengers.

"Then up would drive Bill Millet with passengers hanging on everywhere like flies. Millet would change horses more often than Cobb and they would always be in before him. He used to change at the foot of the range (The Bump) at Reynolds and at Reynolds' again at the Rocky Mowbray, then at Groves' Weatherboards, and again at our place at the Little Mitchell, then at Granite Creek. Ours was the dinner stage going up and the breakfast stage going down. My younger brother Ned and myself used to groom for Millet.

"Almanacks were very popular with business people in those days. McCrae and Millet's almanack depicted a big bulldog representing Cobb and Co., with a big bone. McCrae and Millet were represented as an old crow who had the big end of the bone which was called 'The Bone of Contention.'

"Jack Warner came on to the road about this time to drive for Cobb and Co. I think he was driving previous to this between Georgetown and Croydon; but this was the first time he worked on the Port Douglas Road."

Ned Gallagher was peeved at the patronage the opposition were getting, and the Little Mitchell change was the only one used jointly by the two coach lines. He altered this by moving Cobbs' change to Charlie O'Brien's place not far from Crowe's change. Jim Castles was their groom and Mrs. Castles kept the dinner and breakfast stage.

Until this happened, the Little Mitchell change was a busy place on the old Port Douglas Road. There were the homesteads of the Crowes, O'Briens, Louis Burgarlet, and Ardah, and a Chinaman's garden which employed half a dozen Celestials. Cobb and Co. drivers not previously mentioned included Bill

(79)

Hutchison, and Bob Welch. Another important Cobb and Co. employee was Bob Barry who used to travel the road and do their horse clipping.

The old road provided a livelihood for many. There was George Bell who used to stay at the Little Mitchell for long periods and make yokes for the bullockies, repair harness for the horse teams, and plait greenhide whips for both. Tommy Harris used to travel up and down in his wagonette and keep the hotels and shanties supplied with cordials.

A Chinese named Ah Kee used to hawk vegetables and fruit; he had one horse and used to carry two baskets himself. Sometimes he carried as much as the horse.

Circuses and menageries used to travel the road en route to the mining towns; two companies that Tom Crowe remembered were Ashton's and St. Leon's. And then, of course, there was Annie Bags, an eccentric well educated woman who roamed all the roads to the mining fields from Charters Towers northwards, carrying her possessions in a couple of sugarbags and wearing clothes also made from bags and accompanied by a mob of cats, dogs, a goat, and a cockatoo. She claimed to be a Hungarian countess.

The rivalry between the two coach lines was to last but a short time, for already a far greater opposition to Cobb and Co. was looming: the Cairns-Herberton railway was gradually climbing the range to Kuranda as the last decade of the old century dawned.

In anticipation of its coming, the Government engaged surveyor Alfred Starcke to lay out a few township blocks on the north bank of Granite Creek as long ago as 1887.

Part of the history of the North surrounds the old Granite Creek coach change of the "roaring 'eighties".

The coach from Herberton would come pounding up the rough bush track—Byrnes Street today—amid clouds of red dust, lathered horses, jingle of harness, and creak of bodywork rocking

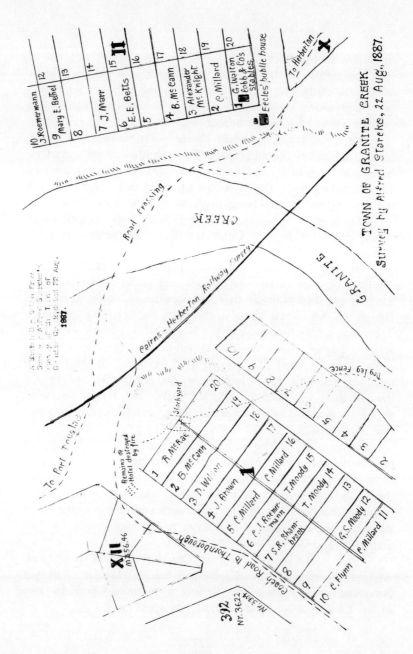

TOWN OF GRANITE CREEK

Surveyed by Alfred Starcke, 22 Aug., 1887.

GRANITE CREEK

To Herbert Inn

Eccles' public house

Cobb & Co's Stables

II
10 J. Roemermann 12
9 Mary E. Bethel 13
8 14
7 J. Marr 15
6 E.E. Betts 16
5 17
4 B. McCann 18
3 Alexander McKnight 19
2 C. Millard 20
1 G. Walton

Road Crossing

Cairns - Herberton Railway Survey

To Port Douglas

A Sketch Map taken from Survey of Alfred Starcke's Part 1 of the T'n of Granite Creek dated 22 Aug. 1887.

Stockyard

Remains of Hotel destroyed by fire

Dog Leg Fence

I
1 R. McRae 20
2 B. McCann 19
3 D. Wilson 18
4 J. Brown 17
5 C. Millard C. Millard 16
6 C.J. Roemermann T. Moody 15
7 S.R. Shambrook T. Moody 14
8 13
9 G.S. Moody 12
10 C. Flynn C. Millard 11

Coach Road to Thornborough

X/11
M. 56.46

392
Nr. 3324

(81)

on leather thoroughbraces.

The clothes of the bearded driver and passengers would be covered in dust; with a swish of skirts, the ladies would cross the rough board verandah in quest of tea and cordials, while the men crowded into the bar.

They would talk of many things — of mines and teams, drivers, and newly-blazed tracks. The roughly dressed teamsters, miners, bushworkers, and nattily attired commercial travellers, the air reeking with Derby tobacco, would talk about the new and exciting discoveries being made in this Pioneers' Country.

Memories of those spacious days have been handed down — the colourful days of Cobb and Co., the packers, and the teamsters.

The late Tom Crowe told me: "When the coaches left the old Port Douglas Road, the carriers and packers also gradually left that old time highway that had seen many happy days, even though we, who lived along it, did have our trials and troubles. There was a lot of sickness in the North in those days, especially fever and ague. We who loved it will never forget that old road — it always seemed like a symbol of freedom. It was a road that led on into mysterious, new country, with always the thought there was something better further out. That was what urged the pioneers on, I suppose. That, and the certainty better times lay ahead."

We can still follow those blazed lines back, and it is not difficult to conjure up pictures of those brave folk who peopled those dim years. Looking at their axemarks on the trees, and the washed out ruts made by iron-shod wheels, one may see in fancy, in the van of them all, racing neck and neck, two lurching, swaying coaches drawn by phantom teams, one driven by Ned Gallagher and one by Rod McCrae.

Cobb and Co. left the Port Douglas Road in July 1891. By then the railway from Cairns had reached Myola. Surveyor Amos surveyed a road from Myola to Granite Creek by way of the Clohesy River and £1000 was spent on it.

Reproduction by courtesy John Sands Ltd.

Jim Davies was an early settler on a branch of the Clohesy River that now bears his name — Davies Creek. To some of the old timers it is still known as the "Second Clohesy". He opened a shanty and coach change there. Incidentally, it was on the Clohesy River that the first tobacco was grown in the Cairns Hinterland. It was produced by a settler named Burdett in the early 'nineties. It was an indication of great things to come.

There were other coach services which operated independently of Cobb and Co. before and after the railway reached Mareeba in 1893. Harry Chatfield, remembered as a big man with an outsize moustache, ran a coach from Mareeba to Almaden and Chillagoe before the Chillagoe Railway was built. Cobb and Co. still ran a service from Almaden to Georgetown and Croydon when Almaden became the railhead in 1900. Joe Hirschberg, known for his colorful language, was one driver. Another was Robert Croft. In January, 1907, J. S. Love bought the Almaden-Croydon run from Cobb & Co.

Seventy-five years ago Bill Wall ran a coach service from Herberton through Watsonville, Orient Camp, and Montalbion to Irvinebank. That was when Irvinebank was on a "dead end" road from Montalbion and the latter was a flourishing town on the Georgetown Road.

Those who drove mail coaches and mail buckboards between Irvinebank and Boonmoo when the Chillagoe Railway reached the latter point in 1900 were Jack Williams, Willie Arbouin, Manny Borghero, and Willy Warner. Bill McDonald and a son ran coaches in this same area. Some horses and mailbags were lost at Chinaman's Creek five miles from Irvinebank when the horses fell at the washed-out crossing one wet season. Alby Bimrose also drove a coach from Boonmoo, through Irvinebank and Coolgarra to Mt. Garnet before the Mt. Garnet line was opened in 1902. Bill Lees was another coach driver.

The last coach driver on the Herberton-Irvinebank run was Cecil St. L. Holdcroft, O.B.E., later a well known Herberton

(84)

businessman, shire council chairman for many terms, and chairman of the Cairns Harbour Board for years. He drove the coach with from four to seven horses in 1923-24 until he replaced the horses with an International truck — the first motor truck in Herberton. Cecil Holdcroft gave his coach and horses to Fred Westerman who ran a service from Herberton to Silver Valley and Hot Springs. Jim Cook, Mick Larsen, and Fred Moss had it as a packhorse mail which lasted until after World War II.

During World War I., the drivers of the 'Nineties were still handling the ribbons. Bill Wall and Mick and Terry Carr were on the Dimbulah to Wolfram Camp road. In earlier times, Bill Johnson had the coach service with Bill Hambling his right-hand man. After using a coach, then a buckboard for years, and finally a truck, Bill Hambling was the mailman up to about 1950. A pioneer of the district, he was raised on Leadingham Creek just below Northcote where his father, John Hambling, settled in the early 'eighties.

CHAPTER 6

FOLLOWING THE BLAZED LINES BACK

The Carrying Roads — the Teams — Mules and Packers — Early Herberton — "The Wild River Times" — Pioneer Store-keepers.

The carriers and the packers followed roads that were strange to the mail coaches. What is now the Mareeba and Herberton Shires had many of these now forgotten roads. They were not roads in the real sense. They were merely blazed tree lines with a few trees cut down to allow the passage of wagons, with a few cuttings at the creek crossings. As one track became impassable because of either bog or washouts, the teams made another alongside. Because of this, it is still quite easy to follow these roads except where progress in the form of cultivation and fencing have obliterated them.

From the Port Douglas Road in the 'eighties one could turn off at the Little Mitchell and follow the slow moving teams past the Mud Springs where Tom Totten, later Sorensens, lived, then turn off the Thornborough road and go down through the present Paddy's Green tobacco lands (the ruts used to be still quite plain through Cliff Johnson's farm in the 'forties) where Abbott and Fearon had a cattle station, to the swamp country at the Dingo Creek-Cattle Creek junction.

One could follow Cattle Creek down to the Walsh River where the Ganes had a homestead in the early days. Just below here, Jack Cahill's place at Parada was a favourite camp for carriers and packers. Cahill, who had come from the Palmer with John Doyle, had some big teams on the road also.

Crossing the Walsh at Parada the road went down to Price's Bend, then southward by Catherine Creek and so over the mountains to Montalbion. There was poison peach on this old road and the carriers had to be ever watchful.

When Muldiva silver mines, and later Calcifer copper mines were opened in the late 'eighties, the carriers with loading for those centres turned off the old Montalbion road at Cattle Creek, crossed Kimalo Station of today, then through a gap in the McLeod Hills, named for William McLeod who was with Mulligan, and came to McGuinness' Bend on Leadingham Creek. Where Wally Reichardt, later of Mareeba, grew tobacco for many years, there was a big camping ground.

Crossing the Walsh, this road — known as the Chillagoe Road — passed Chinese gardens where horse feed and vegetables could be obtained. There were camping places at Eureka Creek, Eccles Creek, and Emu Creek. The teams crawled through the fine white dust to Oaky Creek where a township arose, called Wadetown after Harry Wade, a popular hotelkeeper, later of Irvinebank. Nearby, the Bamford mines came into prominence during the first decade of this century. The dreaded Featherbed Range was one of the hazards on this road.

The teams crawled on, six, eight, to ten miles per day, past Koorboora wolfram mines and over the Spring Mattress — or was it the Straw Bed — (another rough range) to Ned Ryan's shanty near the site of Almaden. Four miles further on, in the limestone country, was the turn-off to Calcifer and the Tate Tin Mines. Another few miles brought the carriers to Muldiva. Then began the long weary journey back to Port Douglas with silver-lead ingots. Others would load up bagged tin at the Tate, and copper ingots from Calcifer.

In the late 'seventies there was considerable rivalry between horse teamsters and bullockies. The urge for speed was beginning to exercise men's minds, and the horse was faster than the bullock; but bullocks could haul heavier loads. Then came the terrible tick (redwater) plague that decimated the working bullocks as it did the beef cattle. In 1895, the carrying roads were littered with dead bullocks; whole teams were lost in a night. Bullock wagons were forced off the road, and proud horse teams took their place.

"Scratch pulling" was a favourite sport among horse teamsters, and some champions took part in contests. Bill Clelland's grey, Ranger, and Alex Thompson's bay, Tom, were well remembered by old timers. They said that Ranger was the champion leader on the road; he knew every turn in the old Port Douglas Road and to the camps further out, and when called upon to use all his mighty strength in a contest, he would first dig holes for his front feet to get a better grip. Never again will we see the like of those horses, or the men who drove them. Both are a vanished breed.

About forty-two horse teams, forty-four bullock teams, and thirty pack teams were using the Herberton-Port Douglas Road in its heyday.

The first wagon from Port Douglas arrived at Herberton on 11th. September, 1880. Before that, pack teams were on the road, and hundreds of people walked, despite the danger from hostile blacks.

On 20th. November, 1880, a packhorse mail service was started between Cairns and Herberton, (the mailman was Bob Croft, later a coach driver) over an incredible mountain trail — now followed in part by Gillies Highway — cut through the jungle and over the mountains to the Mulgrave River Valley by James Robson, another of that shadowy band of "men who blazed the track".

The packers contributed a great deal to the progress of Herberton, and saved Cairns from extinction by Port Douglas. It is recorded that on 24th. July 1880, eight hundredweight of bagged tin ore arrived in Cairns by pack team from Newell and Jack's propecting claim at Herberton.† The packers may have followed Atherton's track down the range from Tinaroo. A more direct link was needed. An old record of 1884 states that "the Cairns road" turned off the Port Douglas Road at Scrubby Creek (Carrington). This was the track cut through the jungle and

---

† Ruth Kerr believes, from her research, that the first tin ore to arrive in Cairns from Herberton was one ton from Woodburn and Stubley's claim, carried by packer, Bernard Hynes.

over the ranges by James Robson.

Associate of John Atherton on the Tinaroo tinfield, Robson stuck to the field to the last. When a track was needed to link Cairns with Herberton, he rose to the occasion. In a short time he blazed a route that passed in the vicinity of Kulara, traversed the almost impenetrable Boar Pocket scrub, and descended the range by a steep, winding track down the Mulgrave spurs — the Gillies Highway was constructed over part of the route in 1924-26. But Robson's feat was one of unsurpassed bushmanship through that dense, dark rain forest still peopled by Aborigines who had had no contact with white men.

One of the most important outcomes of the opening of this pack track was the idea, born in Cairns, of linking that seaport with Herberton by a railway. Cairns owed a great debt to the valiant Scot, James Robson. On January 1, 1884, forty-eight citizens of Cairns signed a testimonial and presented him with a gold watch. Considering that over a quarter of a million pounds' worth of goods were conveyed over this track by pack teams during the next few months, a gold watch does not seem much compensation.

Tinaroo was the home of Robson and his brothers, David, Alick, and Joey. James Robson used to cross the Barron River by dinghy to get his mail at Tolga, and on one trip during the wet season of 1903 the boat capsized and he was drowned. He was buried alongside the grave of his mother at the old homestead, Glen Atherton.

Soon after it was opened, Mr. Macrossan, the Minister for Works, and Frank Stubley, M.P., rode up Robson's track and were greatly impressed by the fact of being able to travel from Cairns to Herberton in a single day on horseback.

The drivers of the pack teams, laden with bagged tin and tin ingots, enthusiastically turned their horses' heads away from the beckoning Port Douglas Road, and plunged into the primeval scrubs eastward.

(89)

Up Robson's track in 1880, rode and walked some of Herberton's earliest pioneers. Small children were taken up sitting in boxes on either side of a led packhorse. One family engaged a Chinaman to carry their two children up the track in his baskets.

This latter method may have been the safest if one considers this story by the late Bill Gallogly:

"On a frosty morning long ago at Nigger Creek near Herberton, a teamster named Jack McCann stepped out at early dawn to round up his team horses. He saw a straying packhorse among his draughts with a kerosene case pannier-fashion on either side of the packsaddle. McCann caught the packhorse intending to retain it until a claimant turned up. Hearing a noise in the boxes he looked in, and rubbed his eyes. In each box there was a baby, wrapped in a blanket. That was the way the pioneers took their children over the range." Mr. Gallogly did not elaborate further concerning the babies, but he said the story was quite authentic. Jack McCann was the grandfather of Mrs. Cecil Holdcroft. He was killed when his wagon ran over him.

In the wet season the track was almost impassable being dangerously slippery. Foodstuffs, furniture, corrugated iron, and mining machinery were carried up the pack track, mainly on mules. From 1880 to 1930, mule teams were part of the life of the tinfields around Herberton, for even after railways were constructed they packed ore from the mines to batteries and sidings.

*   *   *   *

The following is an extract from the diary of Dr. Gilbert White who became the first Bishop of Carpentaria in 1900. For many years prior to this, he was a Bush Brother at various places, including Herberton. This extract, published in the North Queensland Diocese Jubilee Book, is dated 1887.

My sister and I left Herberton on Monday afternoon for

Cairns. We started about 2 p.m. and rode leisurely down to Scrubby Creek, about ten miles, where we stayed the night at the house of a selector named Gordon who lives on the edge of the scrub.

I rode Nugget, a very strong little horse that I have had for some months, and my sister, old Tom, whom I bought for her. He went steadily but was unfortunately slow.

Next day I woke early, before five a.m., and the moon was shining brightly as I sat on the balcony of the house and watched the heavy mist over the ground, plainly showing the advantage of a two-storey house.

After awhile our host awoke and we finally got off by 6.30 a.m., and after riding a mile, plunged into the scrub. The road was fair for a mile or two and then became very bad. Imagine a path cleared through a high impenetrable jungle through which the sun hardly ever reached the road, the sides lined with a dangerous stinging tree fatal to horses, trees and logs lying about anyhow. The road(?) a mass a glue-like mud of uncertain depth and ploughed by hundreds of packhorses into deep furrows on top of which the "new chum" horse invariably tries to tread, whereas the only safety consists in treading down into hole after hole.

Even our steady old horses, though not "new chums", got frightened at times amid the mud and roots and plunged about wildly. Fortunately we escaped the stinging tree, though we got a solemn lecture from an old packer for deviating a little from the track. "Keep in the mud as much as ever you can," was his parting advice.

At last we came to the Barron bridge. The bridge (?) consists only of a stony causeway under water and is very dangerous when there is much water in the river.

At 11.30, we got to Boar Pocket, a little inn in a "pocket" or clear space in the scrub, and here we waited an hour while we gave our horses a feed and had dinner ourselves.

The next four or five miles were terribly bad and just as we

(91)

got to the end of the worst part we met Mr. and Mrs. R. on their way to Herberton. They innocently remarked that the scrub they had come through was terribly bad (there was not really a bad place in it), and we left them wondering what they would say by the time they got to Boar Pocket.

At last we got to the top of the range and began the three miles of steep descent. For a mile and a half we had to lead the horses, and on reaching the bottom we took off the saddles and gave the horses twenty minutes' spell while we took some cake and tea.

As we went on again along the banks of the Mulgrave River it began to get dark very rapidly, long before we were out of the scrub which arches overhead in many places and is as black as a coal mine.

I trusted to my horse for some time, my sister following my white coat which was just visible, but the road became at last so bad I had to get off and keep striking matches to keep out of danger, as there were some very nasty turns and gullies.

It was 7 p.m. when we got to Alley's, and very glad we were to get there. We had ridden over perhaps the worst road in the world.

*   *   *   *

Before and during the time the railway was slowly climbing the ranges towards Herberton, it was the era of the packers. Without them, development of this vast mineral district would have been impossible. Well remembered are the teams of mules and sure-footed horses that wound their way down the mountainsides. Remembered, too, are the hardy packers. Manny Borghero was probably the last of them, for he bought the remaining mules when the Irvinebank Mining Company's famous pack team was broken up. At one time Barney Lesina, with a hundred mules, had the largest team on the road. Donald McDonald had forty-five horses and mules.

Bronzed, bearded men were these packers, as tough as an ironbark tree. Loading and unloading forty or fifty mules

(92)

night and morning was child's play to these giants of the past. It was possible for a team to carry a total of ten tons of loading.

The mules were tough like their owners. Famous was the mule that Borghero bought with sixty-five others from the Irvinebank Mining Company in 1919. This was Jumbo, an honest and intelligent animal who knew exactly what was required of him. Old timers tell how he loved to lead the team, arriving at his destination an hour ahead of the others. He could amble all day with five hundredweight on his back, up steep hills and down, one old timer told me.

It was said Jumbo knew his destination by the kind of load he was carrying. On one occasion, the team was at the packer's camp at Riverstone at the foot of the range, but Jumbo was at Yungaburra, called Allumbah Pocket in the early days. The team at Riverstone needed corn, so Jumbo was loaded with four one-hundredweight bags and put on the track down the range, at mid-day. He traversed the track alone and arrived at the camp at midnight.

Then there was little Gipsy who regularly carried eight "fifties" of flour from Cairns to Herberton. There was Pompey and Spider who carried 350 lbs. each — more than their own weight. The small mules were the strongest. When packing ore to the batteries the teams often did not follow any road; the mules would climb around the hillsides on kangaroo tracks or anywhere they could get a footing. The leading mule picked the way, and accidents were rare.

Most of the Northern stations bred mules for the packers. Some of the best came from the Valley of Lagoon, VLI brand. Others were the 6LN from Woodleigh, the 9WD from Cashmere, and the F2H from Fossilbrook. The packers developed harness to their own design, such as the "Port Douglas" packsaddle, with bags especially designed for mules. With the advent of mechanised transport and good roads the mules were doomed, but it was after World War II before the last of them were turned loose, to wander old and grey, around the old camping

grounds. Jumbo died at Eccles Creek at fifty years of age —
mules are noted for their longevity. They deserve an honored
place in our history.

*   *   *   *

Things brightened up for young Tom Crowe wondering
how he could fill the gap the coaches had left, when a bullocky,
Jack Bailey, stopped at the Little Mitchell with two bullock
teams and needed a "spareboy" and Tom got the job at "ten
bob a week and tucker, and you gotta pull your weight." Dave
Riordan (his nephew became an Arbitration Court Judge) was
the driver of the second team. It was the year of the "bank
smash" — 1893 — and prospects were decidedly gloomy.
Bailey was on his way out to Muldiva to load silver lead; it
would be the first to go over the new railway to Cairns, the line
then being operational to Biboohra, five miles from Mareeba.

Dave Riordan left Bailey's employ at Montalbion and
George Bell was taken on as driver of the second team. This
was the man who had travelled the old road as a yoke and
whip maker, but he was a handy man and could drive a bullock
team equally as well. He and his family lived in a tin cottage
by the bank of the dam in Montalbion. His daughter Georgina
married one of the Swindleys who were also bullock teamsters
on the Port Douglas Road.

Bailey's teams followed the Georgetown Road for a few
miles then ran Emu Creek down to where Petford is today,
coming on to the Chillagoe Road, or Muldiva Road as it was
then called. They crossed the Featherbed Range, the Strawbed,
and the Spring Mattress, and eventually pulled into Muldiva
where they unloaded the stores brought from Port Douglas and
camped at Ned Atherton's slaughteryard. Three weeks later
they unloaded the silver ingots into railway trucks at Biboohra,
then a busy township. The big steel railway bridge over the Barron
River had just been completed and to the teamsters from the
Outback it appeared as grand as the Sydney Harbour Bridge.

Impressive to them, too, was the puffing-billy engine, the

(94)

Yankee Pioneer locomotive with its bell-shaped funnel and cowcatcher. It was afterwards used as a shunting engine at the Chillagoe smelters after doing yeoman service on the Cairns Range railway construction. Tom Crowe remembered that Smallwood and Blundell were driver and fireman, Jim Smith was cleaner, and Harry Harris was guard. The first mechanical monster had arrived to oust the coaches; two more had yet to appear before the horses and bullocks finally gave way — motor vehicles and tractors.

Thus Tom Crowe came home to his mother at the Little Mitchell along a road where dozens of carriers would be passed before the Iron Horse came, and now he did not pass one. The old Port Douglas Road as an artery, had been severed.

A few days later Tom heard that a packer, George Pritchard, wanted a boy, so Tom rolled his "cigarette" swag (one blanket and one change of clothes), mounted his horse, and rode to the Barron Bend below Biboohra, a favourite camping place for packers. Pritchard had already left on his way to the Tate Tin Mines, and Tom caught up with him camped at Cattle Creek.

Next morning, with frost on the ground, Tom did as he was expected — got a billy of water, lit the campfire, got breakfast ready, took down the tent-fly, folded the pack covers, lined up the thirty packsaddles, and did a few other things while George the packer mustered the mules.

In his loading were four two hundredweight cases. One mule named Andy carried two of them every day. Two other mules carried the other two cases on alternate days. Altogether, there were four tons of goods to be loaded and unloaded night and morning. As well as this, George was breaking in several mules as he went along. But Andy was the champion of the team, quiet but full of life. He was loaded last every morning and would lead the team all day; he was the first to be unloaded at the next camp. The loads were so heavy that it was a feat of strength to lift them on to the packsaddle and when one side was loaded forked sticks were used for support while the other side was loaded. How one man handled fractious mules with such loads on his own, Tom Crowe did not know.

He wrote years later: "I often look back on those days and think of the hard task the packers had to keep people supplied with the necessities of life and take the minerals back to the seaboard. The bullocky was the gentleman of the road; after his five or six mile stage was done, providing there was grass for his bullocks his day was over. The horse teamsters did not have such a good time as they had to feed their team twice a day as well as having to brush their horses down every morning and very often at the night camp having to tack on shoes. But it was the packer who had the hard job. Pack transport was the fastest on the road (apart from coaches) . . . . "

George Pritchard packed for Fischer Bros. of the Tate Tin Mines; they owned a store and a big tin sluicing plant which they later sold to John Moffat's Irvinebank Mining Company. Discovered in 1879, the Tate Tinfield was greatly dependent upon pack transport in its early years, and the miners who worked claims there were particularly hardy types; many had their own pack teams.

Some years ago, an old time mining man, the late Ernest White, remembered two Tate miners, Paddy Cagney known as "Paddy the Native", and Mick Galvin, a wonderful bushman. About 1892 Mick heard the call of the West Australian goldfields and he and a mate whom he had known in his native Kilkenny, Ireland, and who had just arrived at Port Douglas, set out for Coolgardie. Mick had a good plant of horses so he loaded up with supplies and he and his friend set out on the journey across Australia — first across to Normanton, then around the Gulf of Carpentaria to Borroloola, Katherine River, Hall's Creek, Derby, and so eventually to Coolgardie, a ride of 2500 miles. Mick's mate died on Coolgardie and he did not stop to look for gold. He rode back across the continent to the Tate Tin Mines and resumed work on his old claim.

The Vallely Bros. were other Tate miners who rode to Coolgardie and later returned to North Queensland. Earlier, in 1886, when word reached the Tate that gold had been found at Hall's Creek in the Kimberley district of Northwest Australia, the Power Bros., Harry and Ned, who had a good pack team, joined in the rush. They had no luck at Hall's Creek and rode back to the Tate. Then early in the 'nineties they again crossed the continent on horseback, lured to West Australia a second time by gold on the Murchison field. Again their luck was out and they returned to the Tate tinfield. Harry Rose, another great bushman, also took his pack team from the Tate to the Murchison, won a little gold, and returned to the Tate.

It is of interest to mention here that the discoverers of Coolgardie, Arthur Bayly and W. Ford, were among the early prospectors on the Croydon field in 1886. They too rode across the northern portion of Australia in the mad gold rush to Hall's Creek. They were no more successful there than they had been on Croydon, but working their way south across mainly desert country for some eighteen hundred miles they eventually made their big strike at Coolgardie.

The Irvinebank Mining Company won 3500 tons of tin from the Tate; Donald and Hughie McDonald packed one thousand tons of this on their pack team to the Irvinebank smelters.

Two Chinese packers are remembered, but there were many others: Ah Tye and Ah Lum took hundreds of tons of silver bullion from the Montalbion smelters to Port Douglas, their back loading being principally horse feed.

In a pamphlet published in Herberton in 1884, the Tate is described as being "sixty miles from Herberton" and the main centre for stream tin, over 100 tons being won during the previous year from the reward claim alone. Hann, Mulligan, and others had noticed the presence of tin on the Tate. In 1879, however, the field was opened by hardy prospectors named John Dow, John Williams, John Hogsfleisch, and Harry Hammond.

They took up a sixty acre reward claim. It was rich. Tin was found in the grass roots and down to fourteen feet. But prices were low — £70 per ton at the most — and it had to be packed to Port Douglas in the early times. Later, a wagon road was opened. The discoverers therefore made little out of their rich find.

Harry Hammond and John Williams tried mining elsewhere, while the others went in for hotelkeeping which was more lucrative than mining. When Herberton boomed, Hogsfleisch opened the Cosmopolitan Hotel there, John Dow opened an hotel at Newellton (Silver Valley) and later had one between Irvinebank and Montalbion at a place which became known as Dow's Flat.

Like all prospectors, John Williams doubtless dreamed of striking it rich one day, and his hopes were high when he found a pocket of gold twenty miles north of the Tate. A number of men rushed to the spot and a little township of tents and bark huts called Williamstown after its discoverer existed for a brief period. The largest nugget found weighed forty ounces. Harry Hammond worked various tin mines around Watsonville for years. We will hear more about the Tate and its pioneers later.

* * * *

The wealth of .Herberton lay in its lode tin, but it was soon found that stream tin existed also — in the famed Deep Lead, discovered in 1882 by J. McDonald. The Deep Lead was an ancient river bed running from Wondecla to beyond Tepon, adjacent to the Wild River. In early times some of the tin assayed as high as 72.5 per cent metal, and in the 1883-1903 period, the Deep Lead produced most of Herberton's £200,000 worth of stream tin. In 1885, Marsterson and party drove a tunnel which attained a record length of 2900 feet. Thousands of shafts and dumps in this area still remain, indicating how intense was the activity.

In January 1881, the first machinery arrived at Herberton to treat the tin lodes. It was for the Great Northern Battery.

(98)

A team of eighty-one bullocks hauled this tremendous load up The Bump from Port Douglas, then up the Herberton Range. With its arrival, the future of Herberton seemed assured.

Steadily the first tents and bark huts were replaced by wood and iron buildings on both sides of steep streets up hill and down, the Wild River's once clear waters running discolored and shallow from the cradles of hundreds of miners, and from the battery's sludge, the throb of pounding stampers echoing around the age-old hills — hills rudely awakened from their eons of slumber.

On 21st. August 1880, Warden Mowbray from Thornborough laid out the town. On 30th. October, he issued the first mining licenses at Herberton. Previously prospectors had to ride to Thornborough to obtain them.

The first wagon arrived at Herberton from Port Douglas on 11th. September 1880, but before this, teams had come from the Hodgkinson. R. Bimrose had brought his family by wagon from Northcote and opened the first hotel in Herberton. Woodward had the first butcher's shop, and the first stores were those of William Jack, F. W. Merry, and Foy & Collins. On 20th. November, 1880, a packhorse mail was inaugurated between Cairns and Herberton. The mailman was Robert Croft, later a coach driver.

On December 31st. an open air meeting was held for the purpose of establishing a School of Arts. A collection of fifty pounds was taken up. W. C. Ranson was appointed secretary. On 8th. January 1881, a block of land was bought for eighteen pounds ($36.00) and a fortnight later Herberton's first cultural centre was opened in a bark hut.

On New Year's Day, 1881, the pioneers held a picnic on the bank of the Wild River and, as an old report has it, "the only music were the bagpipes operated upon by Hugh Harrison."

By the middle of 1881, Herberton had two newspapers. The first was the "Wild River Independent" which had been the "Hodgkinson Independent" at Kingsborough, and was edited by

(99)

Marcus Greene. It appeared in September, 1881. The first issue of the "Herberton Advertiser" came out on 16 November. The latter had been previously published in Cairns as the "Cairns Advertiser", but due to the decline of Cairns in those early times, the publisher, Dr. Edward Myers who had been in the Hodgkinson rush and was the first doctor in Cairns, took it to Herberton. Dismantled, the plant was taken up the pack track on a mule team. Dr. Myers was a remarkable man, considering he was a paraplegic. He had been a doctor on the Palmer Goldfield and at Cooktown, and apparently was interested in journalism as well.

On 15 May 1882, the first issue of "Jenkins' Wild River Mining Circular" appeared. It was but a single sheet printed on one side only. No doubt the proprietor-editor was the same indefatigable "Mr. Jenkins" who had been the newspaper correspondent at Thornborough and at Port Douglas when the latter was founded.

John R. Boyett, who had been editor of the "Hodgkinson Mining News" at Thornborough, came to Herberton and established yet another paper, "The Herberton and Western Miner" in July 1882.

In January 1883, the first issue of the "Wild River Times" appeared, and soon afterwards both the "Mining Circular" and "Miner" ceased; Boyett took over as editor of the "Wild River Times", and it became one of the best known newspapers of the pioneering days.

John Boyett was a Londoner and had been in the Palmer rush. He ran the "Times" for twenty-two years until his death. Harry Jerrold then conducted the paper for Boyett's widow. As the "Herberton Times" it functioned until the early 1930's.

A hundred pre-paid subscriptions of sixpence per copy was sufficient capital in the early days to start a newspaper. Advertising was usually half-a-crown (25c.) per single column inch.

Old copies of the original "Wild River Times" that survive

(100)

gives one a good idea of life on the tinfields in those early days. At first, the "Times" occupied a building next door to Madrid's house in Grace Street; later it moved further up to a building next door to Wieland's butchery of today.

Some of the other tin discoveries close to Herberton were just as rich as the Great Northern, but unlike it they did not live to any depth.

Between 1880 and 1896, the Wild Irishman mine, for instance, discovered by a man from the Emerald Isle named Macgillicuddy, yielded tin worth over £100,000. At today's prices for the metal it would represent over one-and-a-half million dollars.

Another of the pioneer miners of 1880 was Donovan who discovered the Band of Hope. Other rich mines were the Phoenix owned by M. Fox, and the Monarch worked by Trembath and Adcock. The descendents of some of these pioneers are still in the North.

The St. Patrick was one of the richest of early mines, discovered by another Irishman, Dan Lavery. He also discovered the Bradlaugh; it was later worked with great success by John and William Collins and Tom Mannion. One of the owners in recent times was the late Jim Stenhouse, son of one of the North's prominent prospectors and pioneers, William Bruce Stenhouse.

Then there was the New Bradlaugh, worked by Jack Ferris. Ted O'Malley, and Bill Eton were later associated with it. A famous mine in the early 'Eighties was the Ly-ee-moon, named after a coastal ship of the period.

*   *   *   *

In 1880, William Jack opened the first store in Herberton in a bark hut 16 ft. x 12 ft. Though he directed his energies to storekeeping, he remained a partner all his life in the Herberton Tin Company which operated the Great Northern Mine and battery.*

His business soon had a turnover of £3000 per month,

_____
* Ref: Research by Ruth Kerr, Brisbane.

despite Jack's opposition to alcohol. It was his proud boast that contrary to the practice on most mining fields, not a drop of liquor was ever sold by him. He could have made a fortune as a wine and spirit merchant, no doubt.

William Jack was born in Paisley, Scotland, in 1834. His mother was a cousin of Sir Walter Scott. He and his family sailed for Australia in 1858, and his wife died on the voyage. Landing at Brisbane, Jack went to Stanthorpe where tin had been discovered. There he met John Newell from County Down, Northern Ireland, and another Scot, John Moffat from Ayrshire.

In 1873, Jack and Newell came north to the Palmer and like thousands of others, joined in the rush to the Hodgkinson three years later. Jack's two young daughters were cared for by his brother, Graham, and his wife. Graham Jack, a Crimean War veteran, managed a sugar plantation at Tinana, Maryborough. When Willie Jack went into business in Herberton, his daughters joined him there; they rode up on horseback from Port Douglas in a convoy of other travellers.

The girls were frightened of the wild blacks sighted along the road. Mrs. Allen wrote: "Neither Mr. Jack nor Mr. Newell ever had anything but friendly relations with the Aborigines and had no hesitation in entrusting their children to the care of black nurse boys or girls."

In 1882, John Newell joined Willie Jack in the business, and thus the well known firm of Jack and Newell came into being. About three years later, Jack left the business in John Newell's care — he married Jack's daughter, Janet — and went off to the Celebes in what was then the Dutch East Indies, looking for minerals and stayed there for eight years. He died in Cairns on 18th. May 1910.

An era in North Queensland history ended when Jack and Newell closed their original store in Herberton at the end of 1977. Built of pit-sawn cedar planks in 1882, it had changed little in appearance. Until the last you could buy almost anything there — quartpots, camp ovens, and even miners' dollypots and moleskin trousers, it was said.

The people of Herberton, determined not to quite lose this link with the past, formed a co-operative, the old building was renovated and it is being progressively re-opened as a general store. The original fittings, including massive cedar counters, have been retained.

In the pioneer days when Jack and Newell, with 26 stores in the mining towns of the Cairns Hinterland, were "universal providers", moleskin trousers, red flannel shirts, cabbage-tree hats or "American felts", Blucher boots and elastic-sides, were the standard working dress of the menfolk. And Jack and Newell provided for the ladies, too, with bolts of gingham, calico, flannel, chemises, and bonnets. In 1884, Jack and Newell advertised in the "Wild River Times" that they had for sale "moleskin trousers, merino vests, cushions, and cosies" which had been "bought for cash by our Mr. Jack."

Stories are legion of how popular old John Newell "grub-staked" the miners and of how, when some of them got too old to work, he assisted them. There were rheumaticky old tin scratchers who lived on his credit at his store until they died. At Irvinebank and other places, Jack and Newell were tin ore buyers. Another firm, Armstrong, Ledlie, and Stillman, were robbed of tin ore one time when a couple of smart operators got under the building in Irvinebank and bored augur holes into the bags of tin stacked above.

Recently the present managing director, Mr. Rod Newell of Mareeba, presented Jack and Newell's old ledgers to the history department of the James Cook University of North Queensland, Townsville. The figures in the ledgers and the entries in copperplate handwriting detailed how miners in this Pioneers' Country were helped by this firm which was itself such a part of the country.

For fifty years John Newell was managing director of the Great Northern mine, and led any move connected with the progress of the district. He helped institute the Herberton

(103)

Show, first held at Wondecla in 1885; it was only the second of its kind in North Queensland — the first show was at Charters Towers in 1882. The Herberton Show was held every year until 1932.

In 1896, John Newell was returned to the Queensland Parliament as Conservative Member for the seat of Woothakata which he retained until 1901. When Herberton, base for a huge mineral district, became a municipality in 1888, it was natural that John Newell should be elected the first mayor of the town he helped to create. He died on July 4, 1932. His wife, Janet, died in 1947.

Other mayors of Herberton during its brief life as a municipality were William Macadam Bonar, (1890-92 and 1893), Herman Selig (1892), and James Noonan, 1894.

W. M. Bonar was an expert mining man. He was in turn manager of the Great Northern mine and the Bischoff Mill on the Walsh River. He came out from England in a sailing ship when a teenager, and became a shearer on Outback sheep stations in the pioneering days. He gained his mining experience in the Herberton area. My late friend, Gus Waddell, once of Irvinebank, had mineral specimens dated from early this century with notes in Bonar's handwriting. He died at Herberton in 1925.

His wife who lived to be almost a centenarian, showed typical pioneering spirit. Even when 94 years of age she won sixteen prizes for jams, jellies, cakes, and scones at the 1959 Atherton Show. Her memories encompassed all of Herberton's history. The future Mrs. Bonar landed at Port Douglas, being carried ashore from the lighter as was the custom, and travelled by Cobb and Co. coach to Herberton, and then to Nigger Creek (Wondecla). She married W. M. Bonar in Mrs. Jack's home at Watsonville, then they set off on horseback to spend their honeymoon, riding with packhorses and cattle down the range to Cairns. Theirs is a story typical of young married couples in the tough pioneering days.

(104)

CHAPTER 7

THE VALIANT BREED

James Arbouin — William Mazlin of Atherton — George Clarke — C. O. Garbutt — Christie Palmerston — Mulligan goes exploring again — Halpin's expedition.

James Arbouin was one of the many migrants who, though little remembered now, helped to make North Queensland, and in particular the slice of Pioneers' Country that lies over the mountains inland from Cairns.

I am indebted to one of the old pioneers, Mike O'Callaghan of Cairns, for the following information on the Arbouin family. Part of a paper he prepared for the Cairns Historical Society reads as follows:

The Arbouin family had originated in France and about three centuries ago were prominent wine manufacturers in Bordeaux, but with the revocation of the Edict of Nantes of 1698 the family fled from France and became British subjects.

Charles Arbouin was born in England on December 20, 1777. In 1808 he left England to take up residence in Jamaica, British West Indies, and in that same year he met and married Catherine Susannah Davies, daughter of an Irish lawyer in Jamaica. Charles died in Jamaica on November 20, 1839 at the age of 62, and his wife died there several years later, both being buried in the churchyard of the Parish Church of St. Andrew, Half-Way Tree, Jamaica. They left a family of two girls and two boys. James of this article was the youngest of the family.

James became a school teacher in Jamaica. But with the finding of gold in Victoria in the 1850's he and a man named Taylor, who later became his brother-in-law, chartered a boat to take them to Victoria and the goldfields. They made no fortune in Victoria so moved on to New South Wales to a gold discovery at Bathurst, but again had no luck; so they moved on to the tin-fields of northern New South Wales where they appear to have fared better.

At this time James married Martha Taylor at Parramatta — a sister of his prospecting partner. Thereafter they made their home at Tenterfield where he again took up the role of school teaching. Here too his family of four boys and three girls were all born. The boys were James Oliver, Charles, William Taylor, and Edward Robert, and the girls were Emily, Kate and Martha. In the early seventies his wife died in Tenterfield.

It was during 1873 that James Venture Mulligan and party had found gold on the Palmer River, and in 1875-76 on the Hodgkinson River. These discoveries must have proved attractive to the ever adventurous Arbouin. He travelled on the "Blackbird" to Cairns with his four sons and three daughters, in the latter part of 1876. He conducted an Auction Mart in Cairns during 1877 and early 1878, then with the opening of the road from the Hodgkinson to Port Douglas, James moved his business to that Port. Two sons — James Oliver and William Taylor — now moved off on their own to the Woolgar Goldfield, and the third son Charles accepted employment with Dermot Henry, a storekeeper at Thornborough. Jack, Newell, Brandon, and party had discovered tin at Herberton early in 1880, so, in September 1880 James Arbouin and the balance of his family were again on the move, this time to Herberton, centre of the newly discovered tin-field.

The transport of the family on this epic trek from Port Douglas to Herberton consisted of one saddle horse and one pack horse. The three girls Emily 14, Kate 11, and Martha 9 years, took turn about double-banking on the saddle horse, whilst James and his son Ted 12½ years took turn about leading the pack-horse which carried their goods and chattels. The Aboriginals had been troublesome in the area so old man Arbouin carried a rifle for defence purposes. The lighting of fires had to be restricted so that raiding Aboriginals would not be attracted to their small party. Progress was slow, particularly over the

"Bump" section, but the road was well defined for coach travel as far as Granite Creek. But from there on to Herberton it was only a "blazed tree" trail.

The son, Ted, walked ahead to locate the track, the father followed leading the pack-horse, with one girl walking and the other two girls on the saddle horse. From Tolga to Atherton, through the scrub the track was cut only just wide enough for a loaded pack-horse. The journey of about eighty miles took seven days to accomplish, and fortunately no Aboriginals were met.

On arrival at Herberton it was found that only one family had reached the place ahead of them — the Bimrose family. Of course several prospecting parties had quickly followed the original prospectors.

The Arbouins lived in Herberton for several years and were joined by the other three sons, James Oliver, William Taylor, and Charles. James Oliver engaged in timber getting in the Evelyn scrubs; Charles and William Taylor prospected on the new field; and James senior and son Ted took up casual occupations around Herberton. It was during this period, while prospecting, that Charles located the fine tin show some four miles to the north-west of Watsonville that became known as The Arbouin. It was subsequently acquired by the Stannary Hills Mines & Tramway Company.

At the dawn of the present century, the family name was also given to a copper mine twenty miles west of Mungana, opened by Charles and William Arbouin. During his varied career, Charles managed Jack and Newell's stores in Irvinebank and Stannary Hills. In between, he went prospecting to the desert goldfield of Tanami in Central Australia and almost perished of thirst. At Wolfram Camp in the boom times, he partnered Alex Gillian in an ore buying firm.

James' elder son, James Oliver, was killed by lightning at Charters Towers. His widow returned to Watsonville and married a miner, Harry Bradshaw. Her son Charles Arbouin, enlisted in World War I and became one of the first soldier settlers on the Atherton Tableland. He died in Atherton in May 1972.

His sister Janet married Charlie Strattmann of Mareeba, and Kate married Nat Absell of Koorboora.

Ted, the youngest of James' sons, was employed by John Moffat and the Irvinebank Company, and later by the State Government when they acquired it, from 1887 to 1936, engaging in tin mining and milling all his working life. He died at Atherton in 1950. Ted's second daughter, Agnes, married Mike O'Callaghan at Irvinebank.

*   *   *   *

William Mazlin was another of our pioneers. His name is perpetuated in Mazlin Creek in Atherton, a town of which he was virtually the founder.

Born in Parramatta, N.S.W., away back in 1857, he and his brothers Jim, Tom, and John, were typical Colonial lads whose adventurous spirits brought them to the northmost frontiers in the late Eighteen-seventies. In 1881, the four Mazlin brothers were cutting cedar in the scrub near the future site of Atherton. The nearby forest clearing was known as Prior's Pocket.

Their camp was about where the Atherton ambulance station was later built. Teamsters, Herberton bound, camped at Mazlin's clearing, and the erection of a roadside shanty by a Scots couple, William McCraw and his wife, naturally followed. Thus did Atherton begin its life in the same manner as scores of other country towns in pioneer days. But until the railway came in 1903, Herberton, and not Atherton, was the business centre of the Tablelands. Mullock from the Great Northern mine was used to construct the main street of Atherton, for years a boggy stretch of the Port Douglas-Herberton road where the laden wagons ploughed through, hub-deep in red mud.

The Mazlins erected crude dogleg fences across openings in the surrounding rain forest to keep bullocks and horses in check.

The brothers' cedar and kauri pine was transported by team to Herberton where it was in steady demand for building purposes. The Mazlins themselves had several teams on the road. On the edge of the scrub at Carrington, they and others had pit-sawing works cutting this timber into planks and beams. In 1884, E. P. Williams had a steam-powered sawmill on Scrubby Creek. Among the early timber men were Thomas, Loder, and Nixon.

Walnut was not considered to be of much value and when the early selections were cleared, it was burnt in millions of feet. Tom Mazlin sent a flitch of Walnut to London to have it valued. Wondering Englishmen valued it at six shillings per cubic foot, but the brawny bushmen laughed and continued to stoke fires that blazed in lonely jungle clearings with timber worth a fortune. Chinese, anxious to get in crops of corn in the rich virgin loam between the blackened stumps of the the world's finest cabinet timbers, did likewise. European owners allowed them 35 shillings for each acre of scrub they cleared.

William B. Kelly opened a store at Prior's Pocket in 1882. Kelly had come to Cairns in 1877, and went to Herberton in 1880. Another man whose name does not seem to have come down to us, almost beat him for the Atherton building site. In those days, mining leases were the main form of tenure. Kelly rode at night to Herberton to lodge his application ahead of his rival, at Warden Mowbray's office. Later Kelly raised a petition to get a township surveyed, and at last, on 23rd. February 1886, the first sale of town allotments was held and Prior's Pocket officially became Atherton. Kelly was the first chairman of the Tinaroo Divisional Board.

About ten years ago a man who said he was the first white child born on the Barron River on the Atherton Tableland, recorded some of his reminiscences in a newspaper interview. He was Albert Creber Barron Putt, and his daughter, Mrs. Eileen Bryant, has made the material available for this book. Mrs. Bryant now lives in Parramatta, N.S.W., but her sister,

Mrs. C. Cater, still lives in Mareeba.

The father of these ladies was born on Portion 48, called Providence Farm, on May 12, 1888. His father, Edward Creber Putt, had selected the block in 1884. In 1886 he was the first white man to settle his family on the upper portion of the Barron River. He built a house of slab walls with a shingle roof.

Mr. Putt said that J.B. Kelly was the first man to select land on the Tableland. In 1881 he selected Portion 1 where the Peanut Board buildings were later erected.

The next selector was Jules Freddreich, a German, who took up a block in 1882 on the Barron River, known later as Picnic Crossing. The Aborigines were hostile and a force of spear-armed warriors came and chased him away. Some time later the block was re-selected by a man named Giblet.

Mr. Putt recalled: "My father and his family lived in constant danger from the wild blacks. They would throw spears and boomerangs at the house whenever they saw anyone walking around the place. He applied to the Government for protection and they sent up a Constable Hansen from Brisbane with a supply of rifles, revolvers, and ammunition. He taught all the older girls to shoot.

"Hansen took a party comprising Edward, Ted, and Bill Putt, William Colley, and Peter Jackson, out into the scrub where they shot a number of Aborigines. That 'civilised' the rest. Lake Barrine, was, I believe, discovered by constable Hanson and Ted Putt.

"Atherton was first called McCraw's Forest Pocket. Later it was called Kelly's. Prior's Pocket was another of its names.

"One night in May, 1900, about fifteen or more of the old pioneers, including John Atherton who had come up from Emerald End, held a meeting. They had a load of half green wood, a tin of kerosene, and built a bonfire on the side of the road where the A.L. & S. store (now the Big A Supermarket) now is. Also in the equipment was a case of whisky, a kerosene

(111)

tin of water, and two empty porter cases for tables near the fire.

"They started the fire going with a gallon of kerosene at about 8 o'clock, and everybody settled down to some solid drinking and speechmaking. Finally, they got around to the purpose of the meeting. Someone stood up and said: 'Well, Mr. Putt, we are having this open air meeting to give this town a name.'

"Edward Putt turned around and touching Mr. Atherton on the shoulder, said, 'We will call it Atherton.' And that is how Atherton got its name. Robert Street was named after my father's father, Robert Stone Putt.

"The first shire council, called the Tinaroo Divisional Board, was formed in Herberton, with fourteen members — nine from Atherton and the Barron River, and five from Herberton and district.

"At first they held their meetings at Herberton, until finally my father moved a motion that it would be better for those five members from Herberton to come down to Atherton instead of nine members riding fifteen to twenty miles to Herberton. The motion was carried. Neil McGeehan was one of the first maintenance men. His earthmoving plant comprised a wheelbarrow and pick and shovel, and an axe, and with this poor equipment he performed a wonderful job."

*　　*　　*　　*

It is a well known fact, however, that Neil McGeehan owned and occupied the first house in the town of Atherton. The family has been actively associated with Atherton and Kairi ever since. Other early settlers were William and John Marnane who were well known packers.

One of the old timers, Wally Weare, told the writer recently:

"I came to Atherton in 1903 with my parents, from Mt. Garnet. My father opened a butchery opposite Moses' Hotel. The other hotels were Brazier's, the Commonwealth (Halloran's), where the Grand is now, and Bill McCraw had the Barron Valley. The saddlers were Jim and Bob McHugh. I remember

(112)

Blackley's store — Armstrong, Ledlie, and Stillman had not then opened. The main street was not terraced as it is today, but was steeply sloping. The houses were very scattered with bush all around.

"The first farm going towards Herberton was that of A.A. Loder who was dairying. Then there was Chinatown around where the old josshouse still stands. The Junction Hotel — Tom Purcell's — was on the road out, where the pack track turned off to Cairns. Jim Thomas' sawmill was nearby.

"At Scrubby Creek, officially Carrington, the Williams family then lived. I remember the Williams boys — Ned, Paddy, Fred, Bert, Jack, and Harry. They helped their father look after cattle and horses. The family also ran an hotel, store, and butcher's shop. Other settlers were the Hemmens and Morleys."

Wally Weare went to school at Carrington. There were eight in the Weare family. The school teacher was Lizzie Cameron. The school-teacher in Atherton was Mrs. Taylor, and her husband was then shire clerk.

The Weares lived in Robert Gordon's original two-storey house, built of red cedar. The Weares engaged in dairying — all hand milking in those days. The milk was made into butter and sold to the stores in Atherton.

Wally Weare's mother, Clara Page, was born in Charters Towers and her sister became Mrs. Robert Gordon. They came to Port Douglas and then by dray to Herberton. Clara's father was the first baker in Herberton. Wally recalls that the Golden Grove butter factory was opened by W.C. Abbott, first at Wirpoo. He then shifted it into Atherton, and later to Malanda.

Thomas Peake built the original Barron Valley Hotel. W. F. Logan, Atherton's first commission agent, was also the first clerk of the Tinaroo Divisional Board. Robert Logan was a blacksmith. Robert Young was the town's first plumber.

The Loder family were pioneering selectors when dairying began early this century. It is said they introduced the first separator and also manufactured butter and cheese. George Windhaus grew and manufactured coffee in the 'nineties. Charlie Tucker who had a farm where the golf links were later laid out, introduced sheep to the Tableland, but they did not find favour.

Other selectors around Atherton were Michael Halloran, George McKeown, Charles Ballinger, Rockley, Thomas Pink, Henry Corbett, John Butler, Maher Bros., Henry Jewett, William Ure, Peter Ford, Patrick Courtney, James Templeton, John Clark, John and Jacob Allen, and others.

Phil Garland, the beche-de-mer sailor who had fought the blacks on the site of Cairns two or three years before there was any settlement and had named Smith's Creek, "Battle Creek", turned to bullock driving after Port Douglas was founded. As a selector and teamster he lived at Scrubby Creek, or Carrington as it was officially called. Matt Petersen had an hotel there and Thomas Purcell had another where the pack-track to Cairns branched off the Herberton road. Blacksmiths were as important then as motor mechanics and service stations are today, and a man named Chappel had a strategically situated smithy at Carrington.

William Mazlin was one of the first selectors to go in for mixed farming on the Tableland on a large scale. In March 1883, he took up 160 acres in the Evelyn area, later adding other blocks. He called his property Orange Grove and built a homestead of pit-sawn cedar. He disposed of his farm to E. Harte years later. Mazlin grew oaten chaff, then worth £7 per ton, which was quickly bought up by the packers and horse teamsters. Butter, selling at half a crown (25c) per pound had a ready sale in the nearby mining towns. Delicious honey was also produced from an apiary of about a hundred hives.

Mazlin is said to have been the first to successfuly grow paspalum grass on the Tableland; the grass was to become the mainstay of this great dairying area until recent times when better pastures were introduced. It all began with three roots of grass that John Newell, when Member for Woothakata, gave James Mazlin.

William Mazlin ranks among the great bushmen of his time, for he made many journeys of exploration, seeking new ways through the dense tropical jungle that clothed most of the country between Evelyn and the coast. In 1887, he was cutting cedar on the headwaters of the Johnstone River. Mazlin blazed a track from Evelyn to the Millaa Millaa Falls. Carrick and Sons obtained the contract to clear the scrub to make a track eight feet wide so horses could get through.

In 1831 Mazlin found cedar near the later site of Ravenshoe—hence Cedar Creek, the town's first name.

Mazlin also blazed a track from Evelyn to Carrington. It was inspected by a surveyor named Longland, and Longland's Gap on the later-named Evelyn Highway (now part of the Kennedy Highway) was named after him. About 1899, Mazlin blazed another track, this time through forest country, from Evelyn to Archer Creek on the way to Mt. Garnet, when searching for a railway route to the latter mining town. But the line was built from Lappa on the Chillagoe Line instead.

Evelyn and Woodleigh Stations were the first pastoral properties taken up in the Herberton Shire. Frank Stubley who made a fortune out of mining on Charters Towers but later lost all he possessed, took up Evelyn Station in 1880 or 1881. He first put Willie Joss of Herberton in charge, and later his friend, George Clarke.

The pioneer cattleman, Charles Overend Garbutt, took up Woodleigh on the Herbert River about 1882, and he has been considered as the discoverer of the unique Innot Hot Springs. He was on the track of some wild blacks who had been spearing his cattle when he saw steam rising from a creek bed. He thought it was smoke from a native camp and he expected to find some of his prime beef being cooked over the Aborigines' campfires.

Cautiously, with rifles at the ready, Garbutt and the two

men who were with him, crept up to the creek bank. Then, to his amazement, he found that the supposed campfire smoke was steam rising from hot springs. These springs contain valuable mineral properties and at one time the spa water was bottled and sold. Possibly the springs have potential as a tourist attraction or resort.

The Methodist boarding college in Herberton has taken its name from the early station — Woodleigh. Garbutt sold Woodleigh to the Grant Bros., and Munro, Gordon, and Co. owned it in the 'nineties.

C. O. Garbutt died beside his campfire on the road between Mareeba and Chillagoe in 1905. Charlie Jenkinson, once a well known journalist later living in Mareeba, recalled he was setting out from Kuranda for Chillagoe in a buggy when C. O. Garbutt rode up with a packhorse carrying prospecting tools. He offered to pilot Jenkinson to Mareeba as the old coach road, (now the Kennedy Highway) was badly washed out at the crossings of the First and Second Clohesy (the latter is Davies Creek today). Jenkinson said his night camp was enlivened by Garbutt's reminiscences of his time on Woodleigh and later at Muldiva.

A few days later, the old pioneer was found lying dead in his camp. A son, Ernest, was butchering at Gurrumbah and later established a well known family business in Townsville and Ingham. Another son, Arthur, drove a coach between Biboohra and Mt. Molloy before the railway was built.

George Clarke managed Evelyn Station for about five years until it was sold up by Stubley's creditors, and then returned to mining.

With Fraser and Mosman he had discovered the richest goldfield in Queensland — Charters Towers — in January 1872. In 1886, he and Christie Palmerston discovered payable gold on the head of the Russell River. Clarke cut a path through the jungle from the foothills of Bellenden Ker and over the main range to Boonjie on the Tableland. He and Willie Joss found gold there in 1889.

In 1890 it was reported Clarke had cut a track from Herberton direct to the Russell Goldfield, a distance of 28 miles through the jungle. Two complete crushing batteries were packed, dismantled, on Jack Kane's mules from Mareeba (then nearest railhead) to Boonjie (Towalla Goldfield) in 1894. The loading included steel rails, huge pulley wheels, stampers, and galvanised iron. There seemed to be nothing that those men of old could not put on a packhorse or mule.

In 1894, Clarke was a cattle buyer for Munro and Gordon at Cattle Camp, near Carrington. Soon afterwards his friend, Alex Munro, died, and Clarke decided to go prospecting again — to the wilds of New Guinea this time. Gold had been found on the Mambare River in Papua and dozens of schooners were being fitted out in Cairns, Port Douglas, and Cooktown to take adventurous diggers to this new frontier. In 1895, George Clarke, one of our great prospectors and bushmen, was fatally speared by natives on the Mambare River.

In 1884, Alex Munro of Herberton sponsored the Cairns Range pathfinder, John Doyle, to blaze a wagon road from Herberton, through Coolgarra, and over the later site of Mt. Garnet, to Junction Creek, and so to Georgetown. "Doyle's Track" is still shown on some maps. This was the era of great bushmen.

On September 2, 1884, the "Wild River Times" newspaper of Herberton reported on the opening of a "dray road to the Etheridge" (Georgetown):

"We are indebted to the courtesy of Mr. John Doyle for the following detailed account . . . . Starting from Herberton on the 5th ultimo, after examining the country between California Creek and Fossilbrook and Return Creek junction, determined on taking a centre line between the two routes on account of there being better water and less obstacles to overcome; and commenced, when reaching the woolshed at Fossilbrook, to blaze the track which crosses Noe, Fairyhoe, Warrigal, Mulligan's

(117)

Sandy Creek (Sandy Tate?), and several other creeks, to a reach in Return Creek near Mt. Garnet, and from thence to the Victoria Machine at Coolgarra.

"Mr. Doyle estimates the distance from Coolgarra to Fossilbrook at about sixty miles at most, and considers the route he has marked as a good natural road, passing through good grass and well watered country. As few men have had more experience than Mr. Doyle we congratulate the Divisional Board, that gentleman, and the residents of the Etheridge and Herberton . . . . "

The "Herberton Advertiser" in its issue dated 7th January 1885, published a list of donations towards a one hundred pounds' bonus to the first and second teams carrying three-and-a-half tons each which would travel from Herberton to Georgetown via Doyle's Track. The paper reported that eight teams were being loaded at Port Douglas en route for Georgetown within a period of two weeks.

The newspaper added: "Port Douglas was originally the port from which Georgetown drew its supplies, but on account of Normanton being forty miles nearer, it has been given the preference. At the present time, however, the road from Normanton to Georgetown is blocked in consequence of the heavy rains."

On 4th March 1885, the same paper reported that the Etheridge Gold Escort would shortly travel over Doyle's Track by way of Herberton to Port Douglas. The Divisional Board engaged John Doyle to accompany Mr. Fox's teams over the route.

On the 11th March, the paper said that Inspector Islay of the Native Mounted Police, met Fox's teams about eight miles east of the junction of two tracks, and found the wagons were bogged. It stated the track went on 21 miles to Mulligan's Creek, with good travelling to Munro Creek (25 miles), then eight miles of rough basalt to Old Cattle Camp, then one mile to the "crossing of the junction", and four miles to Firth's old woolshed.

On April 28, the teamster, Fox, said the road was "almost the best" he had travelled on and he expected to reach Georgetown in another two weeks.

The "Cairns Post" chimed in on July 2, 1885, to say that Mr. Fox had "conclusively shown that goods can be conveyed from Cairns to the Etheridge at a cheaper rate than any other port." Cairns was already anticipating the Cairns-Herberton railway by means of which it expected the wealth of the interior to be funnelled into Cairns. But just over 25 years were to pass before the railway reached Herberton and during that time many changes occurred. The railway was to reach Forsayth before it reached Herberton.

Back in 1885, news of the opening of a new wagon road, despite bog and "rough basalt" was of the utmost importance. The pioneers greeted the blazing of a wilderness track with as much joy as we would the opening of a bitumen road today; blazed treelines were the highways for the bullock and horse teams.

*   *   *   *

The late J. W. Collinson, a Northern historian, wrote in "In the Path of the Pioneers" (1952):

"On May 1, 1882, Sub-Inspector Douglas of the Native Mounted Police, under instructions from the Government, left Herberton with a party of twelve to try to find a practical track to Mourilyan Harbour, the nearest point on the coast in a direct line. With Douglas were Jack McLellan, H. Redman, five Chinese, and four native troopers. After a long and arduous trip through precipitous jungle country, and without food for the latter part of the journey, Douglas reported that such a route was impossible.

"On October 31, Christie Palmerston, a wonderful bushman and explorer of the Northern jungles, left Geraldton (Innisfail) with two Kanakas, two Johnstone River Aborigines, and an Etheridge native, for Herberton. He followed the south bank

(119)

of the North Johnstone, crossed the Beatrice (which he named), and reached Herberton by way of Nigger Creek on November 12, through sixty miles of jungle without a break.

"Palmerston returned by practically the same route on December 21, reaching Geraldton in ten days. The Johnstone Divisional Board of the day had promised him £400 to find this route, but all he ever received was £20, and he therefore did not open the track. It was a superb feat of bushmanship. The Palmerston Highway follows part of this route today."

John Newell and A. S. Cowley left Herberton on horseback about the same time and reached Geraldton next day, but whether they followed Palmerston's route or not is now unknown.

*   *   *   *

The tangle of rough ranges in country dry and barren compared with the rain forest eastward, fascinated the early prospectors. From both Herberton and the Hodgkinson they probed its mountains, creeks, and gullies, in quest of minerals and at the same time, exploring.

It attracted James Venture Mulligan like a magnet. A business life in Thornborough was not to his liking, so it was probably with enthusiasm that he gave it up because of financial failure, and gathering a few mates, loaded packhorses and rode off into this almost unknown region.

With him went James Gibbs, Jack Moran, and William Bruce Stenhouse. They left Thornborough on 14th. March 1881 and made their first camp at George Jackson's homestead on Leadingham Creek. (See Chapter 4). Mulligan reported that "Mr. George Jackson has a very comfortable homestead, a number of cattle and horses, and has twenty-one milch-cows which are milked every morning. The dairy is the most complete of its kind yet seen in the North. All Mr. Jackson's butter finds a ready market, and he cannot supply half the demand. The dairy is sixteen miles from Thornborough . . . . "

Crossing the Walsh at Parada, Mulligan and his three mates rode across to the Planted Tree Crossing, and then over the range between the Walsh and Herbert waters, arriving at Herberton on 16th. March. On the way, Mulligan noticed that "Watson and others" were prospecting the "Great Western District" with good results. They camped at the Chinese Gardens two miles below Herberton until April 1st. because of rain. The Wild River rose in flood.

The "Queenslander" newspaper, Brisbane, dated 6th. August 1881, described "Mulligan's Latest Prospecting Trip":

"Mr. Mulligan was very much surprised to see such a town (Herberton) had sprung up in twelve months . . . . Beef is supplied at threepence per lb. of excellent quality. Mr. Mulligan describes Mr. Denny's laboratory at Herberton as very interesting, containing a large number of specimens of various kinds of ore — cassiterite, copper, galena, iron, manganese, etc. The copper had just been found outside the belt where the tin is being worked at present, and seven miles from Herberton.

"A visit was paid to the prospectors' claim (Newell, Jack & Co.) They have an immense lot of surface tin . . . . Mr. Mulligan then describes Mr. Moffat's machine, and the different claims on the field . . . . "

On April 3rd., Mulligan's party reached Evelyn Station which was described as a comfortable and convenient place with a fine garden and fruit trees, and running about 7,000 head of cattle. The real prospecting trip began at the Herbert River on 7th. April when a tree was marked M over I, and each succeeding camp numbered. Continuing southward, Mulligan reached Blunder Creek near where Kennedy emerged from the scrub in 1848. The leeches were a nuisance here; they filled the men's boots with blood and even got into their beards.

The next few days found them in open forest in country later comprised in Wooroora, Glen Gordon, and part of Gunnawarra Stations. A horse died after a fall over a precipice and another was drowned in the Herbert River. On 29th. April the party reached Garbutt's station (Woodleigh) where stores were replenished for which the Garbutts refused payment. "The latest newspapers were also kindly given to the party by Mrs. Garbutt."

Crossing the Wild River, Mulligan camped at his old campsite of 25th. June 1875. It was now 29th. April 1881. Stream tin was found next day after a day's ride westward. "This gully might pay for working", Mulligan said. This was prophetic as Mulligan was in the vicinity of either Return Creek or Smith's Creek near the present Mt. Garnet. Scanning the country from a high hill, he decided it was useless looking for gold (his main interest) as the country was as he put it, "only fit for blacks and wallabies". In succeeding days he found a big deposit of iron ore, and stream tin in California Creek. The prospectors crossed very rough country between the Lynd and Tate divide and Mulligan named a high mountain, Mt. Gibbs after his mate. Another peak was named Mt. Stenhouse. Jack Moran also had a mountain named after him. Other rugged peaks in this uninhabited country were named after Hodgkinson pioneers — Mt. Byers, Mt. Jackson, and Mt. Reynolds. Mulligan was taking a zigzag route around the mountains south of the Walsh and wrote in some disgust — "Plenty of tin, but only colours of gold in the creeks."

On 25th. June so much tin was found that even Mulligan could not pass it by to chase gold. In this creek they obtained up to 4 lbs. of stream tin to the dish. The creek in which this tin was found was named Emu Creek because four emu eggs were found in a nest on the bank. Two of the eggs, preserved, became prized possessions of the late Jim Stenhouse of Herberton. He was the son of the man who was with Mulligan. To the south, a copper lode was found. Perhaps it was Mt. Garnet. Mulligan predicted that "this will be a great mineral country, and there will not only be tin and copper but probably other minerals yet un-noticed." The expedition returned to Thornborough on 30th. June 1881 because of shortage of rations. Mulligan reported payable tin on Emu Creek. This was the same creek that Kennedy had followed down to the Walsh in 1848. Also on Kennedy's tracks, Geoffrey Weate found small quantities of gold deep in the scrub on the headwaters of the Tully River.

While Mulligan was out prospecting and exploring, another expedition was in almost the same area, unknown to each other. It was a party led by an old time prospector and cattleman, Con Halpin, then living at Kingsborough. Little has been written about him, and his expedition is forgotten today. Few people know that he was the first white man on the later sites of Irvinebank and Stannary Hills, soon to be populous mining towns. Old Irvinebank and Montalbion residents remember the Halpin Bros. as butchers in those centres in the 'nineties — even then white-bearded men who rode in from their station near the junction of Chinaman and Emu Creeks.

Halpin's report to the Minister for Mines, Mr. Macrossan, was published in the "Queenslander" but it is difficult to delineate the route as no names were given to his discoveries. Halpin uses the old time namings — the main Walsh River was called the "Northern Walsh" (some people pronounced it "Welsh"); Eureka Creek was the "Middle Walsh" and Mulligan's Emu Creek was the "Third Walsh". Halpin also does not name his companions on this trip.

He set out from Kingsborough on 25th. February 1881 and rode first to Reynolds' shanty and cattle station on the head of Cattle Creek on the road to Port Douglas where the party stayed salting beef. From here they headed for the ranges south of the Walsh River, turned westward, and reached Eureka Creek.

They followed it up through the gorges and then crossed south-westward to Emu Creek or "Third Walsh" as Halpin called it. It was then the 18th. March, and they were hampered by wet season rain and horses getting bogged. On the 13th. April, they prospected the creeks finding some colours of gold and plenty of tin. The day after they struck payable tin in a creek (probably California Creek), two prospectors came to their camp. They were the first white men they had seen in the area. They were Black and McIntyre who said they also were on payable tin. As there were no access roads, getting the tin out would be a problem and the price was very low. That was why gold had the greater allure.

The Halpin party prospected the country between what was later Lappa Junction and Ord. Tin was everywhere, but only colours of gold. Early in June they were prospecting down the Einasleigh, passed a tree marking one of the Jardine Bros.' camps of 1864, and riding in a semi-circle, prospecting as they went, the Halpin party crossed the head of the Tate River and returned to Emu Creek. Two of the party (probably Con Halpin and his brother) made an excursion across country to the creek they had prospected in April and marked off a claim.

They arrived back in Thornborough on 14th. July 1881 and reported their discoveries to Warden Towner. The expedition had travelled 700 miles and been out in the wilds for twenty weeks with the loss of only two horses.

Apparently Mulligan did not apply for any ground, his expedition having been financed to the extent of £180 by the Government.

It seems that Con Halpin's camp of 15th. March 1881 was on Eureka Creek near the later site of Stannary Hills. The next day he went south over rough mountains and through a gap, camping "on a small creek with good feed for the horses." This creek must have been Gibbs Creek, and it is reasonable to assume that Con Halpin and his party were the first white men on the future site of Irvinebank, possibly six months before Gibbs, McDonald, and Party made their discovery of lode tin — the Great Southern mine — on this spot.

Halpin Creek and the land parish of Halpin are all there is to remind us of a shadowy figure who rode the trackless mountains long ago in quest of mineral riches. In the ghost town of Kingsborough there was once a Halpin Street.

CHAPTER 8

SILVER AND TIN

John Moffat — Montalbion and its Pioneers — Silver Valley — Miners of Long Ago.

When J. V. Mulligan rode across from Thornborough to Herberton on the start of his expedition in March 1881, he passed close to the Great Western mine opened only a couple of weeks earlier by an old mate of his, Bob Watson. This was the first big tin discovery in the ranges just west of Herberton. Watson had with him two mates named Dougherty and Connelly. Mulligan wrote that Robert Watson was a genial man, very generous, and well liked by everyone. He put back into mining, or in helping others, all that he made.

He came North at the time of the gold rush to the Gilbert, in 1869. His sister, Mrs. Edward Mytton lived on a nearby station, Oak Park. Watson opened a general store on the Gilbert in 1870 and when the Palmer broke out he was one of those who joined in the rush. The Alex Watson who was with Mulligan was probably his brother. Bob Watson ran a store and a gold buying business at Oaky Creek on the Palmer field.

One of the townships on the Hodgkinson field was named Watsonville — whether after Alex or Bob is not clear. It was situated on Cornish Jimmie Creek a few miles down the river from Thornborough. The name was later changed to Woodville. The Government Geologist, Dr. R. L. Jack, visited Watsonville, six miles west of Herberton, at the end of 1882. The principal mine then was the North Australian, owned by two Irishmen, Casey and O'Loan. Dr. Jack reported that 600 tons of ore had been raised, estimated to go sixty per cent black tin. Casey and O'Loan won £60,000 worth of tin from this mine when top price was £30 per ton; it would be worth millions of dollars today. The owners sold their mine for £30,000. The outcrop stood several feet out of the ground and blocks of ore weighing several hundredweight each lay on the surface.

(125)

Casey, a "flash" miner, lost a lot of his money at the early-day race meetings in Herberton. He owned a good horse called Finnigan and matched him against another horse called Baldy. The first wager was £1000, later increased to £4000. Baldy won from the barrier rise and there is a story that a man was posted behind a tree about two furlongs from home with a revolver, and if Finnigan had been leading at that stage he would have been shot.

The Great Western mill and the Bischoff mill on the Walsh River — the latter was the only hydro-powered mill in the North — began crushing early in 1884.

Meanwhile, there had been big developments in the hills about twelve miles to the south-west.

A party of seven prospectors found rich tin in a mine they called the Great Southern. The party was Jimmy Gibbs (who had been with Mulligan), Jim McDonald, Bill Eales, Andy Thompson, David Green, Jack Green, and Jack Pollard.

John Moffat who had bought into the Great Northern mine at Herberton and erected the battery and dam on the Wild River in 1881, became interested in the new discovery by Gibbs and party.

There are few better known names in North Queensland's mining history than that of John Moffat. He became a legend in his own lifetime, and since then the legend has grown. There are still old timers in the Cairns district who knew him personally, and all agree that he was a man of sterling character.

Randolph Bedford, the old time writer, wrote of John Moffat: "He respected all men, quarrelled with none, gave to every man his chance, lived cleanly, spoke evil with none, and whenever he came to a stile, he looked for the lame dog."

He wa s born at the Loudoun Mill, on the bank of the River Irvine, near Glasgow, Scotland, in the year 1841. As a young man, in 1865, he sailed for Australia in the full-rigged ship, Whirlwind, (Captain Bullybrand). For some years he followed station work and all sorts of odd jobs, and later had a drapery store in Stanley Street, South Brisbane in partnership with Robert Love. The latter became a well known resident of Mareeba years later, and was manager of Jack and Newell's store for a long period.

John Moffat went to the Stanthorpe tinfield in the early 'seventies and there became interested in metals and mining. With John Holmes Reid he was a leading figure in the establishment of the Glen Smelting Company at Tent Hill. From here he went north to Herberton. With the Great Northern mill under way, crushing tin ore from the early Herberton mines, Moffat went home on a trip to Scotland. He sailed from Cooktown in 1882 on the Chybassa, one of the old British India Steamship vessels which took the Torres Strait route. He visited the tin mines of Britain and modern treatment plants and smelters in Germany. Full of energy and new ideas, he returned to Australia in the steamship, Cuszco, one of the earliest steamers of the Orient Royal Mail Line.

Arriving back at Herberton in 1883, Moffat found that the main thing everyone was talking about was the sensational tin discovery by Gibbs and party in the hills to the west. Moffat immediately became interested and negotiated for the purchase of the Great Southern mine for, it has been said, £6,000. After ninety-five years, this mine is still producing tin. Other early mines were the Comet, Adventure, Freethinker, Homeward Bound, Ibis, and Tornado.

Moffat moved from Herberton to Gibbs' Camp as it was known, situated in a valley in the hills where two creeks met. They had been named Gibbs Creek and McDonald Creek after the prospectors. It was Moffat who named the locality and the town that came into being on this site, Irvinebank, after his birthplace in Scotland. It was to be Moffat's home and headquarters of his many activities for the next thirty years.

Of the original prospecting party of seven men, only one stayed on the site of his discovery. He was Billy Eales who died in Irvinebank in 1913. Jimmy Gibbs became a publican

(127)

in Watsonville and died there in 1906. His son went prospecting to the Northern Territory and became a station owner. Jim McDonald became one of the early farmers near Tolga, growing horse feed for the carriers and packers. Andy Thompson heard the call of gold at Coolgardie in Western Australia in the 'nineties. David Green became a journalist and rose to be editor and managing director of the North Queensland Newspaper Company, first at Charters Towers, then in Townsville. What became of his brother Jack, no one seems to know.

John Moffat immediately began construction of a battery and a dam. The dam, built of logs, impounded an area of about thirteen acres at the junction of Gibbs and McDonald Creeks. He built his homestead and office on a hill overlooking the dam, and the battery close by. This was only a five-head battery at first. It caused an influx of prospectors and many more mines were discovered. Moffat also began immediate construction of a smelter. By the end of 1884, both plants were in full production. The smelter, greatly enlarged, operated until 1920. The present State Treatment Works which still pounds away on Irvinebank tin ore, is on the site of John Moffat's original plant which was eventually enlarged from five to forty head of stampers, with the addition of a ball mill.

One hundred men were employed at first, and the town of Irvinebank grew steadily. On May 12, 1884, the first white child was born — John James Irvine Bethel. By 1907 Irvinebank was at the peak of its prosperity with a population of around two and half thousand, with every hillside and the whole valley covered in houses. John Moffat was employing 600 men. Irvinebank had rail communication, in the form of a tramway from the Chillagoe Line, three years ahead of Herberton, although agitation had begun in Herberton for a railway in 1882.

The prospectors were pushing still further out. Tin was discovered at Stannary Hills in 1884, and silver-lead at Montalbion in 1883.

It was on the rugged hill of Mt. Albion in country more

level than at Irvinebank, four miles to the east, that the Prentiss Bros. made their strike. An old time geologist described the hill as "a great lonely-looking mass with bold and majestic outlines rising 600 ft. sharply above the surrounding country."

Mt. Albion still stands as it has ever stood since Time began among miles of leafy ironbarks, stony ridges and coarse grass that hide a few signs of man's unrest. There are house blocks in the grass, some weathered cypress pine posts, broken bricks, foundations of part of a smelter, and a few bits of iron. Here, three-quarters of a century ago, a thousand people lived and worked — and died. Only their debris, and their graves are left. This was once the flourishing town of Montalbion. For a few years it was a coach change on the important arterial road from Port Douglas to Croydon.

Mike O'Callaghan of Cairns remembers seeing Cobbs' coach come in and stood close by as the horses were changed. He learnt his "three R's" in the long vanished school by the dam. Only a few brumbies, kangaroos, and station cattle drink at what was once the town's water supply. A few stones, some broken and defaced, and a few rusted iron railings, mark where some of the pioneers — and their children — sleep: Rose Mary˙Lily Foy who died at the age of ten years on 27th. November, 1886; John Joseph Graham died 6th. October 1889; George Gaspar Mihr died 4th. February 1900.

Before the rise of Irvinebank, Montalbion was the largest town on the tinfields outside Herberton, but its glory was brief. For less than twenty years the smokestack of the smelters belched forth volumes of smoke and fumes over the town. When the smoke drifted away so did the town and its people, all of which revolved around the smelters and the mines. Montalbion was the headquarters of the Walsh Divisional Board (shire council), the only post and telegraph office and hospital. All these facilities were moved to Irvinebank when Montalbion died around 1905.

The first hospital was built of canvas and calico tied on to saplings, and only the crudest facilities were available. It speaks volumes for the healthiness of the climate — and the stamina of the patients and staff — that no epidemics occurred. But at least one mining settlement further out — Muldiva — was decimated by typhoid.

Matron Montgomery and her husband, in charge at Montalbion, moved to the Tate Tin Mines where conditions would not have been any better. Matron A. Morton was in charge by 1889 when a substantial cottage hospital was built. A well known matron was Matron McCarthy whose daughter Mary was to become matron of the Townsville hospital for twenty years. Her mother left Montalbion to open an hotel at Calcifer, the pioneer copper mining settlement that pre-dated Chillagoe. When Montalbion hospital was moved to Irvinebank, the doctor was Dr. Alex Jack, the last in Montalbion, and Dr. McDonald was the first in Irvinebank.

Early shire clerks of the Walsh Divisional Board at Montalbion were John. Cairns and Billy Rawlings. During the time the latter was M.P. for Woothakata, Archie Morton was clerk. It is recorded that in 1889, A. W. Richards was chairman, and Michael Henry was the Irvinebank representative.

In the late 'eighties and early 'nineties, Montalbion had seven hotels — some idea of its size and importance. They were conducted by George Mihr, James Murphy, Ben Joy, Jim Jennings, Sam Bennett, "Red Jim" Tait with the ginger beard, and John Quill. Mihr's hotel was the last to close, in 1903. Mike O'Callaghan recalls that Mihr's, Murphy's, Jennings', and Joy's hotels were all situated in the main street and Tait's and Bennett's were in a street called Espina Street which faced the smelters. Quill's was on the edge of the town.

John Langtry re-opened Murphy's hotel briefly during a slight mining revival in 1899. He had had a large bullock team on the Port Douglas Road but had seen it wiped out in the terrible tick plague. Many of the hotelkeepers ran other businesses while their wives looked after the hotel. For instance, Jim

(130)

Murphy had a butchery, Ben Joy was a blacksmith, and Jim Tait was a carrier. Old timers say that George Mihr was a man of many parts. He had been a medical orderly on a German immigrant ship and in Montalbion he often assisted Dr. Stewart. He died in Montalbion in 1900.

The Peters family were well known citizens. Wilhelm (Willie) Peters was a carpenter and landed at Cardwell with Dalrymple's party which founded the settlement in January 1864. His first son was named Cardwell as he was the first white child born there. The other sons were Percy and Billy. At Montalbion the sons engaged in mining.

Mike O'Callaghan recalls that Cardwell, who never married, was an expert with the accordion and concertina and, as he says, "many a campfire gathering on the mining fields was brightened as a consequence."

Good fortune came Cardwell's way in 1908 when he and the two Roos brothers, Fred and Theodor, found one of the richest tin mines in the back country — the Tommy Burns near Sunnymount on the Mt. Garnet line. They sold out to a mining company floated in Irvinebank; George Davis was an early manager. Cardwell retired to Mareeba where he died; his father is also buried there, as is his brother Percy. The latter went in for cattle raising and butchering. Billy Peters worked silver lead and tin mines around Montalbion and Irvinebank most of his life, one of the richest and long lasting being the Rainbow near Irvinebank.

The Queensland National Bank opened in Montalbion in the late 'Eighties, and James Allison, manager, and a teller named Coomber, are recalled.

"Red" Jim Tait was another man of pioneer days whose descendants still live in the Cairns district. He had a saw-pit in Irvinebank in the very early times where local cypress pine was laboriously cut by hand into building timber. He opened the Commercial Hotel and when Montalbion boomed he sold out and took over the Smelters Hotel there. He was also a butcher, storekeeper, carpenter, and carrier in the old mining town. He was a member of every committee and was universally popular.

When Montalbion declined, Jim Tait went carrying with a seven-horse dray. He would also cart maize to the mining fields from Chinese growers at Atherton. He joined in the mad gold rush to New Guinea in the 'Nineties and died there.

The pioneer storekeepers were Jack and Newell who opened a branch in Montalbion around 1885. Tom Blackley was their manager for many years until the store closed in 1901 and he was transferred to the firm's Watsonville branch. When the railway reached Atherton in 1903 he went there and opened a store on his own account. John Henry had a large store in Montalbion also, and he ran it until his death in 1896. J. McIntosh was another storekeeper. A Chinese, Tye Lee, had a store on the outskirts of the township.

During Montalbion's prosperous days, all stores had to come by wagon or packteams from Port Douglas, and later from Mareeba. There were no butter factories in the Cairns district in those days. Butter was a luxury, beef dripping being universally used. Joe Marsterson rode up the range from Mutchilba on the Walsh with his home-made butter packed in stone jars on either side of a packhorse, at regular intervals. Hans Wieland had a dairy on the Irvinebank road.

Butchers were Jim Murphy and the Halpin Bros. Those who followed were George Hume, Jack Mollett, and in 1900, the Day Bros. of Watsonville.

The town dam was built of stout ironbark logs and local clay, a structure that has stood for ninety years, so the workmanship must have been first class. Residents of Montalbion had to cart their water from this dam in casks in a spring cart or in canvas bags on a packhorse. For the people of the mining towns in those days there were practically no amenities or labor saving devices which today would be deemed essential.

A woman, a strange wanderer of the back country settlements, occasionally came to Montalbion. This was "Annie Bags". No one knew her real name, nor would she divulge it, but it was said she was a German or Hungarian countess who had fallen on evil times and preferred to live the life of a hobo. She wandered on foot from one mining town to another accompanied by a retinue of dogs, cats, a cockatoo, and a goat. She carried all her worldly possessions in a couple of sugarbags.

Montalbion had a large Irish population. The centenary of the Irish rebellion of 1798 was celebrated with a great sports gathering, and a photo of the organising committee is still in existence. Race meetings were popular events, the Montalbion racecourse also catering for Irvinebank.

As well as the Walsh District Amateur Turf Club, Montalbion had a flourishing rifle club back in the late 'Eighties, and a cricket club also. Cricket matches were played regularly with the other mining towns. Old timers recall one big match that took place at Montalbion in 1899 between the Irvinebank team and the survey party then at work on the Chillagoe Railway construction between Boonmoo and Petford. Harry Thornloe Smith, the chief surveyor, was a good cricketer but nevertheless the crack Irvinebank team which had good bowlers like "Snowy" McKinnon and Ted Arbouin, severely trounced the surveyors on the old Montalbion ground. Ted Arbouin made 51 runs that day. Old timers also remember the Aboriginal wicketkeeper, Albooma. He was also a fine athlete, but met his match in Charlie Wessells of Watsonville, a renowned footrunner.

The little pack mules, Spider and Pompey, have already been mentioned. (See Chapter 6). They were owned by a Canadian packer, Davey Thom, who had a string of ninety mules. He also used Spider and Pompey in a buggy, and it was one of the sights of Montalbion to see Davey and his fiancee bowling into and out of town with the two tiny mules going at a hand gallop. Before returning to Canada a few years later, Davey sold his team to the Irvinebank Mining Company.

The Montalbion smelters were erected by Moffat and Young in 1885. Limestone for fluxing was obtained from Newellton, Silver Valley, and iron oxide from the Wild River. That year 2028 tons of ore were smelted for a yield 193,653 ounces of silver then worth £37,000. In 1887, over 272,000 ounces were won and Moffat and Young sold the plant to a London company for £170,000. The Montalbion Silver Mining and Smelting Company was formed. It had varying fortune from year to year; much of the silver ore could not be treated because of galena. In 1890, the recovery of silver improved under "Captain" Rodger's supervision, and 66 men were employed at the mines.

In 1891 the company collapsed, and despite a reconstruction the following year, the works closed in 1893 due mainly to the fall in silver prices because of the economic depression at the time. Arthur W. Richards staved off the company's liquidation by re-opening the smelters and making a small profit; 64,000 ozs. of silver were produced in 1894. In 1895, a "Cairns Argus" correspondent praised Richards highly for his management and stated he had taken over the company's properties on tribute. By 1898, however, only a few small mines were working and when Richards had re-treated all the discarded mullock, the smelters closed in 1899 for good. The plant was dismantled and carted away on wagons to Mt. Garnet where copper had excited everyone's fancy.

A brief revival occurred at Montalbion in 1900 when the Kitchen Bros. opened a silver-lead mine, the Victoria Extended, but the town was finished. By 1906 it had virtually ceased to exist.

*   *   *   *

In 1881, J. V. Mulligan, James Newell, and William Bruce Stenhouse were prospecting the ranges west of Herberton. Camped on the Dry River they indulged in some target practice with their rifles on the bluff opposite. Investigating the result, they found their shots had exposed a lode of native silver.

Thus was Silver Valley found. It was one of the earliest discoveries of silver in Australia, and years before Broken Hill. The township that sprang up was named Newellton after James Newell, brother of the more famous John.

Some of the silver claims returned 150 ozs. to the ton when a small waterjacket blast furnace was erected by a Melbourne syndicate. Most of the ore, however was transported in drays to Montalbion with two teams of horses to negotiate the ranges. Limestone from Silver Valley was transported in the same way. In the days before cement as we now know it, lime mortar was used, obtained by burning limestone in limekilns. Limestone from Silver Valley was used in the kilns at Irvinebank.

William Lees, a mining writer in "Queensland Country Life" in 1907 stated that the country for two miles around Silver Valley was seamed with lodes carrying up to 800 ounces of silver to the ton. Some of the lodes were ten feet wide. Lode tin and alluvial was also won in vast quantities, and there is still tin there. J. V. Mulligan found the Magnum Bonum, a very rich tin mine in the early years. The depression of the 'Nineties ruined silver mining here also.

Crushing of tin ore began at Silver Valley before Irvinebank, and old records reveal that the battery erected on Thompson's Creek only worked from 20th. March 1883 to December 1884 when it was dismantled and transported to Irvinebank for John Moffat. The North Australian Mining Company had built this battery and also a dam on Thompson's Creek. Silver ore sent to the Sydney Mint from McFadden's claim, Paddy's Hole, returned 104 ozs. to the ton. Jack Pollard, Jim Newell, and McLean had the Caledonia, and other early mines were the Silver Streak, John Bull, White Star, and Rainbow. Jack Pollard was one of Irvinebank's discoverers, and lived around Montalbion in the boom days.

Australia then had no smelters to deal with complex ores so as with Montalbion, the silver of Silver Valley was passed over in favour of the tin. Much work was done at the Irvinebank smelters to obtain a pure metallic tin, and this could be done by mixing in high grade stream tin from Emu Creek, the Tate, Nettles Creek, and other places as the years passed.

Up to World War I., Silver Valley produced huge quantities of tin, but figures and totals are not available, and in this story of the pioneers we are trying to avoid too many statistics which are wearying.

German buyers were interested in the complex ores of Silver Valley. Harrod's Hadleigh Castle mine where 80 tons of ore was picked up on the surface, was on the slope of the range above Newellton, 2955 feet above sea level, and two miles away was the Lancelot, also owned by Harrod in 1895. F. E. Clotten from Frankfurt-on-Maine formed a company at Herberton and bought the Lancelot and other mines. A battery was erected and the more complex ore, after the best of the tin was extracted, was sent to Germany. Old timers remember a Dr. Edlinger who wore thick pebble glasses, looked rather like old Emperor Franz Josef, and studied grasstrees and their resin. He and all the other Germans disappeared when World War I. broke out in 1914.

The Hadleigh Castle and many smaller mines continued working, but the prosperous days were over, for the First World War sounded the deathknell to the type of mining the pioneers knew. Some of the old mines are still being gone over. In 1951, Harry Thompson, then of Mareeba, reconstructed the old Lancelot, or Silver Valley, battery, and reopened the Westward Ho silver lead and copper mine, but the revival was brief.

Up to fifty years ago, big tonnages of ore came to the Lancelot by packteams and horse drays; Gus Arnott and Dan Rawlings ran the battery for years. Other hard working miners of the area were Harry Oxten and Jim Plant who found Mt. Nolan, and Alf Lenton, George and Gus Furlong, Bert and Ted Putts, and others over the years. In 1918, Hubert Barrett bought Mt. Nolan and ran the battery. Fred. Morris and Dan Rawlings struck it rich and sold their mine for £1500, then considered a high price.

Morris Barrett and George Crow had a mine on the Dargo Range, and one day a delayed charge of dynamite exploded in George's face. Morris Barrett brought him to the surface by means of the windlass and bucket, saddled a horse and rode for help. Bill Peterson — who tells this story — his brother George and a mate, Archie Thorbourne, returned with Barrett on foot, made a stretcher out of bags and saplings, and carried the terribly injured miner over the mountains for five miles, but he died before medical aid could be obtained.

Mr. W. H. Peterson, who lived at Innot Hot Springs for years, was on the Ebagoolah Goldfield at the beginning of this century, and has a fund of memories about the old mining days.

He recalls there was quite a township at Silver Valley 60 years ago. The main suppliers of foodstuffs were another firm of "universal providors" in the mining and farming districts inland from Cairns — Armstrong, Ledlie, and Stillman. Frank Wieland had a butchery and was the last owner of the Silver Valley Hotel; he pulled it down and built his home in Herberton from the materials. Then there was Tom Miller the packer who was also a champion buckjump rider.

W. H. Peterson wrote in the "North Queensland Register" (August 17, 1974): "The old spirit of mining is not around today. I clearly remember the original pioneering atmosphere of Silver Valley when it was a new and lusty mining baby, alive and active in its faith in the future. But that was long ago . . . . "

An example of the initiative of the old time miners and their capacity for hard work, can be seen today in the remains of a water race which they built to take water from the Wild River to the Dry River. The water was conducted by gravity from a waterfall along the sides of rocky hills and across gullies in viaducts of hand-placed rocks fitted together without mortar. The channel cut through rocky outcrops, and was quite an engineering feat.

(137)

CHAPTER 9

ABORIGINES

Hostile Natives — Death of a People.

The Barbaram tribe roamed from the Clohesy River area south-west to the Upper Walsh, Irvinebank, Mt. Garnet, and Almaden regions, while the Ngatjen were scrub-dwellers from Atherton eastward to Malanda and Millaa Millaa. The Djirubal possessed the country from the Herberton Range south to Ravenshoe, Tully Falls, and south-west to Cashmere. The Hodgkinson area was the country of the Muluridji.

It was inevitable that the early miners in the Herberton area should clash with the natives, as had John Atherton to the north. Harry Reade, writing in the "N. Q. Register" dated March 1, 1975, recounted a story told him by Mr. Ray Hood of Mareeba, a recently retired executive of the pioneer firm of Jack and Newell at both Herberton and Mareeba. He told how his father, in the early days of Herberton found a party of five Government surveyors whose camp on the Wild River had been attacked by Aborigines. Four of the white men were dead, but the fifth man was still alive; he had a cruel barbed spear through his stomach.

Mr. Hood's father broke off the shaft of the spear and putting the barely conscious man across the pommel of his saddle he mounted and set off for Herberton as fast as his horse could go over the rough country with its double burden. Harry Reade described it thus:

"Some of the country he crossed is impassable even to four-wheel drive vehicles. The wounded man's blood drenched the saddle. Heartbursting climbs up the steep slopes were followed by wild plunging descents down the other side. A mile from the town the horse foundered and died under them. Mr. Hood's father carried the wounded man the rest of the way on his back. The doctor cut out the spearhead — and the man lived."

There is an old report that miners were speared at Nigger Creek — hence the name, this derogatory term for the Aborigines then being in general use — in the early days of the rush to Herberton.

Dr. R. L. Jack, the geologist, reported in 1882 that the Spear Claim and the King of the Ranges at Watsonville were owned by Gillespie and Scouller, and the former owner was killed by the Aborigines. Scouller was also speared, but not fatally, while working the King of the Ranges.

Old timers say two men were working a claim, later called the Spear, when a crowd of natives approached and speared the man on top. When the man below came up to see what had happened, they speared him also. Their names do not seem to have been recorded and no one knows where they are buried.

In 1977, Dr. Noel Loos of the James Cook University, Townsville, completed an exhaustive study into the relations between the Aborigines and Europeans in North Queensland from 1861 to 1897. The following is an extract.

"Herberton was only a year old when the citizens discovered their vulnerability to ambush and sudden attack. In January or February 1882, three miners were speared, one fatally, while in April a pony express contractor was surrounded and killed in broad daylight only one mile from the small mining town of Nigger Creek and three miles from Herberton. A petition signed by 265 people pointed out their inability to protect themselves from ambush and requested that the Aborigines be driven from the district by the Native Police. The Police Commissioner was instructed to respond accordingly. A detachment of Native Police was moved to Herberton and two other detachments were ordered to patrol the district. In his recent research Professor Dixon referred to 'the almost instant elimination' of the Barbaram tribe situated on the Herberton tinfield . . . . considering the petition of 1882, it is not surprising. Later that year, after two more spearings and a spate of camp

(139)

robberies, the 'Herberton Advertiser' remarked:

" 'Verily we live in troublesome times and can hardly bring ourselves to consider the Black Police as the most effective instrument possible for the suppression of myalls . . . .' "

The "Cairns Post" of 11 April 1888 reported: "A rifle and revolver are as necessary to the miner as a pick and a shovel."

Dr. Loos noted that "Roads from Herberton to Cairns and Port Douglas became dangerous trade routes and requests for police protection were frequent. Some settlers . . . . were killed and the Chinese were reported working for security in groups of twenty on the Johnstone River. In fact, the local correspondent to the 'Queenslander' reported 'the scrub and the blacks are terrors . . . .' "

In 1884, the "Wild River Times" said that raids by Aborigines had become of such a frequent occurrence "in the neighbourhood of the scrub in the vicinity of Herberton (being indeed of almost daily occurrence) that their recital wearies us as well as our readers, and it is only the more sensational cases that now find any interest outside the victims of their thieving, destruction, and bloodthirsty propensities."

The Native Mounted Police whose camp was formed at Nigger Creek (probably after the surveyors were killed) were sent out to "disperse" the natives. All the warriors escaped so the police are said to have shot all the women and children they found in the camp. A map drawn by Peter Moffat in 1884 shows a spot a mile south-west of Irvinebank as being the "Scene of massacre of Aboriginals by black troopers." It is between Graveyard Gully and Fireclay Gully, in the high ranges.

Seventy years ago, Jim O'Hara, one of the pioneer miners of Coolgarra, told Bill Roberts, who provided the writer with much valuable information, the following story.

One day in 1884, Jimmy rode into Herberton to register a claim at the warden's office. Mounted on a big 16.2 hands thoroughbred with a very hard mouth, he was on his way home to Coolgarra when near Watsonville the horse suddenly bolted and Jimmy could not control him for some distance.

Looking back, Jimmy saw several naked blacks coming out of hiding near the track. His horse had probably saved his life as the natives were undoubtedly lying in ambush ready to spear any travellers.

This incident led to the miners combining to drive the Aborigines from the district, Bill Roberts was told. Tony Linedale, an associate of John Moffat, also told him that he was at Emuford when the blacks were banished from Watsonville.

It was near sundown, and from his camp he heard a strange and disturbing noise from a ridge west of the camp; then the blacks came into view, silhouetted against the sunset.

The wailing and screeching came from these people and it transpired they were the ones driven away by the miners of Watsonville. They were allowed to settle around Emu Creek, and Con Halpin, who had a cattle run there, periodically slaughtered a beast for them, hoping thereby it would prevent them killing his stock, and the idea worked.

The settlers in the scrub country around Atherton also used peaceful methods after the Native Mounted Police had failed to bring peace to this Northern frontier of the 1880's. Their horses were useless in the rain forest, which provided ideal protection for the native guerillas.

They constantly speared the Mazlin Bros.' horses and thieved from timber-getters and teamsters. At the Woothakata Divisional Board (Shire) elections of May 1888, it was reported that the presence of a large party of hostile blacks around Atherton — already settled for about six years — prevented forty men from voting. This was one of the few occasions the primitive spearmen held up the process of constitutional government, albeit unwittingly.

A settler near Atherton wrote to the "Herberton Advertiser" in 1890 describing how he and his neighbours had to always carry firearms with them even while felling scrub as they risked being speared or tomahawked at any moment. (Quoted by

H. Reynolds in "Lectures in N.Q. History", James Cook University, 1975).

Dr. Loos writes: "The selectors near Atherton urged the Government to try to conciliate the Aborigines. As a result, a policeman known for his concern for, and skill in dealing with the Aborigines, Constable Hansen, was sent to make contact with the rain forest Aborigines. When this was affected, it was found that the Aborigines were starving, or would have been, if they had not robbed the settlers. Food was provided for the Aborigines on the understanding that they stopped their raids.

"The scheme was an immediate and dramatic success. Depredations ceased almost entirely. Selectors were able to clear more land and profit by the harvests, and very soon Aborigines were working for the settlers and providing a plentiful source of cheap labour . . . . Soon a number of food distributing centres were set up in North Queensland to pacify the Aborigines of other districts. This policy was continued beyond 1897 when the first Protection Act was passed . . . ." This policy, while more humane than the Snider rifle, nevertheless was to contribute to the annihilation, through degredation and sickness.

Mr. W. Johnston, president of the Cairns Historical Society, wrote in the Society's bulletin No. 106, February 1968, concerning the treatment of the Aborigines in the Eighteen-eighties period near Cairns and in the back country:

"Poisoned flour left in prospectors' camps . . . . the shooting of Myalls on sight, these are some of the stories handed down. The armed bands and 'nigger hunts' which wiped out men, women, and children at Bones Knob and at Evelyn . . . . retribution, which was seldom a matter for boasting . . . . (At Cairns) within a decade, the tribesmen had been subdued, and a camp established on Lily Creek, with mia-mias built of bags, old kerosene tins, and bark. There they lived mainly on charity, degraded, diseased, nondescript, issued with one blanket each year by the police. In return for this gift, the once proud warriors gave a war dance upon demand . . . . "

Old timers remember "blanket day" at Irvinebank, Thornborough, and other places in the 'nineties and early this century, when Queen Victoria, represented by the local police, gave of her bounty to her lowliest subjects, one blanket a year being poor and bitter compensation to a people left dispossessed and hopeless.

On the Tablelands, no mission stations were established. Near Kuranda, the Seventh-Day Adventist Church established Mona Mona in 1912. On the coast those at Cape Bedford near Cooktown, at Bloomfield River, (both 1886) and at Yarrabah near Cairns in 1892, helped to save the Aborigines from extinction. Around Mareeba and the Tablelands, the influenza epidemic of 1919 almost wiped out the remnants who had survived the carnage of the early days.

A few years; ago there were old timers still living who could tell tales of narrow escapes from the blacks; men like the Dickson cousins, founders of Bolworra Station in 1878. It is on the Lynd and Tate Rivers, a locality then noted for the hostility of its cannibal tribes. The Jardine expedition was attacked in this area several times in 1864.

About 1880, when camped at a lagoon on Bolworra, the Dicksons were attacked and had to fight for their lives. The spears fell like rain and the men's Snider rifles cut a swathe in the ranks of the warriors, but still they came on and the pioneers were almost overwhelmed. One had received a spear through his arm and another in his thigh and he gasped to his mate, "Shoot the tall 'nigger' with the rusty hair or we're done!" The tall native who was obviously the leader and showing great courage, fell to the pioneer's deadly rifle and the attackers melted away into the bush.

Robert Peter Dickson died in Chillagoe in 1913. He sold Bolworra to the late Freeman Lawrence in 1904. Dickson also formed Dagworth on the Einasleigh River.

The late Ted Henry spent his youth in Irvinebank. His

(143)

father and uncle were saddlers attached to the Queensland Mounted Police and were first stationed in Port Douglas. Ted's father Michael Henry made trips with the gold escorts to and from the Hodgkinson and Croydon. On one occasion signs of Myalls were noticed so after having their evening meal around the campfire, the escort party unrolled their swags in a patch of scrub a hundred yards away. It was just as well for in the morning a dozen spears were stuck in the ground near the campfire.

In the late 'Eighties, Michael Henry left the police employ and with his wife and children trekked to Irvinebank in a covered cart pulled by two horses, going by way of Cattle Creek, Parada, and then up the range to Eureka Creek (Stannary Hills of later on). Camped at the latter creek, the wild blacks surrounded the camp at night, unknown to the Henrys. They were asleep under the cart when six spears landed through the canvas top.

Michael Henry, a fearless bushman of fighting Irish blood, leaped up, a long-barrelled "Frontier Colt" revolver in each hand. His wife had a new "Winchester 73" and knew how to use it. They fired six shots from each weapon. Henry sat up on guard the rest of the night, but the attackers had been frightened off by the fusillade.

When the Wieland family established their farm between Irvinebank and Montalbion in the early 'eighties they constantly had their cattle speared by the blacks.

A carrier named Watson was carrying on the Port Douglas Road when the front axle of his wagon broke on the Herberton Range. He had his wife and young son with him, the latter acting as "spare boy" for his father. Watson packed the broken axle on horseback to Herberton for repair, leaving his wife and son with the wagon.

Next morning they were startled to see five naked clay-daubed Aborigines, each mounted on a fine draught horse, riding up the road. One was smoking a Chinese pipe evidently taken from a murdered Chinaman. Mrs. Watson had a rifle, but she was relieved that the blacks passed by, staring insolently, and disappeared into the scrub.

A short time later a carrier rode up on horseback; the horses had been stolen from his team, but it would have been suicide for him to try to recover them alone. The blacks often stole horses and hid them until they needed them for food but in their wild state they seldom rode them as they were usually frightened of the animals. The carrier told the Watsons they were lucky they were not molested as the horse stealers belonged to a war party that had put up a very stubborn fight against the Native Mounted Police at Scrubby Creek a few weeks previously.

Not many people may know that the Aborigines who inhabited the rain forests of the Tableland and were a small people, no more than five feet tall and of slight build, were a branch of the Negritos, the same race that were better known in Tasmania where they became extinct a hundred years ago. Generally they were inoffensive people. Thousands of years ago they came southward from South-East Asia to be eventually overwhelmed by a larger, more powerful and more aggressive race who are the ancestors of most of the Aborigines. Only a small number of the pygmy Aborigines survived by taking refuge in the impenetrable jungles of the coastal ranges of North Queensland, in Tasmania, and on Kangaroo Island. Only in North Queensland have remnants remained to the present day.

Norman Tindale of the South Australian Museum revealed these facts only in recent years. It was a photograph of Tableland natives of small stature, taken by the old time Cairns photographer the late Mr. Atkinson, that gave Tindale his first clue. These were the type of natives Christie Palmerston and others would have encountered in their jungle explorations; they were not just small specimens of Aborigines; they were a different race. Tindale found numbers of them living on a reserve near Mt. Molloy.

As happened practically all over Australia, the natives of the mining fields inland from Cairns acquired a type of civilisation that made them third-class citizens, living in unhygenic camps on scraps and handouts, in cast-off clothes, being the hewers of wood and carriers of water for white "boss" and "missus." There was "King" Maccalate with comic-opera brass plate on a chain around his neck who regularly visited John Moffat's office for a handout, and was never refused. There were the nameless "gins" who helped some of the pioneer women wash clothes and nurse children, being trusted and well fed. And there was pathetic Jimmy Berrigan, once a police tracker proud of his uniform. Discharged, he was allowed to keep it and was given a tent and a rusted-up shotgun without cartridges. It made him an important person among the camp blacks on the edge of town, and he strutted proudly, giving everyone orders.

Jimmy spoke good English and was considered "a flash nigger" by the whites from whom he cadged shamelessly. Most of the white women were afraid of him. Mrs. Michael Henry asked him what he thought of the fireworks display on the occasion of Queen Victoria's Diamond Jubilee in June, 1897. He shrugged, rolled his eyes and said with some disgust, "Only 'nuther way white man play."

A few former warriors who refused to conform and thieved food from prospectors' camps in order to live because all the wild game had been frightened away or shot out, were marked men. They were "outlaws", and were hunted as such.

One of these was called Jacky Norman. He was wanted by the police for stealing from tents and homesteads and for demanding food from settlers' wives with threats of being tomahawked. When Mrs. Langtry of Montalbion courageously refused his demand he threw his tomahawk at the slim verandah post of the hut, bringing the verandah crashing down. At that moment the terrified woman and her children neard horses' hooves and two mounted constables came cantering over the hill. "If they had been acting for the films of later years they couldn't have done it better," Ted Henry told me.

Jacky Norman bolted for the cover of thick bush where he had hidden his spears and boomerang. Constable McLaughlin from Watsonville, and champion athlete of the Northern police, rode him down and grappled with him. McLaughlin had drawn his revolver and the blackfellow fought to wrench it from his grasp.

As Constable Lannigan from Irvinebank raced up, Jacky Norman grabbed the revolver. It discharged, and the bullet struck Lannigan in the heart. Jacky escaped but was later captured and sentenced to life imprisonment in St. Helena gaol near Brisbane. Nowadays he would have received only a short sentence for resisting arrest, for the shooting was clearly accidental. Local feeling ran high as Lannigan was a very popular officer.

He was killed on the eve of his wedding to Minnie Kelly, a governess of Coolgarra. Later she married Jim Tunnie. Edward Lannigan's grave, dated 6th. September 1894, is in the little Irvinebank cemetery.

Another Aboriginal outlaw named Tommy was wanted for spearing a miner as he climbed out of his mine at Silver Valley. Another miner was reading a book by candlelight in his tent when Tommy put a spear through his hand and the book as well. In the eyes of the partly tame blacks in the camps he was a hero. He was proud of the crease in his skull where a Snider bullet had grazed it. He would come right into Irvinebank and used to talk to the lubras working in Jimmy Gibbs' hotel.

On one occasion Manny Borghero the packer saw him go into the kitchen where one of the native women used to give him food. The police trapped him there, and next day he was handcuffed and leg-ironed on a horse led by a mounted trooper and taken to Herberton. A crowd gathered at Jack and Newell's corner in Irvinebank to see them ride by.

(147)

CHAPTER 10

TOWNS OF THE PAST

When Watsonville was the Far North's Cultural Centre — an old timer's memories of Coolgarra and its Pioneers.

Along with Montalbion and Irvinebank, Watsonville is a place that old timers get very nostalgic about. Situated in a valley that was almost devoid of grass and surrounded by rocky hills where only goats could thrive, its people nevertheless had the reputation of being the most hospitable and friendly in the North. It was also a centre of entertainment and sport, from the late 'Eighties to the early 'Twenties.

Seventy years ago all young men within a radius of thirty miles who wished to learn to dance came to Watsonville. They came on foot, on horseback, and by buggy and coach. This then prosperous mining township had good singers, splendid violinists, a brass band, and a School of Arts library stuffed with the best literature of the day. Watsonville was perhaps the cultural centre of the Far Northern mining fields.

In sport, it held its own for half a century. As long ago as 1888, its tug-of-war team was invincible and held the championship for a decade. It was said their anchormen were trained by being pitted against the pin-horses of a team. Watsonville's footrunners were of Olympic standard. Old timers remember the Wilesmith brothers, Charlie Wessells, and Jimmie Gibbs.

But it was at rifle shooting that the Watsonville men really excelled. This tradition has lasted till the present day. Tennis was another very popular sport and one in which the ladies could participate. Hilda Roos held the N. Q. Championship for many years. One of the town's first champions was a tall youth named Speigelhauer. He, like hundreds of young men from the mining fields, gave his life in World War I.

Old timers speak of some of Watsonville's citizens, most of whom made their final homes in other Tableland towns or in Cairns as Watsonville faded. There was Harry Bradshaw, Tom Condon, John Stephens, Jim Donaldson, Barney Lesina, Hughie Reid, Ben Joy, and many families — the Roos, Days, Leinsters, Wilesmiths, Wessells, Putts, Matthews, Hammonds, Toys, Trevennen, Harrods, Borgheros, Dempsters, Aumullers, Tweedies, Cassidys, McKewans, Roberts, and many others. Some of them sleep in the little forgotten cemetery among the barren hills. These were the pioneers who wrested a living from these hard hills with pick and shovel.

The Federation Mine was 3435 ft. above sea level, the Great Western only twenty feet lower. The names of the mines reflect the nationality of some of the miners — the North Australian, Chance, Rose of England, Stewart's T. Claim, Queen of the West, Ben Lomond, Boundary, Pioneer, Bismarck, Caledonia, Ulster, Leinster, Glencairn, St. Patrick, Parnell, Argyle, Victoria, Dreadnought, King of the Ranges, Boulton's Folly, and others. A school reserve was gazetted in 1883.

The Bischoff Mill on the Walsh River was erected by H. W. F. Kayser from Mt. Bischoff, Tasmania. It was owned and managed by Hugh Dempster for many years. My friend, the late Gus Waddell, possessed a notebook of his father's containing a sketch of the Pelton wheel that was turned by water power, also drawings of the mill's stampers, jigs, buddles, tubs, and one of a "Munday" buddle 18 ft. in diameter. The latter was possibly the invention of John Munday, one of John Moffat's plant managers eighty years ago. The notebook which was dated 1906, also contained drawings of the New Era mill and Hardman's Star of the South mill on Chinaman's Creek.

Charlie Wessells, who died a few years ago almost a centenarian, had many memories of old Watsonville. He recalled popular Constable Stubbs who, though a fine horseman, was thrown from his horse and killed. He remembered Ben Joy's lovely daughter, Ann, who married a great athlete from Chillagoe named Arthur Blakey. He became John Moffat's private secretary. Ann was a talented pianiste.

(149)

There were five boys in the Lesina family and one, Barney, had both legs smashed when he slipped and fell under Kidner's bullock wagon which he was driving. Dr. Bowkett of Herberton and Dr. Jack of Montalbion managed to save his legs from being amputated, but they remained very crooked.

Hugh Dempster's brother, Jack who was a champion axeman, formed the Watsonville brass band, and the first members were Charlie Wessells, Harvey Bird, Oscar Roos, Bobby Wilesmith, Harry Howe, Theo Roos, and Charlie Arbouin. Before long there were eighteen players. A professor of music from Melbourne, J. Phelong, happened along on horseback and eventually took over the band and made it one of the finest in the North.

Charlie Wessells recalled how, as a boy, he took his first job at the Bischoff mill and had to start work so early that he had to walk the two miles along the mountain track in the dark with a lighted candle and with dingoes howling all around him. But at ten shillings (one dollar) a week he considered himself well paid.

His father had been a sailor on the old time full-rigged ships that sailed around the world in the Eighteen-'fifties. Later he and his father-in-law tried gold mining at Gympie. When tin was found at Herberton, the former, whose name was Baker, came North. He discovered the rich Monarch tin mine and sent for Charlie Wessell's father. As soon as he arrived he cut saplings and stripped bark to build a rough shack for his wife and family, including young Charlie. They came up to Herberton by Cobb and Co. coach from Port Douglas in 1882. Baker built a tin battery on Nigger Creek. The Wessells moved to Watsonville in 1885 ; it then had seven hotels and five general stores.

In 1910, the Irvinebank Mining Company erected a ten head battery at the United North Australian, and built a dam across Jamie's Creek. Machinery from a 20-head battery at Coolgarra was used. Results were disappointing as the concentrates contained copper and other minerals which created problems at the Irvinebank smelters. The mill closed when World War I. broke out, and nothing now remains of it. Sam Day was manager, James Puxley the mine boss, and Gilbert Petter, later a leading citizen of Herberton, was in the office.

Sam Day was later manager of the Great Northern at Herberton. He brought two famous mines to the notice of the Irvinebank Company — Rowland and Morris' Stella on Cassowary Creek, and the Pompeii at Bakerville. Old timers say the owners of the Stella "gave away a fortune without knowing it." Such is the luck of mining.

Well known hotelkeepers were T. C. Bird, Jimmy Gibbs, and the last one was Jack Leinster. Bird sold Ross's "Belfast Ginger Ale" in an oval bottle with wired cork and top. Jimmie Jack, brother of Willie Jack, had a store in the very early times, and this became merged with Jack and Newell. Halpin Bros. and Willie Dougherty were butchers. James Allison, who later opened the Q. N. Bank in Montalbion, opened the Watsonville branch in 1886. Little remains now to indicate that once a happy prosperous community lived here. The old home of the Roos still stands. Nearly all the other wood and iron buildings have gone and not even the stumps are left. Some tin is still being mined nearby, however, and there is at least one modern residence.

Bakerville, between Watsonville and Irvinebank, is also only a name on the map today. A pioneer miner was Louis Pedersen and another was Joe Matthews. Pedersen's sons are still mining in the area — they have the rich Peacemaker mine — and one son, Cecil, is Herberton's well known saddler. His mother was a Miss Struber whose father found the fabulous Perseverance mine. The Pedersens ran the Bakerville hotel for many years and remained as the last inhabitants of the place when the hotel closed.

Back in 1895, Joe Bradshaw and Alex Renton were associated with the Bakerville Tin Mining Company. Mines were the New Era, Roman, Pompeii, Hamilcar, Carthaginian, Phoenician, Sulphide, Tourmaline, and Bakerville Block. J. M. Potter erected a battery at the New Era. The Reliance mill produced 192 tons of tin from 1100 tons of stone. No doubt Bakerville was named after Charlie Wessell's grandfather, mentioned earlier.

*   *   *   *

Coolgarra is an Aboriginal name, but no one seems to know its meaning. Discovered by prospectors pushing out from Herberton soon after it was opened in 1880, it was established as a tin mining centre by 1884 as that year it is listed in a directory published in Herberton. The place had a crushing mill owned by Delaney and Co. and a police barracks and a "temporary lock-up." Coolgarra was 25 miles from Herberton and sixteen miles south-east of Irvinebank, at an elevation of 3000 ft. above sea level. In its first four years the battery treated 3845 tons of stone for 272 tons of 70 per cent metal. The fall in tin prices in the depression of the 'nineties caused the virtual closure of Coolgarra and its mines, but in October 1899, the Coolgarra Tin Mining Co. was formed and a 20-head battery erected in 1900. This crushed ore from the Alhambra, and other mines. From 1901 to 1903 the Alhambra produced £20,000 worth of tin when the price was £120 per ton.

Other early mines were the Vesuvius, the Fanny Parnell, the Alexandra Lode, the Pillar lease, Tasmanian, Cardigan, and Giblet's Lode. This was found by Ned Giblet, a Palmer Goldfield veteran. He also found the famous General Gordon mine at what became to be known as Glenlinedale. At that time tin fetched only £1 per unit; now it is around $130.00.

Pryor Treweek, a Cornishman, was manager of the Coolgarra Tin Co.: George Bradbury was in charge of the battery, and Ted Arbouin was tin dresser. There was also Evan Thomas, engineer, Archie Turner, assayer, and Arthur Blakey accountant and paymaster. The McAulay and Peter Armagnacq families were Coolgarra township's pioneers and the former stayed

(152)

on to be the last inhabitants of the place. The O'Haras were very early residents, and there was also Dick Baldickie and Harry Kuszner. Bob Anderson was in charge of Jack and Newell's store, and Fred Bimrose was associated with Armstrong, Ledlie, and Stillman's store.

With the closure of the Coolgarra Company's operations in 1903, the Irvinebank Company re-opened the mill a year or so later and crushed stone from other mines. It was supervised by John Murrane, for years a tin dresser at the Loudoun Mill at Irvinebank. J. R. Raleigh, previously manager at Mt. Garnet and Stannary Hills and later at Mt. Molloy, took charge in November 1906. The Irvinebank Company's pack team transported all ore from various mines to the Coolgarra battery. Packers were Bradshaw, Armagnacq, Callaghan, and Frank Wieland.

Bill Roberts remembers a one-armed teamster named George Frowen.

"People were amazed," Bill said, "that he was able to cope, as his left arm had been amputated at the shoulder as the result of a shotgun accident many years before. He harnessed his own team, and anyone who has put the collar and 'kangaroo' hames on a horse knows that still another hand would come in useful. He also shovelled the rough ore, often from off a rough bottom from the ore paddock to the dray, using a long-handled shovel. He could also wheel a wheelbarrow with a sling over his shoulders, but it still required a strong arm to steady it and push it along.

"Horse teams hauled supplies from Mt. Garnet to the cattle stations, and Harry Evans, a bearded patriarch, had a fine team, and was often seen at Coolgarra. I remember on one occasion he matched one of his team to scratch-pull against a pair of buggy horses that Dad was proud of. Harry's horses easily walked away with Taffy and Trinket as Dad's horses were named — a matched pair that had won first prize at a Herberton Show."

Bill Roberts recalls that Tom Kerr had the Mt. Garnet-

Coolgarra coach which was driven by Billy Rees and later by Frank Collins.

Asked about the packers, Bill said that Frank Wieland had a big pack team comprising mules and horses, and at one time a queer character who was afflicted with St. Vitus' Dance was his offsider. Despite his disability, he was a capable packer, and rode well. Wieland rode a fine big stallion called Columbus. Lang Lan Kee was a Chinese packer, based at Gurrumbah.

Nearly all the horses and mules in a team had bells. When a team was strung out, there would be a long distance between the leader and the men driving, and a rogue might wander off, but the bell betrayed him. Recalls Bill Roberts: "One would see a pack team jogging along with its cacophony of bells, and this is something of those days that is symbolical. A packer was known to be a good one if his team had few sore backs, and adversely if the team was plagued with them . . . . When No. 10 Tunnel on the Cairns Range railway collapsed in the heavy wet of 1911, we once again depended on the pack teams to bring supplies of all kinds all the way up from Cairns until the railway operated again."

Old timer, Bill Roberts, recalls that Coolgarra had a succession of well-respected school teachers. The first he remembers is M. M. O'Connor, then Cyril Ward and H. G. Youatt. Both these teachers were first class tennis players and were also Sunday School teachers. They started a school library and fostered a love of reading among their bush-bred pupils. Other teachers were Stuart Stormouth, W. F. McLeod, and L. C. Boyle. A later teacher was Hugh A. Borland, later well known as an authority on North Queensland history.

Coolgarra had two hotels. One, the Thistle-and-Shamrock, existed until 1969 when the last inhabitants, the McAulay family, left. The other hotel was the Coolgarra, owned by Dave Roberts and alternately run by him or Alfred Bowden. The two general stores were Jack and Newell, and Armstrong, Ledlie,

THE OLD "V" BATTERY AT MT. CARBINE

G.PIKE

(155)

and Stillman. Sonny McAulay was a butcher, George Crook had a bakery, and Constable Stephen Creedy was a popular policeman.

Families who went back to the early 'Eighties in Coolgarra were the McAulays — Ellie, Maggie, Sonny, Ada, Theresa, Clarence, Ethel, and Artie. Another big family was that of Peter Armagnacq and his wife — John, Victor, Jeanette, Tom, Josie, Lafayette, and Leon. David and Sarah Roberts included children Lily, Tom, May, Dave, Willie, and Alf.

Other Coolgarra citizens were George Crook and his wife and family; the Emslies, Manleys, Maltbys, Lynagh, Callaghan, Reynolds, Keegan, Corcoran, Jack Crook, Claus Linde, Dick Frazer, Bowden, and many more. There was Alby Murphy, Dick Lampard, Alec McLean, Jim Rooney, Alf Sheppard, Bendon, Green, Stapleton, Barrett, Jones, Larkin, Mitchelmore, Bowes, Martin Devery, Alf Lenton, Matt Fox, Charlie Wessels, Austin Rose, Sam Davidson, Sam Berke, Charlie King, Jim Dwyer, Billie Hansen, Arthur Blakey, Jim Crockett who took over Jack and Newell's store, and Alec Downie who was the last licensee of the Coolgarra Hotel. He was killed in World War I.

John Clancy managed the rich Excelsior mine a few miles out.

The Coolgarra men were very sports-minded, with footballers such as Bob and Sandy Anderson and Jack and Ernest Garbutt who were good footrunners as well.

Seventy-odd years ago there were several pack teams operating around Coolgarra. It was six year old Willie Roberts' task to go out at dawn with frost on the grass to locate his father's horses among the hundreds of animals grazing in the vicinity. They were recognised by the sound of the bells around their necks. Everyone rode horses, and picnics were popular, especially to John Broad's property, Uramo, on the Herbert River.

In those days, miners received a wage of eight shillings per day of 48 hours. Top men and shift bosses received ten

(156)

to eleven shillings. Hotel board was twenty shillings (two dollars) per week; it included breakfast, a cut lunch, and a good three-course meal at night.

Harry Kuzner, a Frenchman, was a carpenter and his wife was a midwife. She attended all confinements in the area for about thirty years, and she also made herself available in Irvinebank, thinking nothing of riding fast over the mountains at night, sidesaddle. Mrs. Kuzner had been a Mrs. Dines previously and members of the Dines family are still about the Tablelands.

In those days, the ultimate luxury in the home was the Coolgardie drip-safe, for refrigerators were unknown. The only cool water came from a waterbag, and in most miners' and settlers' homes the kerosene tin and the kerosene case were conspicuous; butter boxes, too, were prized. From all these, chests-of-drawers, small tables, stools, chairs, kitchen dressers, and settees were made. Great use was made of cretonne material to cover them.

The empty kerosene tin had a hundred-and-one uses. The tin scratcher cut a tin diagonally to make a "banjo" scoop.

Great improvisation went into making a "Jacob's ladder" — a central stick of timber pierced with augur holes with rungs of bloodwood sticks driven through, half on each side to give a hand or a foothold on either side. These ladders could be suspended or raised at will in a shaft when "firing out".

There was a brief revival — the last — in 1918 when Bill Craven, Archbold, and Runge, brought in a new battery from the Georgetown area. The teamsters were George and Jack Camp.

Tin is still being won at Coolgarra, this time by Tableland Tin Company's dredge. Bill Roberts recalled that Jimmy O'Hara, the discoverer of Coolgarra in 1882, was an old man when he knew him, and he liked to talk of the "early days".

Tin was then black in the creekbeds, and tons were obtained with dishes alone. It shows how rich the creeks in the area must have been when discovered by the O'Haras.

CHAPTER 11

THE COMING OF THE IRON HORSE

Old Herberton — Great Rides — Kuranda and Myola — The Third Section of the Railway — Mareeba and Clohesy Goldfields — Jordan Goldfield.

With the rapid decline of Thornborough and the Hodgkinson, Herberton became the most important town inland from Cairns. The pioneers thought of it as "the big place" and "going to town" meant going to Herberton, and it was quite a special occasion. But if you had not been to "The Towers" (Charters Towers) you were not travelled and not seen anything. At the end of last century and the early years of the twentieth, Charters Towers was called "The World". To go to Cairns meant only going "down to the coast" and was nothing special.

In imagination, we will roll back the years to the early 'Eighties and walk down Grace Street, Herberton, from the Wild River bridge facing south. On the right-hand side was the Cosmopolitan Hotel kept by John Hogsflisch, one of the discoverers of tin on the Tate. Next door was the "Wild River Times" office later moved to a building next door to Wieland's butchery. On the site of Madrid's house was Mrs. E. O'Brien Queen's Hotel. Next was a blacksmith's shop, then Jack and Newell. On the next corner was Munro and Gordon's butchery, owned by different parties at different times, and now demolished. Next door was Walsh and Co's general store.

Where the Queensland National Bank functioned until World War II when it became a private house and then J. J. Boyle's commission agency in the 'Fifties there was originally an hotel. Next to the bank was the Apothecaries' Hall (chemist and dentist) where Gilbert Petter's office was situated later on. Further along the street was J. Warby's agency.

The present School of Arts is a building of the 'Eighties. The Criterion was a two-storied hotel kept by James Finnigan which was Cobb's & Co's booking office. This hotel and one next door kept by Mrs. McManus, was burnt down in 1898. Later, Mr. Gilder built the picture theatre on the site.

We cross the street, and on the site of the present post office was O. Barrett's "Corner House" store, established in 1884. Going along the righthand side of the street, facing north, were several small shops, including Sam Denny's assay office, later a tailor's shop. Further along was the Federal Hotel, kept by W. Matthews in the 'Eighties.

Next door was Herman Selig's "Crystal Palace" store. From 1900 until a few years ago it was Armstrong, Ledlie, and Stillman's general store. They had branchers at Irvinebank, Coolgarra, Malanda, Peeramon, and Cairns, with headquarters at Atherton. They opened at Ravenshoe in 1918 and were active at Mt. Garnet from 1902 to 1919. The founders of the firm were originally employees of Jack and Newell. The late John Ledlie of Herberton and H. J. Armstrong, originally of Irvinebank, were staunch businessmen of the mining fields remembered by older residents today.

The Royal Hotel was a single storey building in the 'Eighties kept by Hides and McCall. It was rebuilt in its present form in 1914. Next door was Collins' "Tinaroo Store", and next door was another hotel also kept by Collins. Where Cecil Holdcroft conducted his newsagency for very many years, Airey and Berkley had a jeweller's shop as long ago as 1884. R. Firth had the Post Office Hotel where the Shire Hall now stands. It was advertised in 1883 as being "second to none of the first class hotels in the Colony" — rather a sweeping statement. It was eventually destroyed by fire. In the same fire went Robson's bakery next door.

Adjacent was John Hollway's commission agency, Callaghan's butchery, and the Mill Inn owned by Kilgour and Mihr. Charlie Harding's livery stables were next door. He lived out at Nigger Creek and bred good horses. Close to the stables was the post office in the 'Eighties. Across the Wild River was a butcher's shop and two more hotels. The old West End

Hotel was on the site of the former Church of England Girls' College, now occupied by Woodleigh College.

Out at Nigger Creek (Wondecla) a brewery was started in 1890, and at Deep Lead (Tepon) were two hotels kept by Murphy and Farrelly respectively. At Wondecla was the carriers' camping ground and nearby was the public water-race where the stream-tinners washed their dirt.

To fulfil spiritual needs in 1884 was Fr. J. D. Murray, later Bishop Murray (Roman Catholic); Rev. J. T. Maltby (Methodist), and Rev. J. Wilson (Anglican). The latter's successor was Rev. Gilbert White in 1890 — later Bishop of Carpentaria. The Catholic church was built in 1884, and St. Bernard's Convent was erected about 1910. The earliest Presbyterian minister was Rev. George Ewan in 1894. Around 1890, the Salvation Army "invaded" the mining towns and attracted crowds with their street hymn singing and brass band music.

Prior to 1883 the nearest mining wardens were at Thornborough, but from 1883 to 1894 a Mineral Lands Commissioner was stationed at Herberton. They were William Mowbray, A. H. Zillman, and A. R. McDonald. Wardens were A. C. Haldane, F. P. Parkinson, W. M. Lee-Bryce, P. M. Hishon, and others. Combined with this office was Police Magistrate. In the early days the Commissioners, and then the Wardens, attired like true pukka sahibs, complete with pith helmet, attended by a squad of Native Police troopers, undertook long horseback tours of the mining fields.

At the end of the 'Nineties, the population of Herberton reached its highest peak — about 1500. In 1906 there were 8335 people in the nearby district, but the town had lost population as Irvinebank was then booming.

An important Herberton citizen was Robert Colin Ringrose, a solicitor, barrister, geologist, member of the Royal Society, and a leading man in community affairs. He was president of the Chamber of Commerce for a long time.

(160)

He studied law in England and geology at Edinburgh University. He arrived in Herberton in 1887; its mineral country and rock formations fascinated him, and he was particularly interested in the Hypithamee Crater. Mrs. Ringrose was considered a beauty though it was whispered that she used nothing but powdered starch to retain her peaches-and-cream complexion. They had six children, the first two dying from diptheria in 1889. The home Mr. Ringrose built at the One Mile still stands. His memory is perpetuated in Mt. Ringrose. He died at Herberton on August 4th. 1914, and the family later moved to Brisbane. His youngest son, Edward Colin Davenport Ringrose became Director of External Studies at Queensland University; The Ringrose Memorial Libraries are named after him.

The Tinaroo District Hospital was functioning as far back as 1883 with Dr. W. D. Bowkett and Matron J. Montgomery in charge. The hospital has served the district well for over ninety years and it is a pity it is to be "phased out" and reduced to an out-clinic of the Atherton Hospital, twelve miles away. The Herberton Hospital was strategically situated to deal with accidents and sicknesses as far off as Irvinebank, Mt. Garnet, and the station country beyond.

In pioneer days, the Herberton Hospital was a godsend. In 1887, relays of miners carried an injured mate, Frank Blackmore, on a stretcher from Northcote on the Hodgkinson Goldfield to Watsonville in the middle of the wet season. A dray took him on to Herberton Hospital but he died just as he arrived.

There was at least one record-breaking horseback ride to Herberton to fetch a doctor. This was that of Charlie Dines early this century. He set out from Mt. Garnet on a big bay horse called Hector, owned by James Noonan, and covered the 35 miles by way of Silver Valley in two hours, despite the rough mountainous country.

Doctors were energetic men in those days. He sprang into the saddle and galloped to Mt. Garnet in just over two hours.

Charlie Dines on Hector accompanied him back, the horse covering nearly seventy miles in four hours without a rest.

There were certainly some good horses in those days, and the men were tough also. Rev. Fr. O'Brien of Herberton was called to Chillagoe to tend a badly injured miner, Bill Dunne, of the Girofla mine. Bill McDonald, a well known coach driver of the day, loaned Father O'Brien his beautiful dapple-grey horse, Charlemagne. The horse did the ninety mile journey in six hours over some of the roughest country in the North by way of Irvinebank, Montalbion, Petford, and Almaden.

Being a lifeline to the pioneers, the old Port Douglas Road knew sorrow, too.

A clatter of hooves as a horse, ridden hard at dead of night . . . . and the people at the wayside hotels and lonely home-steads knew someone was in need of medical help, for a lone rider urging an exhausted horse over the rutted mountain road in the darkness meant he was riding to try to save a life — perhaps that of his child, his wife, or that of a mate.

Packers at their campfires would start to their feet as the drumming hooves came closer, a dark figure and a glimpse of a foam-lathered horse in the firelight, and they were gone. "Someone's in trouble," they would say. Sometimes there was rain, thunder, and lightning, and the road slippery and dangerous. "God help a fast rider on the road tonight," they would add.

Hours later in daylight the same rider on a fresh horse would come back up the range, and he and the doctor in bowler and broadcloth, his bag tied to his saddle, would go galloping by — it may be a forty mile ride to save a life, but too often "the doc." was too late.

A nameless bushman was one of many who made such a ride, this particular one riding eighty miles to Port Douglas and back from Granite Creek to fetch the doctor to Mrs. Eccles. But there was little he could do for sunstroke, so the doctor's ride was also in vain.

Bill Gallogly told this story: A youth of some fourteen

years lay dying in Port Douglas hospital. His mother rode from Calcifer, near Chillagoe, to see him. She changed horses at Dimbulah and again at Mitchellvale, John Fraser's homestead. This woman rode sidesaddle and covered the whole one hundred and fifty miles at a hand gallop. There is a tombstone in the Port Douglas cemetery to the memory of the dead youth. History does not say whether the mother's gallant ride got her to his bedside in time.

Gallogly quoted the well known lines about the gallant Paul Revere:

"A horseman sweeps at the dead of night, Through the mountains of Navarre, And headlong is his starlit flight . . . . "

Another for whom help came too late was a Mrs. Mathieson, travelling on a dray en route from Port Douglas to Kingsborough. It was no sort of a journey for a woman in an advanced state of pregnancy, and when near the Little Mitchell she went into labour and complications developed.

This time the horseman who thundered over the miles of rutted track is not nameless; he was Billy Lee. He led another horse to fetch back the midwife — what towers of strength such women were to their pioneering sisters in this land where doctors were rare. The midwife rode back with Billy Lee but she was too late. After long days of agony on the ground under the dray, Mrs. Mathieson had died. In 1961, the Mareeba Rotary Club erected a plaque on her lonely grave "In memory of the early pioneers." It should also be in memory of all those brave souls who travelled the Port Douglas Road and died on the way.

If the age-old rocks and the ancient trees could speak, what tales they would tell of human endeavour, of sweat and tears that were shed on the Port Douglas Road long ago. It was but a fleeting span in history, but one full of pathos and of hardship, only a fraction of which is remembered now as the oldest of the old timers who knew this road pass away.

There are a few people still living in Cairns and its hinterland whose parents and grandparents walked in the dust behind labouring teams up The Bump long ago. Stories of those hard days have been handed down, but as time passes, facts are becoming obscured by legend and garbled memories.

True mateship prevailed on the bush roads in those days. It was a pioneering age, work was hard and pleasures were few, but everyone enjoyed life, more so than they do today. Everyone pulled together, for they knew they were building for the future.

Old timers still talk of Minnie Wieland's ride. The Wieland family's farm was situated midway between Irvinebank and Montalbion and they supplied milk and butter to both towns. The eldest daughter, Minnie, was classed as one of the best lady riders in the district, back in that era of many peerless horsemen and women. Riding sidesaddle, she was unafraid of the wildest horses. Like other bush girls of those pioneer days, she was able to cut out and yard a beast as good as any stockman.

One day in 1891, Minnie was returning home after delivering milk which she carried in cans on a packhorse from house to house in Irvinebank. Passing the wall of the dam, five year old Albert McIntosh called to her and said that little Jimmie Henry had been drowned in the dam.

Leaving the packhorse, Minnie did not wait to hear more, but giving the alarm in Irvinebank, she wheeled her horse and set out at full gallop to summon the doctor at Montalbion. There was then no doctor in Irvinebank. An old timer told me that Minnie had the fastest ride of her life. This time she was not riding to orders as on the day she rode Lovely Nell in the Governor's Bracelet at the Montalbion races. (Lady jockeys are no new thing!) Minnie Wieland married a cattleman, Ben O'Shea of Almaden, and was able to spend most of her life among the horses she loved. (See Chapter 13)

A mate of Frank Blackmore mentioned here, was John McBride. He landed at Port Douglas in 1885, carried his swag up The Bump road and settled at Northcote on the Hodgkinson field. His first acquaintance with the Wild North took place on the way when he met black-bearded Bill Groves, a selector on Rifle Creek, armed with a Snider rifle and two Colt revolvers because of the hostile blacks in the vicinity that were spearing his horses and cattle.

Early in 1887, McBride was working at the Just-in-Time mine near Northcote with Bill Blackmore, when Blackmore's brother, Frank, was terribly injured in a dynamite explosion in a mine called the Publican's Purse. Fourteen men set out to carry him on a stretcher to Herberton Hospital. They followed the telegraph line. George Jackson of Leadingham Creek rode ahead to prepare the camps. It rained continuously and the men's Blucher boots sank into the mud at every step. The Walsh River was running chest deep, but the stretcher bearers did not falter. On the far bank they were met by forty men from Watsonville; they had rallied to help a fellow miner, having received the call by Morse over the telegraph wire. The injured man must have suffered agonies during the long march and the cart ride from Watsonville to Herberton.

John McBride remembered seeing the famous pathfinder and horseman, John Doyle, ride an outlaw piebald stallion to a standstill at John Hambling's place on Leadingham Creek one day in 1889. In 1891, McBride and his wife and family left Northcote and moved to Orient Camp, not far from Montalbion. The two baby boys were transported in two gin cases slung either side of a packhorse. McBride lived twenty years in the Irvinebank area and then moved to Cairns where he died in 1935. He was but another of our little remembered district pioneers.

* * * *

In July 1891, the first Cobb and Co. coach from Kuranda arrived at Herberton by way of Granite Creek. Never again would the coaches come from Port Douglas. With first Kuranda as the railhead, and then Mareeba, Cairns had won the battle as the port for the rich mining country of the interior.

Myola, was the end of the second section — the Cairns Range portion — from Redlynch. The first ballast train ran to the Barron Falls in March 1891, and a month later to Kuranda.

(165)

In May the rails were laid to Myola which was the end of John Robb's contract. Behind him lay a great engineering triumph that would cause a furore if even contemplated today. Great credit goes to John Robb as contractor and Surveyor Monk, engineers Willoughby Hannam, Arthur Downey, and others.

By pick and shovel, dynamite, bullock and horsepower, and a few steam-driven donkey engines, more than a thousand men had toiled for five years to carve a track for a railway up the sides of the Barron Gorge, had thrown spider-like bridges of timber and steel across yawning chasms and drilled fifteen tunnels, to perform one of the greatest engineering feats in Australia up to that time.

The thousands of tourists who travel this line now to view the magnificent scenery, know little of how or when the line was constructed. The second section cost 28 lives, the third section, Myola to Mareeba, six more.

John Robb built sixteen miles 25 chains of line — 3 ft. 6 in. gauge — from Redlynch to Myola under his contract which he was one year late in fulfilling, mainly because of problems with Number 15 tunnel and heavy rain. Alexander McKenzie & Co. were the contractors who built the third section from Myola to Mareeba.

On 15 June, 1891 the second section to Myola was opened for goods and passenger traffic by the Railway Commissioner, Mr. Johnston, without any ceremony.

Kuranda, which had been the "Middle Crossing" on the Thornborough-Cairns track, blossomed into a township with the arrival of the railway. There had been a few settlers there since the 'Eighties, but about 1890 "selections" of 160 acres and more were thrown open, covering the scrub and forest country behind Kuranda and westward to the Clohesy River at Koah. There were valuable stands of timber — kauri pine, hickory, oak, walnut, maple, and cedar — and as the settlers cleared their land the logs were hauled to Kuranda by bullock team and railed to Cairns as soon as the line reached there.

Coffee growing was what these early settlers pinned their faith on. Alfred Street had successfully grown it on his farm at the top of the range on the old Thornborough road from the early 'Eighties, with Kanaka labour. After lying abandoned for decades his Fernhill Plantation is now an orange orchard. Street not only grew coffee but he manufactured it and marketed it in tins, winning prizes at the London and Paris Exhibitions of 1886 and 1889. He also provided the market for the other growers as he bought all their crops.

The first disaster to strike was an unusual black frost at Kuranda which badly damaged most of the plantations. Street's was not adversely affected, but when the Government encouraged tea imports to the detriment of local coffee, what could have been a viable industry in North Queensland faded and died. Coffee trees, descended from Street's stock, grow wild in the surrounding jungle today and are of great interest to tourists who visit the Mountain Grove orange orchard and restaurant in large numbers.

Meyer's was another thriving coffee plantation at Myola early this century. Many settlers left and those who stayed turned to dairy and mixed farming.

Alfred Street was an early storekeeper in Kuranda. Garbutt Bros. had a butchery. The first hotel was Charlie Standen's (later Remilton's) where the Kuranda Hotel now stands, then the Family Hotel and the Barron Falls Hotel. This was owned by Ernie Hunter, a mining speculator around Irvinebank, and later a commission agent in Mareeba.

Some of the early pioneers were W. H. Veivers snr., Sam Crothers, Jack Kelly, Mrs. Fallon, the Veivers Bros. and their families, Hoblers, Newberrys, Fitzpatricks, Warrens, Austins, Leons, Bartleys, and others. Kuranda school opened in 1892, built by R. W. Warren. Mrs. Fallon had been the first white woman to land in Cairns.

The good climate, and magnificent scenery of Kuranda and the Barron Falls began to attract Southern tourists very early in this century. Cairns businessmen built holiday homes there and well-to-do retired people made their homes there. Mr. Dick, a fine photographer, was one of the first to publicise the scenic attractions with photos, and he also established "Fairyland", a jungle park that was enjoyed by thousands over the years. Mr. Duggan had a similar attraction called "The Maze".

Myola boomed briefly with the arrival of the railway. For a time it was a township of three hotels, two stores, two butchers, a baker, and a saddler. Willoughby Hannam secured 400 acres and built a fourteen room home set in a six acre tropical garden. Special trains were run from Cairns to bring guests to the parties the Hannams held there.

As the third section of the railway progressed, many of the business people moved with it to eventually settle in Mareeba. With those from Port Douglas they formed the nucleus of early Mareeba's business community. Only the settlers stayed on their farms at Myola, Koah, Welcome Pocket, and other places along the line. The latter was called Mantaka later on. A provisional school opened there about 1892. The first teachers were Denis Horan and Miss Colman who were transferred to Mareeba when the school opened there in 1893. It is interesting to note that the Mantaka school building is now the "Honey House" in Kuranda.

Early settlers between Myola and Oak Forest were the Russells, Warrens, Harens, Parr, Olsen, Tenni, Driscoll, Gane, Dillon, Matthewson, Anderson, Murchison, and others.

By the time the rails reached the Clohesy River there was already a store and hotel there. The hotel building had already functioned at Camp Oven Creek during the construction of the second section, being run by Mick Boland who was to become a leading Cairns merchant. Paddy Tierney and Mick Whelan bought the building, dismantled it, and sent it by train to Myola. From there it was carted by horse team to the eastern bank of the Clohesy River. With six hundred men working on the construction of the third section, trade would have been brisk for a few months.

The late Bill Tierney stated that he possessed an old invoice dated 7th. September 1893 which showed that Tom Vallely, butcher of Blackwater Creek, supplied 157 lbs. of beef and pork for the sum of £2.9.0., or $4.90. Mrs. John Glendon, who was Nellie Vallely, died in Mareeba in 1970, having lived at Kambul nearly all her life.

The Clohesy River bridge is quite a massive construction of four eighty-foot steel spans thirty feet above the river. James Muir was killed when he fell off the bridge. There were other fatalities: Tom Thome was blown up, and Charles Grant was drowned off his horse while travelling from Biboohra to the Clohesy along the line; he was a bridge painter; his daughter married a railwayman, Bill Murchison, who was mayor of Cairns in the early Nineteen-fifties.

Construction progressed rapidly except for the bridge over the Barron River at Biboohra where trouble was found in finding foundations for the last pier. By September 1892, the contractors' locomotive ran on the line to Biboohra, but it was not officially opened until 2nd. January 1893 to the eastern bank of the river. Lyon and Downey, the sub-contractors who built the bridge, had three of their men killed — D. Daley, R. Patchley, and a painter named Smith. The bridge was completed in May 1893.

James Hughes was an early telegraph station master at Biboohra and old timers recall that he died of a heart attack at his office. Biboohra, once the "Upper Crossing" on the Thornborough road, was another place that throve briefly during the railway construction. It was to boom again later when the Mt. Molloy branch line was built.

The men who built the third section — 22 miles 81 chains from Myola to Mareeba — worked forty-four hour weeks for eight shillings (80c.) per day. The railway was opened to Mareeba on 1st. August 1893 and construction stopped. The rails were still a long way from the destination originally intended — Herberton. The depression of the early 'Nineties forced the cessation of many public works. Unemployment and widespread poverty — no social service in those days — caused nationwide misery for two or three years.

*   *   *   *

Despite widespread financial disasters, Mareeba grew into a town during that period, helped by two small gold rushes which coincided neatly with the arrival of the railway.

The Mareeba Goldfield broke out on Tinaroo Creek. It was more or less accidentally discovered by Duncan Finlayson, an old Gympie miner who had been assisted by Alfred Hort, an early Mareeba businessman, to prospect for tin at Tinaroo. He found gold on the way, on a hill close to the road, that travellers to the tinfield had passed by for about fifteen years.

Leslie Luxton contacted the writer with an interesting story. He believes that his father, Sam Luxton, stumbled on the reef that ten or eleven years later was found by Duncan Finlayson.

Sam Luxton was a groom for Cobb and Co. at Granite Creek. The Eccles were his wife's parents. On one occasion, the coach horses got away and Joe Eccles and Sam Luxton went looking for them. They crossed the Barron River and headed towards Tinaroo, and on a ridge Sam found what he thought was gold. He was an Englishman and was not sure, so he showed it to Eccles.

He just glanced at it and said, "Throw it away, Sam — it's only 'mundic'. Let's get on and find the horses." Thus he may have missed discovering the Mareeba Goldfield.

Sam was not to have any luck at mining. Later he and his wife lived at California Creek where he was still a groom for Cobb and Co. This was on the Herberton-Georgetown road. Sam found an outcrop of iron ore which contained fine gold when dollied. He traced it up a hill now called Mt. Luxton,

(170)

sank a shaft, but lost the lode.

The mine that Duncan Finlayson discovered was to yield £35,484 worth of gold. Alfred Hort named it the Queen Constance after one of his daughters. For the month of December, 1893, it yielded 1659 ounces.

Constance Hort was also to have a principal street in Mareeba named after her. As Mrs. Connie Ross, and well over ninety years of age, she was a well known resident of Darwin up to the time of the tragic cyclone at Christmas 1974; she died in Sydney in 1975. Her son, Graham, is still a leading business-man in Darwin.

In 1896, when the gold yield from the Queen Constance dropped, the company went into liquidation and the mine was sold. The name was changed to the Mareeba Jubilee Mine and it worked until 1916. For a few years the township of Dulbil flourished. George Rice ran the mail from Mareeba, and some of the settlers on the Mareeba Goldfield were Stewart, Brown, Downey, Freeman, Jackson, Pickering, Meyers, Davis, Bourke, and others. There was a brief revival in 1908.

The Clohesy Goldfield came on the scene in 1893 also. It was found on the bank of Davies Creek, then called the Second Clohesy. It only had a brief life. In 1894 there were about a hundred people on the field; a mill of five stamps was erected.

The principal mine was Mackenzie Bros.' Waitemata. They were New Zealand miners. But the gold yield was poor and by 1898 the field was but a memory. A little gold can still be found there, and Goldmine Creek on the Kennedy Highway is a reminder of past days. During this small field's brief heyday, a Mrs. Sandiland conducted an hotel and there were a couple of stores; one storekeeper was named Hooley. J. K. Lawson was one of the early pioneers. In 1910, E. Johnson and F. Gregory again worked the Waitemata but with little success.

Christmas 1893 was celebrated by Mr. and Mrs. Hort with a monster picnic at the Barron Falls and a banquet on the platform at the siding. Guests travelled by special train from Mareeba. No doubt it was their way of bringing pleasure into the lives of others at that hard time and sharing their good fortune on the Mareeba Goldfield.

The first test for the new railway came in the heavy wet season of 1896 when there were several landslides on the range and a bad washaway at Oak Forest. On February 9th. there was a severe earth tremor that was felt in Mareeba, Kuranda, and Port Douglas. Number 15 tunnel was cracked but was quickly repaired.

Another goldfield of the 'nineties was Jordan Creek, in dense jungle adjacent to what is now the Palmerston Highway east of Millaa Millaa. It was part of the region explored by Christie Palmerston in 1882 when he discovered and named the Beatrice and Henrietta Rivers.

O'Leary, Gallogly, and Donaldson were probably the first to win gold on Jordan Creek, a tributary of the Henrietta. There were three mining camps and 200 miners on this field in 1897. Up to 1900, the field yielded 4140 ounces of gold. Dan O'Keefe had an hotel and Scheu and Worth had stores. A crushing mill ran for a couple of years. All supplies were brought up the pack track from Geraldton, thirty miles away.

CHAPTER 12

"MEETING PLACE OF WATERS"

Granite Creek Coach Change becomes Mareeba — Bullock Teams — Streets named after Pioneers — Business Places in Byrnes Street in the Nineties — Early Citizens — Railways Assure its Future.

People who had followed the railway from camp to camp through the construction years, and those from Port Douglas who saw a shortening of the coach roads, all came to Mareeba.

In 1894, Tom Crowe's mother decided to move to the new town also. The best means of doing so was, of course, by bullock wagon. When camped with George Pritchard at the Barron Bend, young Tom heard from another packer, Harry Edwards, that Jack Bailey was on his way up from Port Douglas with his team. Knowing that his mother had been waiting for Bailey, Tom rode all night and reached his old home at daybreak. He and Harry Edwards pulled down the house and when Bailey arrived everything was ready to load on to his two wagons. The material was taken to Granite Creek, on the northern edge of Mareeba, and unloaded. The site Mrs. Crowe chose was opposite where Frank Spurrier lived later.

Harry Edwards rode out and cut cypress pine logs and these were hauled in by Jack Bailey's team and thus Crowe's house was built. House building was fairly simple then, even in town; bush materials could still be used. It was sufficiently large for Mrs. Crowe to open a boarding house. Carriers from Montalbion, Muldiva, Calcifer, Chillagoe, and the Hodgkinson used to stay there until they loaded up again. They turned out their horses and bullocks along Granite Creek.

Carriers working to and from Herberton, Watsonville, Coolgarra, and Mt. Garnet used to stay at the southern end of the town at Mrs. Strattmann's Railway Hotel (where the Graham Hotel now stands). The camping ground used to be opposite where the Foxwood timber mill stands today — for many long

(173)

years it was owned by Lawson and Son. This was a big camp when the Chillagoe Railway was being built in 1899-1900 as the Chillagoe Company's teams used to unyoke there also.

The company had some very good teams on the road, old timers say. Among drivers remembered are Bill Riordan (father of Judge James Riordan), Tom Lee, Scotty Emsley, and Bill Hudson.

Arthur Garbutt, afterwards of Townsville, and Fred Drew conducted saleyards on the corner opposite the Railway Hotel. Thousands of horses were sold there in the late 'nineties. An old timer recalled that those from Cargoon Station, owned by the Annings, were in great demand by the carriers as there was seldom a jib amongst them.

In 1896, young Tom Crowe realised a bush boy's ambition and was put in charge of one of Bill Lewis' three bullock teams. Bill Moloney drove the other team.

The terrible tick plague struck North Queensland about this time, and what happened to Bill Lewis' teams was typical of the experiences of other bullockies.

The first trip Tom Crowe made in charge of a team was from Port Douglas to Montalbion to load silver lead. The three teams climbed the Herberton Range by moonlight. The bullocks did not show signs of sickness until the homeward journey began. Lewis gave each sick animal a beer bottle full of a concoction he was trying consisting of castor oil and saltpetre. No one really knew what to do for the redwater outbreak and all sorts of desperate remedies were tried. But there was no stopping the plague. There had never been cattle ticks before in North Queensland and the animals had no resistance. The parasites had been introduced first into the Northern Territory from Indonesia, and cattle being overlanded into Queensland brought the disease with them.

It broke the hearts of the teamsters to see their best and staunchest bullocks die one by one, in agony, and unable to help them. When Bill Lewis started out he had two teams of twenty-two bullocks in each, and one of twenty. When he got back to Mareeba after weeks of delays caused by the sickness, he had two teams of fourteen bullocks and one of twelve.

"It looked for a time as if the ticks and redwater was going to wipe the bullock teams off the road, which it very nearly did," Tom Crowe said.

Though the sickness was still raging, Lewis decided to build his teams up again and he and Tom rode down to Mitchellvale and Brooklyn Stations where the Hills and the Ords then lived, and bought thirty steers. They were driven to Biboohra where their breaking-in or "coupling" commenced in Matt Petersen's stockyard in that township.

Tom Crowe explained: "After coupling the new steers we took them to Mareeba and yoked up. To couple a steer he was roped and drawn up to a corner post of the yard; a light chain was put around his horns; an old experienced bullock is attached alongside him to this coupling chain. A rope was put around his neck and through the coupling chain. The reason for putting the chain around the other's horns was so the old bullock would have more command over him. In a few days when his horns got sore the chain was taken off and put around his neck.

"We put on thirty hundredweight of loading for Bill Paskins and his mate out at the Lappa Lappa silver lead mines — Paskins had kept the old Terminus Hotel in Mareeba. We took our three teams down Mareeba's main street to Granite Creek. We had six steers each yoked on the off side. When Bill Lewis came to the Granite Creek crossing he pulled up and put his offside brake on.

"Eccles' old hotel on top of the bank, where lived Michael Walsh from Port Douglas, was painted all white and the steers objected to passing it, but the brake kept the pull into the bank and he got down safely.

"Bill Moloney came along next with the load on, but he was unlucky, as his leaders would not stop for him and the

(175)

steers kept bucking to the near side. He managed to escape around the back of the wagon just as it plunged over the bank — right over and up on to its wheels again. The load was scattered over the road and part of the wagon also. I never saw two bullocks get out of the way quicker than did the two polers that afternoon; the team never stopped and when the pole-pin dropped out they got out of the way like two kittens."

Tom screwed up his brake when well back from the crossing and got down the cutting and embankment safely, turned around on the flat on the opposite side and pulled up alongside the wreck, loading the goods on to his wagon. The teamsters spent the next day in the creek repairing the wagon, and they were on their way again. They went right out past where Dimbulah later arose to Emu Creek, then on to Eccles Creek as far as the "strawbed" and loaded up with bagged ore.

Already three or four bullocks had died from the plague, but as soon as the wagons were loaded, they started dying every day. When they got back to Mareeba only four of the thirty new steers were left.

The Biboohra Meatworks had just started operations. Bill Smallwood was the first manager, in 1897. In its closing years Jack Meehan was cattle buyer for a time. Later a well known Mareeba businessman — he was one of North Queensland's finest horsemen in his day. In the 'Nineties, graziers received an average price of 75¢ per 100 lbs. live weight.

Mobs of cattle coming into the works suffered very heavily from the tick plague. So many cattle died along the droving tracks that there were men following behind in drays taking the hides off. It was nothing to see five hundred dead cattle in the meatworks' paddock where a mob was held for a couple of days. Those from Lyndhurst and Oak Park suffered particularly.

It was a heartbreaking time for graziers as well as teamsters. Many courageous pioneers Outback had successfully fought and overcome wild blacks, droughts, fires, and floods, after years of hardship only to be ruined by the ticks destroying almost their

(176)

entire herds.

The plague put finis to Tom Crowe's ambition to own a bullock team as it must have for other young men. He took a turn at coach driving for Rudy Hampe and then his mother bought a horse team and this made him feel very happy and secure. But there were a lot of horse teams on the roads and competition was fierce. He got loading at £5 per ton from Mareeba to Kingsborough and Thornborough; he paid £1 ($2.00) per bag for corn for his horses. He made a few trips to Chillagoe, and George Jackson of Leadingham Creek got him loading. He was on a trip with him just as the old century ended when they heard of a gold rush to Ebagoolah away up in Cape York Peninsula.

Many of the packers had gone to the Coen rush in '79. Now other packers and teamsters, too, set out across hundreds of miles of rough country over the Mitchell and the Palmer to John Dickie's new discovery. Early in September 1900, Tom Crowe and his brother Ned and their mate, Chad Neil, also set out. They were away in the Northern wilds for eight years.

Jack Bailey figured in several carrying feats. In 1892 he and three other teamsters, Charlie Emmerson and the two Greenwood brothers, were engaged to transport the first mill at Coolgarra to New Northcote on the edge of the Hodgkinson Goldfield. There was a ten-ton boiler, heavy flywheels, and other machinery; two bullock wagons were used.

Between Coolgarra and Innot Hot Springs the road traversed very steep grades that made hard work for the bullocks. Afraid that the boiler would capsize the wagon, a trench to take the two near-side wagon wheels was dug for over a mile, in decayed rock.

In 1899, when John Moffat built a sawmill at Cedar Creek — later Ravenshoe — Jack Bailey and John Kidner brought the machinery from Mareeba railhead on their bullock wagons; it was a two weeks' journey.

Like many of the teamsters, when ordinary carrying ceased

(177)

because of competition by motor vehicles, Jack Bailey took on timber hauling, for bullock teams were used in the Cairns hinterland for timber haulage up to 1950 until finally ousted by bulldozers.

When Bailey died in the 'twenties, his wife continued to drive his wagon and did so for several years in order to support her family. She could handle the team expertly in the scrub. This is another example of the courage of our pioneer women.

*   *   *   *

Mareeba is said to have been an Aboriginal word meaning "Meeting place of waters" referring to the joining of Granite and Emerald Creeks with the Barron just below the town, no doubt. It has also been claimed that the word means "curlew". Certainly, the name Mareeba is not unlike the curlew's cry if the second syllable is drawn out, and Aboriginal words were often derived from the sounds of Nature.

White men first called Granite Creek, Abbott Creek, but the name did not come into favour. Possibly the latter was the official name — old maps exist showing it — while Granite Creek was John Atherton's name for it. Likewise Mt. Abbott has become Turkey Hill. Back in 1887, Surveyor Starcke laid out a few blocks for the proposed Granite Creek township on the northern bank near the crossing. The coach change was, of course, on the high southern bank.

The route the railway was to take, then only at the foot of the range at Redlynch, would have influenced the choosing of Granite Creek as a site for a township. Ostensibly, the railway was to go to Herberton but it may have been in the official mind even then to make Granite Creek the end of the first stage.

But it was not until six years later that the decision a town should be established on the present site, south of Granite Creek, took shape. It was Surveyor Rankin who surveyed the nucleus of the present town — three long streets and seven cross streets, with others added as the town expanded. Some of them perpetuate the names of early pioneers, and the Mareeba

(178)

Map of Mareeba Shire

Shire Council has continued this policy throughout the years when new streets have been named.

Early pioneers who had streets named after them were Eccles, Lloyd, Middlemiss, Atherton, Hort, and Walsh. Rankin Street was named after the surveyor responsible. Herberton Street, which for many years ran down to the Doyle Bridge and was the road entrance to the town from across the Barron, was so named because in the original survey it was the street nearest Herberton. Constance Street was named after Miss Constance Hort, and Byrnes Street after T. J. Byrnes, Member for Cairns in 1893.

Michael Walsh and his brother Callaghan were pioneer storekeepers at Port Douglas. The former opened a store in Mareeba as soon as the railway came, but it does not seem likely the street was really named after him, as old timers claim, as Rankin's survey was probably made before Walsh arrived. More likely it was named, like Herberton Street, after the district and the River Walsh.

The big general stores of Walsh and Co. would have been rivals of Jack and Newell in the early times, although Cooktown and Port Douglas were the former's main spheres. Michael Walsh's second wife was a Mrs. Burke of Herberton and both are buried in Mareeba. Callaghan Walsh was the first chairman of the Cairns Harbour Board, established in 1906.

Other pioneers honored in street names years ago were Doyle, Strattmann, Keeble, Sutherland, Love, Moody, Paskins, Hampe, Quill, and Pares. In the last thirty years other residents have been remembered as the town expanded — Peters, Meehan, Lannoy, Foulis, Borland, Dickson, Keneally, Petersen, Couper, Costin, Tilse, Suhle, Fenwick, Riordan, Troughton, Emmerson, Finn, Horan, Smallwood, Kilpatrick, MacRae, Wilson, Chatfield, Royes, Vaughan, Carroll, and others — mostly names well known in Mareeba during the first half of this century.

One of the early hotels in Mareeba was Dillon's Mining Exchange on the corner of Byrnes and Middlemiss Streets, later

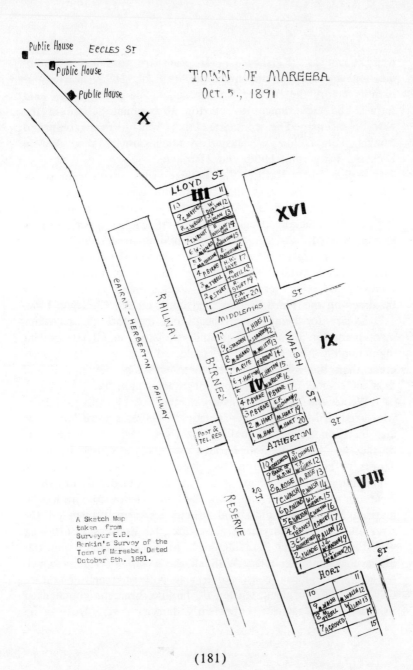

Public House EECLES ST.
Public House
Public House

TOWN OF MAREEBA
Oct. 5., 1891

X

LLOYD ST.

III   11

10
9 G.MAYE5   W. DIXON 12
8 J.WRIGHT   F. BEMAN 13
7 T.W.BINIT E.WILLIAM 14 SON
6 W.J. MUNRO E.ROBERTSON 15
5 E.E. MATHISON E. RATHBONE 16
4 P.BYRNE   H.W. 17 LOVE
3 M.TYRELL   M. TYRELL 18
2 R.STURT   R. STURT 19
                C.A. SHORT 20
1

XVI

ST.

MIDDLEMAS

10   P.HIDE 11
9 C.STANDEN   STANDEN 12
8 M.BOLAND   M.MILLETT 13
7 A.RICE   P.BROWN 14
6 E.T.HATTON J.HATTON 15
              W.WREDE 16
IV   P.BYRNE 17
4 P.BYRNE   P.BYRNE
3 P.BYRNE   E.F. 18 WELCHMAN
2 M.HART   M.HART 19
1 M.HART   M.HART 20

WALSH ST.

IX

ST.

ATHERTON

10 P.   S. 11 MORGENISS AH CHING
9 BANK OF   T.P. 12 N.S.W   McGURK
8 A.ROSE   A.ROSE 13
7 E.WALSH   E.WALSH 14
6 D.ROLLINS W.J. 15 TURNER
5 G.WALDON   G.WALDON 16
4 P.   G.DRURY 17 TIERNEY
3 C.L.   P.ALLAN 18 RUTHERFORD
2 J.WADE   J.C. 19 McMAHON
             J.C. 20 McKINN
1

VIII

ST.

HORT

10   11
9 W.WASH   W.WASH 12
8 M.   W.ALLAN 13 O'DELL
7 A.GROVES   14
                       15

POST & TEL. RES.

BYRNES

RAILWAY

CAIRNS - HERBERTON RAILWAY

RESERVE

A Sketch Map
taken from
Surveyor E.B.
Rankin's Survey of the
Town of Mareeba, Dated
October 5th, 1891.

(181)

well known as "Kershaw's". It was here that an important meeting was held on the night of April 14, 1893, nearly four months before the railway was opened. The meeting was held to ask the Government to open a Provisional School in the new township. The committee that was formed comprised Messrs. Tom Dillon, W. Hastie, Middlemiss, McMahon, Walsh, Dickson, Fitzgerald, Hort, and Hardacre.

William A. Hastie, the builder who erected most of Mareeba's first buildings, had a suitable school building completed by June, and on August 9th. — eight days after the railway was officially opened — the first teacher, young Dennis Horan, arrived. A year later, the building needed additions.

William Hastie also built the Mareeba railway station. The distinctive arched roof covering two sets of rails was only removed in recent years. Hastie erected most of the railway buildings on the Third Section, and later, on the Chillagoe Line.

Except for being the railhead and therefore the transhipment point for a huge and expanding district mainly dependent upon mining, Mareeba had no stable industry in its early years other than the railway. Later there was also sawmilling and then, of course, came the tobacco growing industry.

Wrote the Northern historian, the late J. W. Collinson, who lived in Mareeba in the 'nineties: "Houses were built here and there on ridges overlooking the river. My own home was on the river bank opposite Crouch's on the track used by water carters to bring water from the river. Over the river was the Chinaman's garden where Ah Tin was murdered in 1895. Near our place was a fine home built by Denny McGrath who married Mary Forrest. David Wilson took up a farm on the river and became dairyman. The Mareeba Brewery (Bushell's) was the only other building on the river; thereat was our favourite swimming hole. With all the usual uncertainty which belonged to railway construction and without much guarantee of permanence on the extension of the line, Mareeba commenced its history as a town." Other early dairymen were Durston on the Barron opposite the town, and Mick Kelly some two miles upstream.

Some of Mareeba's early residents came there from the Hodgkinson. Peter Middlemiss was a publican in Thornborough; in 1895, W. Middlemiss was a butcher in Mareeba and a street was named after him. Chas Scherning who made the special "Port Douglas packsaddles" for the packers was one who moved up from Port Douglas and opened his shop in Mareeba. Packers and teamsters arriving and departing for Herberton and further out made Mareeba a busy centre and business was good among blacksmiths, farriers, and saddlers. Dan Collins was a tentmaker who also did a good trade.

There are old timers who can still remember seeing Cobb and Co's coach being loaded with parcels outside Jack and Newell's store, and the passengers being taken on at the Federal Hotel which was apparently near where the Royal is now. Bags of mail were loaded at the post office, on the same site as now, the original building standing until 1949. The postmaster in the 'Nineties was named McLeod. The first stationmaster was L. Courtney. The station yard would have half a dozen horse teams loading up with goods or unloading tin and silver ingots to be railed to Cairns.

We will wander along the one mile section of the old Herberton Road that was Byrnes Street in the closing years of last century, and attempt to describe most of the business premises and name their proprietors at that period in Mareeba's history. The street was hot, bare, and dusty in the dry season, muddy and undrained in the "Wet", and deeply rutted by the iron tyres of the wagons and drays, the feet of scores of team horses trampling it to slush.

On the railway side of the street — starting from the Granite Creek end — was Gates' saddler's shop where Jim Egan and later Alf Grittner carried on the old time trade into the 1950's; then came Peter Berglund, bootmaker, and Albert May, cabinetmaker. Jacobsen's watchmaker's shop was

(183)

a small bark hut tied up with wire to a gumtree for support. At the top end of the Railway Reserve was Norris and Fenwick's blacksmith's shop. All the other buildings faced west towards the railway station.

The post office was situated at the railway station until 1897.

From north to south on the opposite side of the street there was first the historic Royal Mail Hotel of Eccles and Lloyd, where Michael Walsh lived in the 'Nineties. The Terminus Hotel, first kept by Paskin, later by Mick Fitzgerald, was next; this was the second hotel built in Mareeba but is now but a memory. It was an overnight stop for Rod MacRae's coaches.

Then there was John Walsh's bakery, See Chin's store, and W. Dickson's bakery. It was one allotment past the Lloyd Street corner. Then there was an interval of bush to W. Middlemiss' butchery. It was bought by Munro and Gordon and for long years afterwards was Kelly's butchery. Next was Mick Carroll's Carriers' Arms Hotel, a low, verandahed building on the corner of Byrnes and Middlemiss Streets. This old time hotel, built around 1892, was destroyed by fire in 1952 and subsequently the fine brick structure, the Hotel Marsterson, rose on the site. On the other corner was Dillon's Mining Exchange Hotel, as previously mentioned. Early this century, Rudy Hampe was the proprietor.

Next to Dillon's billiard room, Pares conducted an auctioneering and commission agency business. Nearby was the Bank of North Queensland, with Mr. Gabriel the manager, and the School of Arts, later shifted to Walsh Street. J. R. Mayers had a general store next door, and there was also a Chinese shop close by. Hunter's produce store was next door, doing a good trade in horse feed.

Then there was the office of Mareeba's first newspaper, "The Express". It was printed and published by Octavius Lannoy who had run the newspaper in Port Douglas. His assistants were George Martin and Jim Riordan (a Judge of the Arbitration Bench some forty-five years later). George H. O'Donnell later bought the printery and issued the "Mareeba Herald". This was followed by the "Walsh and Tinaroo Miner" produced in co-operation with Ned Martin. The paper had a wide circulation on the mining fields. H. E. Poole was a well known editor around 1909. In 1951 he revisited Mareeba but could not find one copy of the old newspaper. Geo. H. O'Donnell still has his name on a printing establishment in Mareeba, for many years run by his son, W. G. O'Donnell, now retired. The business is now owned by T. Duffy.

Next was Jimmie Richards' barber's shop; old timers recall that he was also a gifted black-and-white artist. A Chinese store was next, then a drapery shop kept by folk named Smith, and later by H. Castor, followed by Danks (a chemist), and a butcher's shop kept by Byrnes Bros. and Pat Callaghan. When they closed early this century, Cummings opened a saddlery business on the premises.

Next door was Peter Byrne's store and his Imperial Hotel — a single storied building that was burnt down about 1901. Eventually out of the ruins rose Dunlop's Hotel. This was again burnt down in 1929, but was rebuilt in its present form. Andy Dunlop came from Mungana.

Next to the Imperial Hotel in the Nineties there was a Chinese shop which later became a drapery store conducted by Anderson where Wilson's drapery store functioned for many years until comparatively recently. Mrs. Fuelling's newsagency was somewhere in this vicinity eighty years ago, and on the Atherton Street corner there used to be the framework of a building called "Hart's Folly" because it was never completed.

Jack and Newell's big store, built by W. Hastie in 1893 with a framework of cedar, stood on the opposite corner until a modern brick supermarket type of building was erected in the late 1950's. Back in the 'Nineties, the manager was Robert Love. The man in charge of the large grocery section was G. J. Carroll and the head draper was John Hurst. Early this century, Peter Berglund moved his boot repairing shop from the Granite Creek end of the town into a shop near to Jack and Newell. Old timers say that Berglund, called in those days "a cobbler", had only one leg, the result of an accident during the Cairns Range railway construction on which he had worked.

Further along the dusty street were other verandah buildings — Walsh and Co's general store which was burnt down before World War I. Arthur Costin's chemist shop was erected on this site — the first concrete building in Mareeba. Next door was Scherning's saddler's shop previously mentioned, then Vaughan's furniture shop, Collins the tentmaker, and Walton's Federal Hotel, booking office for Cobb and Co. all through the coaching days in Mareeba. During the First World War the Federal Hotel was shifted to Cairns, and the block was vacant for years. The late Alf Tilse snr. built shops on it in 1940; these in turn have been superseded by more modern premises.

Captain Foulis lived nearby. He was manager of the North Queensland Timber Company which brought the first traction engines to the North to use for timber hauling. Walter Prior drove the first one up over the Bump Road from Port Douglas. They were not popular with the teamsters or any travellers as they frightened the horses; but they heralded the coming of mechanical transport on the roads.

On the corner of Hort Street was Mrs. Strattmann's Railway Hotel, now the Graham Hotel. In the early days it was only a single storey building. The next block was vacant. It was the carriers' camping ground. When the Chillagoe Railway was being built, that company's teams also used to camp on this spot, shaded by many box and bloodwood trees. Arthur Garbutt and Fred Drew conducted big horse sales here during the 'Nineties.

At the southern corner of this block, at the Rankin Street intersection, was the Court House and police station; the latter was moved to Walsh Street early this century, and the old

Court House, now long gone, was still there in 1942. It served as an ordnance store for the United States Army. Mareeba's first policeman was Sergeant Orr; his successors were Sergeants McGuire, McBride, and Clynes.

Opposite the camping ground was John Fenwick's blacksmith shop. There were some fine specimens of box trees standing here until Lawson's sawmill expanded in the 1950's. It is probably fitting that a motor garage and showrooms — Hansen-Ford — should be on or near the site of Mareeba's old time smithy.

The last business premises in Byrnes Street, and the first met with coming in from Atherton or Herberton, was Sullivan's Royal Hotel, afterwards kept by the Brown family. Portion of this hotel was subsequently used to build the present Royal Hotel in the centre of town. Beyond Sullivan's hotel, the rutted coach road to Herberton wound between the trees and basalt boulders.

This is an overall picture of the business section of Mareeba during the last decade of the Nineteenth Century and the early years of the Twentieth. There were some changes during that time as some business people moved into different premises, and some did not stay for long. For instance, in early times there was Hardacre the plumber; Foster, a blacksmith; Best who had a chemist's shop, and Anderson who was a draper.

On the old sports ground near the hospital, good athletic sports were held between 1895 and 1900. David Love was a champion runner and Jimmie Brown was champion of the hurdle and jumping events. Racing was popular from 1895 onwards. A Turf Club was formed and an Annual and a Christmas meeting was instituted. A horse named Hendon won the double in 1895. Kirrama and Fitzroy won the big events the next year. Royal Mail, owned by Charlie Gillies, won the double at Christmas 1896. Royal Purple and Galore won the double at the 1897 Annual. A special train ran from Cairns, and all sorts of horse-drawn conveyances plied between the town and the course.

The first hospital was erected in 1894, with Matron Orme in charge and Dr. Thomas an early superintendent. It was very small at first and additions were made gradually, helped by such bequests as those of Phillip Maguire of Wolfram Camp, the Returned Servicemen's League, etc. The first section of the modern hospital dates from 1937.

Along Walsh Street, and back towards the river were scattered homes. In Constance Street lived the Pares, Vaughans, and McElhinneys. The McLaughlins, Jennings, Troughtons, Petersens, Whites, and later Harry Chatfield, lived around Lloyd Street. Jack Swan, who drove Chatfield's coaches, lived for many years on the site of Chatfield's home and stables, and his son Vernon, a well known plumbing contractor, lives there today. Louis Petersen lived nearer the hospital, and below it was Mareeba's first brickworks, erected by Tom Mann and in operation about 1895.

Across the railway line in Keeble Street, Walter Jamieson erected a sawmill just after the railway came. His large old-style home on the Strattmann Street corner is now owned by Mrs. Maud Hyde. It is a fine example of the craftsmanship of the old time builders and also shows that Mareeba's early citizens did not live in shacks. Many good homes were built, and still stand.

The Chillagoe · Company erected another mill during the Chillagoe Railway construction somewhere opposite the Herberton Street-Byrnes Street intersection. During 1909, Lawson and Son built and opened their mill, and it is only in recent years that it has been taken over by Foxwood. Mr. Doug Lawson recalls that the big bluegum bedlogs used in its construction, and the bluegum that was the first timber milled, was hauled in by bullock teams from Emerald Creek. The first private logs from the Tableland was maple from "Daddy" Keogh's farm at Kaban. It so happened that during World War II. when the authorities needed maple airscrews for trainer planes, Lawson's mill cut them from first class logs of over 19 ft. girth that were commandeered

(188)

from Keogh's farm. Lawson's original mill was destroyed by fire on Christmas Eve morning, 1925, but was rebuilt and enlarged.

There were only a few scattered homes on the western side of the railway. There was no official land survey there until 1907. Over Granite Creek lived the Finns, Wards, and Moodys. At the north end of Walsh Street was Albert May's home; he later moved to Chillagoe. Sam Hardacre lived on the corner of Middlemiss Street; opposite was the Cummings' home. Further along was Rudolph Hampe, the cordial maker; Fred Wilkinson (plumber), also Mr. Hort's dwelling. Near Albert May's home was Mareeba's first football ground. Soccer was played until 1898 and Mareeba had some fair talent.

At the school which was soon raised in status from Provisional to State School No. 653, James Dowie succeeded Denny Horan as headmaster and held the position for twenty-five years. He has been described as a very good teacher and "a handsome Scottish gentleman." Assistant teachers were Miss Pares and Miss Scherning — local girls. Pupil teachers were H. Carthew and Miss Nelly Fuelling. In 1901, there were 200 pupils on the roll, making Mareeba School equal in size to Herberton and Irvinebank at that period.

A well known and popular figure in Mareeba in those days was John Atherton, riding in and out of town on a diminutive donkey. Atherton favoured the red shirt and cabbage tree hat popular among bushmen of the period. Mrs. Kate Atherton passed away in 1902, and John Atherton passed away in 1913, after over 36 years at Emerald End. Both are buried in the family graveyard there.

In 1897, meatworks were established at Biboohra. The first manager was Bill Smallwood. The works only functioned spasmodically.

Near the railway station, Edward C. Earl built trucking yards, forerunner of later yards at Floreat.

Some of Mareeba's citizens of 1893-1903 can be found among a list recorded by the late Hugh A. Borland, who knew many of them personally later on: Shearer, Ashman, Hughes, Broadley, Murray, Perren, Kearney, Healy, Stewart, O'Neill, Flanagan, Cahill, Norris, Thompson, Malone, Prior, Casemore, Hallam, Duffy, Barr, Gordon, and others. Between the Boer War and World War I. other came: Moody, Pollard, Templeton, Downs, Spurrier, Egan, Robins, Trevarthen, Roberts, Wallace, Muhldorff, Geaney, Ferguson, Waddell, Royes, Hastings, Crowe, Shepherd, Mason, Riordan, Tolcher, Wilson, Petersen, Peters, and many more.

Just prior to World War I., Mareeba had two good brass bands — the Town and Volunteer. Mr. Menadue conducted the Town Band and Mr. Davis the Volunteer. The old bands were a feature of the Annual Shows, instituted about 1909 and discontinued after 1939. The Show Society was a live body and did good work. Some good riding was seen in the ring events with lady riders like Mrs. Galloway and Minnie O'Shea (nee Wieland) competing, sidesaddle, at the early shows. The young people of Mareeba enjoyed themselves between sixty and seventy years ago with sing-songs around pianos at the homes of friends, amateur theatricals in the School of Arts, with visits by travelling shows such as Corricks and J. C. Williamson the highlights, and there were dances, and balls in aid of the hospital and other charities. There was also a skating rink, and of course, band recitals every week, and regular concerts. Before the days of radio, cinemas, and television, people made their own entertainment. Many people had horses, and they provided sport as well as transport. Travelling circuses like Baker's and Hunt's passed through on tours to the mining towns.

In 1907 a Rifle Club was formed under the captaincy of George Donald. Some of the early members were Andy Smith, Charlie Couper, Arthur Page, Tom Barrett, Arthur Lilley, Bill Murchison, and Alex Borland.

There was no town water supply, but the railway tank was

(190)

filled by pumping from the Barron River near the hospital. Ted Troughton, Bob Male, and Jim Dodd carted water in casks and 100 gallon tanks in their drays for people whose rainwater tanks were not equal to their needs.

From December 1890 until 1919, Mareeba and the Kuranda area was in the Barron Shire with headquarters in Cairns. Mareeba had two representatives; those remembered are Messrs. Dunlop and Hampe, and in 1907, Charlie Strattmann was a councillor. At one time Messrs. Warren and Street represented Kuranda.

The first church services in Mareeba were held in a small hall adjoining Peter Byrne's hotel, probably about 1893 or 1894. Two churches were soon built; one was a Catholic church and the other was shared by the Methodists and Presbyterians. Early-day Anglican priests who visited and held services were Revs. Gribble, Hurd, and Thomas. Early Methodist-Presbyterian clergymen were Revs. King, Shenton, and Patterson. Catholic priests made long horseback tours, calling at Mareeba on their way to the mining towns, and Rev. Frs. Bucas, Doyle, Dempsey, O'Brien, and Sugrue are some of those recalled. A new Catholic church, also a school and convent were built in 1909, and the Sisters of Mercy contributed greatly to education in Mareeba as they did in Herberton. The present Catholic church was built by Doyle in 1937.

The Anglican church was built by the Brims Bros. voluntarily, and Mrs. C. Strattmann donated the bell. D. G. Brims had opened a joinery works during the first decade; it was the forerunner of G. F. Smith's factory, well known in Atherton Street and finally taken over by Northern Builders Ltd., who moved it to Keeble Street.

Other small industries came: Andrew Couper opened an iron and brass foundry in 1909. Soapworks were started by a man from Croydon, named Bechtel, and Pearce ran a maize-crushing mill. When mining was booming, an assay office functioned in Mareeba. and the little building is now an historic landmark.

So life went on, through the days of the Boer War and the birth of the Commonwealth in 1901. When war broke out in South Africa in October 1899, scores of young Northerners — sons of pioneers in a pioneering age — went off to join in what they thought would be a great adventure; they rode and fought with distinction in the old Queensland Mounted Infantry. But at home, Chillagoe and its railway was to put Mareeba firmly on the map and assure its future.†

---

† On 31 December 1893, A.R. Macdonald, Mineral Commissioner for the Walsh and Tinaroo Mining District, reported the following populations: Muldiva 247; Tate 299; Koorboora 38; Montalbion 203; Irvinebank 347; Coolgarra 117; Watsonville 200. In Atherton there were 146 men, 78 women, 127 children, also 260 Chinese and 100 Kanakas, total 711. Mareeba . had 579 inhabitants, including 180 men, 123 women, 246 children, and 30 Chinese. In Herberton there were 920 persons, comprising 100 tin miners, 150 other men, 250 women, 350 children, and 100 Chinese. This was ten years before the tinfields began to boom. in 1893, 1600 tons of tin ore and stream tin returned £72,000, at £45 per ton, or only $90.

In the year 1911, 1585 tons of tin were won on the Herberton Mineral Field. It was then worth £147,480. Of this, the Vulcan at Irvinebank produced 408 tons of tin.

The population of the Herberton field in 1911 was 6440 Europeans and 433 Chinese.

CHAPTER 13

CHILLAGOE

Copper at Chillagoe — Calcifer, Zillmanton, Muldiva — Life on the Mining Fields — Boom Days of Chillagoe and Mungana — The Smelters and the Chillagoe Railway — O. K. and Almaden.

William Atherton took up Chillagoe Station about 1887, and as had happened with his father at Emerald End ten years before, his discovery of minerals in the area led to the establishment of a town nearby. However, Malachi McGrath was in the area ahead of Atherton; he may have discovered the caves.

William Atherton and Tony Linedale, brother-in-law of John Moffat of Irvinebank, discovered rich copper and silver-lead lodes in 1888. No doubt Linedale had gone to investigate the area after Atherton had contacted Moffat. The names of Garbutt, Delaney, and Hull have been given as co-discoverers.

Silver lead was also found in the desolate Dargalong Ranges to the south-west. In 1891, E. F. Sandeman worked mica at nearby Mt. Wandoo, and J. V. Mulligan and Alex Riddle mined for gold.

The discovery of Chillagoe copper was part of the natural spread of prospecting out from earlier discoveries such as Irvinebank and Montalbion. The discovery of Muldiva led the way to opening up Chillagoe. This silver lead find was situated four or five miles from the later site of Almaden. We have already mentioned the road the carriers followed, fairly close to the route the railway followed later. The township of Zillmanton preceded Chillagoe township and Calcifer came into being in 1894 when the smelters opened. They would have been rough mining camps formed as headquarters for prospectors, most of them employed by the Irvinebank Mining Company at first.

Muldiva was discovered in June 1890, according to the report of Mineral Lands Commissioner, A. H. Zillman, of Herberton. Obviously Zillmanton was named in his honour.

(193)

In describing the Muldiva silver mines in a report dated October 25, 1890, Edward B. Lindon, a geologist, described the new field and the various lodes and added that he "advised the Muldiva Company to take over the property, and believe by the time a smelter is erected, sufficient high grade ore will be raised to keep the same in constant operation." It was in a lonely desolate spot among ironbark ridges, but there was a permanent spring of water in the creek nearby. Construction of the railway, then at Kuranda, gave hope that soon the area could be more easily reached by horse teams from Granite Creek instead of from Herberton.

The Muldiva Company, another of John Moffat's investments, went ahead with the erection of a silver lead smelter which produced, in 1893 at least, 187,571 ounces of silver despite the difficulties of isolation, transport, and low prices. When the price fell still lower, the Herberton warden reported that "the Muldiva Company was forced to apply for a respite and for a time at any rate, has closed down both mines and smelters." The smelters never opened again and so after but two years of prosperity, Muldiva ceased to exist. The smelters were dismantled and taken on the horse teams of Jack Tunnie and Tom Hooper — Irvinebank Company employees — to the Girofla copper mine near the later township of Mungana — known as Girofla at first. The Muldiva smelters had originally come from Newellton. It was amazing the way heavy machinery was pulled down, mandhandled on to wagons, and transported over terrible roads from one mineral discovery to another. With the passing of time, it is quite bewildering for the historian to correctly place all these movements, sometimes.

At Calcifer, in 1894, 1261 tons of ore was treated for a yield of 212 tons of copper valued at £7000; it was the first smelted copper from the Chillagoe locality.

There were 149 men, 38 women, and 60 children living at Muldiva in 1893. Their dwellings, mostly bark huts, bough sheds, and tents, with a few rough buildings of corrugated iron,

FENWICK'S BLACKSMITH'S SHOP, MAREEBA, BEFORE 1900

made conditions such that would not be tolerated today. Typhoid fever reared its ugly head and half the population was carried off in a tragic epidemic. Dr. Robert Broom and two or three local women acting as nurses, did what they could. Today, a forgotten cemetery with only a few of the graves marked, bears witness to the tragedy. In 1895, only half a dozen miners were still hanging on to the place.

The botanist, Mrs. Ellis Rowan, was a courageous Victorian lady who made a trip to the wilds of North Queensland, along the coast and inland, in search of botanical specimens in 1891. In her little known book, "A Flower Hunter in Queensland and New Zealand", (Angus and Robertson, 1898), she described her visit to Muldiva on her way to see the Chillagoe Caves. Mrs. Rowan* was probably the first "tourist" to visit the caves and undoubtedly was the first woman traveller from the South to do so. Her description of Muldiva shows the typical mining camp of those tough days:

"I am gradually nearing the Caves, but what a journey it has been! In spite of the many warnings I received I was determined to come, and here I am, sitting now, as I write, in a corrugated iron house in the principal street of this newly found mining town of Muldiva . . . . Opposite me is the police station, which fact is painted in red letters on a piece of canvas. It consists of two diggers' tents and a sort of verandah made out of branches of gum-trees. The general store is a tent on forked sticks with a wall of branches on all sides; the proprietor's name (probably Tom Templeton) is written in huge letters upon it, and a counter with glasses and array of tins proclaim his calling. The thermometer is 120 degs. F. in the shade.

"Next comes a real bush bark hut, of which many are

---

* This was the married name of a titled lady — Lady Eileen Knox, the younger daughter of Lord and Lady Ranfurley. The former was Governor-General of New Zealand at the time. As Mrs. Ellis Rowan, she made her home in Melbourne. Her delicate and painstakingly accurate paintings of botanical specimens were unearthed from storage in the Melbourne Museum only a few years ago.

studded about in every direction; then another tent, a bakehouse, one or two more stores, and two bough shelters that call themselves hotels. A man sits under an awning in the principal street (which is still full of felled trees and stumps) with the air of an Indian potentate, guarding a keg of beer, tumblers, matches, tobacco, pipes, etc. Here and there a native goes by, more or less in a state of intoxication. The butcher's shop is a green arbour of boughs. Stores just now are "out", and a pound of flour for the time costs a shilling.

"Everything is full of life and activity. The new chum that you meet is reticent, the old hand communicative . . . . Miners are wresting the metal from beds of rock, burrows in hillsides, and along the bed of an apology for a stream, whose waters are so full of lime that everything becomes encrusted with it, and even your clothes from the wash are powdered. John Chinaman goes by with his packhorse, for already he is pioneering with his garden stuff; where his garden is I do not know; everything seems baked and parched up, and the poor miserable gum-trees do not look as if they could cast a yard of shade. All around are the bare rocky hills, and just beyond the town is the great Muldiva mine which at present shows every sign of a prosperous future . . . . which promises (so many people say) to be hardly second to Broken Hill. (Footnote: It has since that time not realised such high expectations) . . . . The manager took us all through most of the different claims of the Company. Every tunnel we went into had rich silver-bearing stone, some of it giving over 500 ounces to the ton. At one shaft, the Paisley, we went down a perpendicular ladder 180 ft. . . . .

"It is Sunday, and the day seems as if it would never come to an end. Not a breath of cool air anywhere, not a book to read . . . . I could not get away from that fierce heat; then I went back to the hotel and into a little hut next door where I sat and fanned a child dying of fever . . . . I had something besides my own worries to think of. Evening came at last, and I went for a walk with the housemaid from the hotel up to a hill overlooking the town. She gave me a most ghastly description of life in a mining town . . . . The thought of that journey back hangs over me like a hideous nightmare . . . . "

All rather terrifying to a Victorian lady who had come from gentle, ordered surroundings in a Melbourne suburb, but neither unusual or frightening to the hardy folk in the North Queensland bush in the 'Nineties where hardships, and not comforts, was what they naturally expected.

Mrs. Rowan had boarded Cobb and Co's coach at Herberton, bound for Georgetown and Croydon late in October, 1891. She said she had undertaken many rough drives but none compared with that which brought her to Muldiva over "the roughest road in Australia" she was told. In places the coach, when descending the hills, dropped from one boulder to another, the so-called road as rough as a creekbed full of rocks. The coach had left Herberton at 5 a.m. and reached Montalbion at ten o'clock — "the barest and most miserable looking place I have ever seen" — and Mrs. Rowan went on to Muldiva in a buckboard; on this 45 mile journey she was smothered with dust under a torrid sun without shelter and had to hang on for dear life as the vehicle bounced over the boulders on the Featherbed Range, through the mining camp of Koorboora, where horses were changed and there was only strong black tea with which to quench her thirst, and so into the night with only the starlight to show the track. The candles in the lamps had long since melted. The horses were half broken and bolted twice, but at 2 a.m. Muldiva was reached.

Mrs. Rowan went on to Chillagoe Station in a sulky and was guided through the caves by "Mr. A." — William Atherton, no doubt. "They struck me as larger, grander, and more imposing than any of the Jenolan caves in New South Wales . . . . It is not yet known for how far the caves extend; I believe about thirty miles have been explored," Mrs. Rowan wrote.

The Chillagoe Caves are becoming, 90 years later, a major

(198)

tourist attraction in North Queensland and must grow in popularity, bringing publicity and progress to old Chillagoe.

*   *   *   *

All the railways to tap the mining fields west and north of Mareeba between 1899 and 1907 were constructed by private enterprise, and were therefore private railways. Of these the Chillagoe line was the longest — 103 miles — and most important. As the late Hugh Borland has put it, "The Chillagoe Line fertilised a territory." It was probably the longest private railway in Queensland at that time. With Chillagoe as the railhead at first, it was soon extended ten miles to Mungana to serve the big copper deposits there. The line, built between 1899 and 1901, cost £381,902 to construct. Archibald Frew was the contractor for the line for the Chillagoe Railway and Mines Company.

It had been John Moffat's capital that had proved the richness of the Chillagoe area copper mines at Calcifer, Zillmanton, and Girofla, and put the field on the map. But it was all small-scale, and more capital was needed, so in 1897 Moffat sold the bulk of his interests to the Chillagoe Company. This was formed in Melbourne, its leading men being C. W. Chapman and J. S. Reid. The latter had been a pioneer newspaperman in the North, establishing newspapers at Ravenswood and Thornborough in the 'Seventies before going to Broken Hill and making a fortune in mining speculations. In December 1897, the Queensland Government gave the Chillagoe Company approval to construct the railway to Government specifications. The company rushed ahead to erect smelters and develop its leases but spent too little time and money on prospecting and testing. The report that half a million tons of ore estimated to yield 17,000 tons of copper, 1500 tons of lead and a million ounces of silver lay waiting, caused a boom on the Southern stock exchanges and a rush of men and their families to Chillagoe. Within a matter of months, there was a bustling township among the craggy limestone bluffs on the bank of the

(199)

permanently flowing Station Creek.

The railway opened in August 1901, and the smelters began production on September 12th. Ores from Ruddigore, Girofla, and Redcap were the first to be treated.

Erection of the smelters was under the direction of R. Sheppard and J. Higgins. E. A. Weinberg, an American, was a supposed mining expert. The adverse publicity he gave the field almost caused its abandonment before work properly began. His statement that reserves of copper ore did not, after all, exceed more than 173,000 tons, caused a panic among shareholders and a slump on the stock exchanges. Many mines closed when capital was withdrawn, and there was an exodus of people from the town. However, in 1902, the New Chillagoe Company was formed and confidence was restored mainly because of the fine reputation of a major shareholder and the "father" of the field — John Moffat of Irvinebank. It is said he could have sold his shares during the stock exchange boom for three-quarters of a million pounds but knowing this would not be honest he had refused to do so. Now his financial integrity saved Chillagoe from collapse.

Other Chillagoe smelter managers were, in turn, A. Stewart, T. J. Greenway, P. Brander, and James Horsborough. Fred Back was general manager in 1907. Moule, Kunze, Lloyd, Millar, and others played a major part in the running of this large concern — a company which brought £600,000 worth of capital to the region behind Cairns. They had their own jetty in Cairns, and for years the private railway throbbed to the roar of loaded ore trains, and Mareeba benefited greatly. More and more it became a base so strategically situated it was bound to prosper and unlike a mining town, be permanent.

In 1901, the Chillagoe-Mungana Company came into being when it acquired five mining leases from the Chillagoe Railway and Mines Ltd. for £85,000 in cash and shares. The leases were situated ten miles west of the smelters and included the rich Girofla and Lady Jane mines. Discovered in 1888 by

William Atherton and Tony Linedale, there were then great masses of copper ore in huge outcrops. Atherton continued his fondness for the theatre by calling the creek at Girofla, Opera Creek. Thus the township of Mungana was put on the map. Four miles away was the earlier settlement of Zillmanton, already a ghost town, but a revival came in 1907 when the Chillagoe Company reopened the mines employing about eighty men with Arthur Nichols as mine manager. However, Mungana could supply all the extra ore the Chillagoe smelters could handle; the Zillmanton mines flooded and were finally closed for good in November 1911 and another mining town disappeared.

Mungana had the reputation of being one of the wildest towns in Australia close on three-quarters of a century ago. On pay nights it was not unusual for two or three fights to be going on simultaneously in the main street.

The three hotels in the main street were kept by Ernie Markham, Mrs. Dett, and Tim Toomey around 1911 when Gordon Hay, now of Dimbulah, went to school in Mungana. He recalls the well-liked schoolmaster, Mr. Brock, later Commissioner of Queensland Police. In Mungana at that period there was also Brady's general store, McIntosh's bakery; Lisha and Karooz, drapers; Bill Beard's restaurant, and William Atherton's butchery. There were two more hotels at Redcap, a rough mining settlement four miles from Mungana. It had a brief existence during the first decade of this century.

Writing about the impermanent mining settlements like Zillmanton, Calcifer, Mungana, Redcap, and O.K., Dr. K. H. Kennedy in one of the "Lectures on North Queensland History" series, James Cook University, describes them as bawdy brawling townships that owed their reputation as much to the potency of the liquor and to the excitement of the gambling schools, as to the wealth won from the mines. Railway navvies, miners, and smelter hands stormed the many hotels on pay nights to drown their grievances with adulterated spirits and to mix with fellow workers at the 'two-up' games, which often climaxed in stand-up

(201)

fights and brawls . . . . "

Insanitary conditions and poor water supplies caused periodic outbreaks of typhoid and at Chillagoe the water was full of lime. Dr. G. C. Bolton in "A Thousand Miles Away" (A. N. U. Press, 1970) quoted "an observer" of the time saying, it didn't really matter as "Chillagoe-ites don't drink water as a rule" !

Storekeepers in Chillagoe around 1907 were Jack and Newell (who still function there, in a fine modern building), B. J. Magee, Peter Byrne, and Tom Templeton. All the latter three were also bakers; Templeton had come from Muldiva. Peter Byrne also had the Imperial Hotel which is still in the Byrne family. Building contractors and cabinetmakers who erected most of the buildings in the locality were Bulling and Co. and A. May. In 1907 the school had 100 pupils, and E. X. O'Gorman was headmaster.

Chillagoe also had three churches — Methodist, Church of England, and Catholic. In the small mining towns, spiritual needs were more neglected. Dr. N. Trenow was in charge of the hospital in the 1907 period. In those days of the horse when such men were important, P. Mahoney was the saddler and A. Hamilton and F. W. Davis were blacksmiths and coach-builders.

Some strange things happened in the boom days, old timers recall. Like the time a local medico, Dr. McLaughlin, had a boxing bout on a vacant allotment with Tommy Burns in 1909, the year after he lost the world heavyweight title. Burns was with a vaudeville show visiting Chillagoe at the time. Vaudeville troupes and concert players, also travelling circuses, included Chillagoe in their tours. Here it is interesting to recall that it was in the historic School of Arts at Irvinebank that the famous opera singer, the late Gladys Moncrieff, gave one of her early concerts before she went overseas and achieved world fame.

William Lees, a mining writer who produced supplements for "Queensland Country Life" of Brisbane wrote in one of them, "The Copper Mines and Mineral Fields of Queensland", about his visit to Chillagoe towards the end of 1907:

"Although there are hotels and some houses near to the railway station at the foot of the steep limestone bluffs, rising a hundred feet above the road, the township of Chillagoe proper is about half a mile distant, to and from which cabs regularly ply.

"Here a main street contains several excellent hotels, among which may be specially mentioned Torpy's and Chris Millar's. The former was my home for my short stay, and I can but add my praise to the compliments made by all the travellers for the comfort and homeliness here found. On the opposite side of the street is the fine store of Jack and Newell, the offices of Mr. Green, late Brownlee and Donald Ltd., and the Bank of Australasia, under the management of Mr. Smith, while adjacent to Torpy's Hotel is the office of Mr. Norman Pace, share-broker, etc.

"The post and telegraph office at Chillagoe is one of the busiest in North Queensland, and at the time of my visit was in charge of Mr. G. L. Berry, relieving postmaster . . . . A fine public school, well attended with adjacent playground, is under the charge of Mr. E. Doran. There are also two papers published in the township, the 'Chillagoe Miner' and the 'Chillagoe Standard', each containing a large amount of matter relative to the affairs of the district.

"The caves lie a short distance from the township, and an excursion at particularly cheap rates can be arranged, either with the livery stables proprietors or Mr. Freestun, bookseller etc., who takes a keen interest in the preservation of the beauties of these caves; an interest and care that visitors could well emulate."

"The Standard" newspaper was run by George H. O'Donnell who later took it to Mareeba to produce the "Walsh and Tinaroo Miner". It has been claimed there were as many as five thousand people living in Chillagoe, Mungana, and their immediate surroundings in the brief boom times. When the smelters, Government controlled since 1919 when the railway

(203)

was also acquired, closed for good in 1943, Chillagoe went steadily down hill, being only kept on the map as a supply base for large cattle stations to the north and west. Tourism has injected new life into the township and caused the erection of new buildings and town improvements.

Mungana, on the other hand, has completely disappeared except for a trucking yard. Cattle are brought up to 200 miles by road transport to be railed to coastal meatworks and but for this traffic the railway would probably have been closed.

The old time Chillagoe Railway when run by the Company, maintained a high standard of efficiency. Some of the surplus steam locomotives were sent to Darwin in 1942 to haul troop trains on the Darwin-Birdum line and for years after the war stood, rusting and forgotten, at Katherine until finally sold to Japan for scrap. A familiar sight in construction days was the little Yankee Pioneer loco of 1870 vintage; such engines made the famous Union Pacific possible and they were just as successful here.

Some of the engine drivers — they had their homes in Mareeba — were: Harry Fuelling, Bill Garthwaite, Mick Woods (later M.L.A. for Woothakata), Morrow Bros., Sam Cameron, Jim Riordan, and Ralph Hastie who was very well known. Among the guards were Bill Gee and Darby Riordan, later M.L.A. Paddy McDermott was traffic manager for years, followed by Arthur Hastie. A. C. Stirling was a maintenance engineer, Wallace and Foley were connected with bridge construction.

The railway caused development of other mining fields and townships such as Almaden and Koorboora. Almaden was named, because of its silver mines, after an ancient silver field in Spain. When the railway reached there in 1900 it represented the nearest railhead to the Fossilbrook and Tate tin mines, Einasleigh copper mine, Georgetown and the old Etheridge Goldfield. It meant that the old Georgetown Road that the pioneers had known, first from Port Douglas and then from

(204)

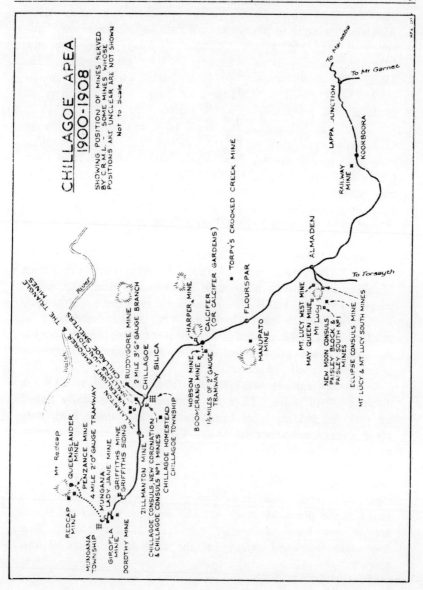

CHILLAGOE AREA
1900-1908

SHOWING POSITION OF MINES SERVED
BY C.R.M.L. — SOME MINES WHOSE
POSITIONS ARE UNCLEAR ARE NOT SHOWN

Not to Scale

Mareeba, had gone forever. The coaches now plied from Almaden through to Croydon. Within eight years they disappeared here, too, as the Chillagoe Company constructed the Etheridge Railway from Almaden to Forsayth, opening it in 1908. The rich copper ore from Einasleigh could now be worked and railed to Chillagoe smelters. The transport of cattle is now practically the only traffic.

Had the Etheridge line been built beyond Forsayth to Georgetown, and then to Croydon which was, in 1908, still a busy gold mining centre, there would have been a railway from Cairns to Normanton and the Gulf Country would have benefited enormously. With rail transport to markets there could have been an agriculture industry on the Gilbert River to replace mining, and it would have helped fishing in the Gulf in recent years.

Back in 1907, other railways were planned to serve the mining fields. One was to run 23 miles north-west from Mungana to Cardross, also called Arbouin and Klondyke, where copper, silver, tin, and wolfram was mined by a force of 100 men. The Irvinebank Mining Company was actively interested in this field. The railway extension never eventuated, though possibly the mines were not worked out; in many cases it was low prices that caused abandonment.

Another railway was planned from Mungana to O.K., a distance of 46 miles. Here the mineral belt practically linked up with the gold reefs of Limestone on the Palmer field, only about twenty miles beyond O.K. Copper had been discovered by John Munro in 1900 when copper and tin, more than gold, was exciting the public. He is said to have named his claim after a brand of jam then in use and the township that arose close by carried this strange name. Few people now have heard of the place, yet there are still just one or two old timers around who have affectionate memories of this isolated little town that flourished briefly for the first dozen years of this century.

One of those who remember it well is Gordon Hay of Dimbulah. He went to school there in 1910. It was a busy place, he says, with five hotels; they were kept by Mick Brown, Bob Amory, Lizzie Matthewson, Kitty Breen, — Burke, and — Orchard. Mick Brown had been on the Mareeba Goldfield, and after leaving O.K., kept the Railway Hotel in Cairns. O.K. was known as a wild town and like Mungana, noted for its street fights on pay nights. Jack Hay had a store, but later sold it to a man named Kingsbury, and returned to carrying. There were many horse teams and about twelve traction engines hauling wagons to and fro between O.K. and Mungana, from 1905 to 1911.

A coach plied regularly to and from Mungana; Stewart's coach change was on Elizabeth Creek. Drivers were named Frousicker and Titmarsh.

Some of the teamsters Gordon Hay recalls were Jack Rosington, Bill Penprase, Jack Woodruffe, Ah Kum, Jack Hay, Rolls Bros., Subby Carroll, and Jack McCarthy. Traction engine drivers were Walter Prior and his two sons; also Woods, and Maxwell.

O.K. was a rough and primitive place; the homes were mostly shacks built of bush timber, with iron roofs and walls of bags or calico, and antbed floors. The school had 47 pupils at its peak, and the teacher was Mr. Adam.

The Bourke Carrying Company owned by an Afghan named Abdul Wade, came to North Queensland in 1900 and camel teams were used to carry coke from Lappa Lappa on the Chillagoe Railway to Mt. Garnet smelters, returning with copper matte. After the branch railway was built, the camel teams were transferred to the O.K.-Mungana road, much to the disgust of the teamsters.

Gordon Hay said: "Dad told me how the teamsters hated those camel teams as horses could not stand the smell of camels. Teams often bolted, and at night time the horses scattered everywhere. It took hours next day to muster the team horses and it was hard to get them back to the wagon as they could still smell the camels.

"Anyway, the camels ate the ironwood bushes and died. I think that's what happened at Mt. Garnet, too. When the first storms came and the gullies ran, the ironwood leaves had accummulated in the gullies and the camels drank the water which was dark brown colour, and the camels died like flies.

"However, old Abdul got traction engines then and was still a thorn in the flesh to the teamsters as the chimneys had no spark arrestors on them and they set fire to the grass and so there was no feed for the horses. The traction engines burnt great quantities of wood. They couldn't have been a great success in the wet weather as Dad told me he often hooked his team on to an engine to pull it out of a creek."

Another memory of Gordon Hay's: "I met a chap a good few years ago who told me he bought his working clothes in Dad's store at O.K. The whole outfit — shirt, trousers, hat, and boots cost him a 'quid' ($2.00) for the lot and Dad threw in a handkerchief as a bonus. How different now!"

Clergymen were rare in the Outback those days and those who did visit the isolated mining settlements had to be as tough as anyone else. Such a one was the Rev. Wilkinson, a Church of England minister who used to travel all through the back country with a team of packhorses, a blackboy his only companion. The parson was universally well liked and no doubt admired for his toughness for he was elderly and not robust. He was also very deaf and used a huge ear trumpet which, unfortunately, terrified the small children. Gordon Hay remembers him visiting his home at O.K. a few times. He had his headquarters at Laura.

One of his most amazing patrols was equal to an explorer's journey. In 1913-15 he rode from Laura to Normanton, then to Darwin, south to Alice Springs, and back to Laura, covering 7500 miles on horseback with packhorses. The station owners gave him brumbies and he would break them in for packs.

BY ALEX HARDAKER

ABDUL WADE   CAMEL DRIVER

(209)

During that long ride the valiant parson was to run short of provisions, lose horses, and almost perish from thirst. He spent his sixtieth birthday on the track. He carried a medical kit as he was often ill with fever, and he was thus able to save the life of a drover he found lying sick in his camp on a Northern Territory stock route.

Bishop Gilbert White wrote of Rev. W. M. Wilkinson in his book, "Thirty Years in Tropical Australia":

"With no home save a little iron room at Laura on one side of which he keeps saddlery and bags of horse feed, he rides ever from daylight to dark through some of the loneliest country in Australia . . . . I well remember my first trip with him.

"He was up before daylight looking after his horses, and adjusting the weight of the many packbags. There was no mention of a pause for dinner on the first day, or the next, or any day after . . . . Supper, the best meal of the day, was salt beef and damper, with a tin of jam added as a special concession to my weakness. I don't know what he lives on when he is not travelling with jam-requiring bishops. The total income derived from his living (?) does not cover horseshoes and horse feed; but he's been doing it for ten years, and still buys fresh horses."

"Deafy" Wilkinson as he was affectionately known, was a byword throughout threequarters of a million square miles of the Carpentaria diocese for many years.

In 1907, the main O.K. mine was producing 1600 tons of ore yielding 160 tons of copper each month, worth £15,000. During the five years it had been working, the mine produced 4000 tons of copper, and shareholders had received £76,000 in dividends. The company, the O.K. Copper Mines Development Syndicate, had John Newell, chairman, and the other directors were G. C. Willcocks, C. A. S. Andrews and J. W. Ashcroft. The general manager in 1907 was R. Shepherd, and H. Twynan was mine manager. The cost of producing blister

OK. SMELTERS 1906

BY ALEX HARDAKER

(211)

copper at the O. K. smelters — which, incidentally, had come from Mt. Garnet — was almost £41 per ton, a dangerously high figure for those times when copper prices never rose about £95 per ton and all mineral prices were unstable. Some of the copper lodes in the area were seven feet wide, and hopes for the future were optimistic.

O.K. had a small hospital where Matron Damm presided.

But by 1911, O.K. was completely deserted, the mines closed and the smelters dismantled. The Hay family were the last to leave. It has been said that home owners, hotelkeepers, and storekeepers just packed a few personal belongings on wagons, carts, and packhorses and left all their furniture behind, even pianos. Such was the fickleness of mining. Mainly it was politics and economics which caused the downfall of these small fields, and not always because they were worked out.

Jock Hay went from O.K. to the Batavia gold rush in Cape York Peninsula in 1911. While he was away, his wife — Gordon Hay's mother — had to bail water with a windlass from a sixty-foot deep well every day to water twenty team horses.

The mail came from Cooktown being brought from Laura by the packhorse mailman, Percy Parsons, who lived at Maytown, once a month. After this, Herb Doyle, son of the pathfinder, John Doyle, was the packhorse mailman from Mungana to the Palmer and back.

Limestone was another ghost town about thirty miles further north towards the Palmer. Gordon's father, Jock, found the only inhabitants in 1911 were an improverished family of small children. He assisted the father to take them on his pack team to O.K. where the Hays looked after them for a time. The children were transported in the old time manner, in kerosene cases either side of a packhorse. The family's main means of sustenance was a herd of goats. The children had never seen butter or bread; they had only ever used mutton (goat) fat on their damper. Life was indeed hard for poor folk in those days; they had no social service to fall back on.

(212)

At Almaden, Ted Torpy was the leading mining man. He and T. C. Tait, of Broken Hill, had a silver lead mine on Crooked Creek, a Walsh River tributary. Torpy and Anderson also had the Maniopoto mine.

The Wieland family moved from Montalbion to Almaden about 1900 when the railway came and opened the Carriers' Arms Hotel which Mrs. Bridget Wieland conducted. Her husband and sons had horse teams, and there was plenty of work. When Almaden became the railhead, wagons went out with stores to newly opened mining camps; there was Einasleigh and its big copper mine, also Angor, Gallala, and Fossilbrook. Gallala was a wolfram field. Fred and Peter Petersen discovered it when taking stores and tools on a big team of packhorses to the Angor tinfield. Roy and Jack O'Sullivan, only very young men, won three-and-a-half tons of tin in as many days, one old timer recalls, and this gave them their start in life.

All the ore from these fields was brought into Almaden by wagon. The first copper from Einasleigh where smelters were erected was brought in by camel teams, later by traction engine. This was around 1902. Cobb and Co's coaches ran from Almaden to Georgetown and Croydon; well remembered drivers were Joe Hirschberg and Robert Croft. The latter's daughter, Mrs. Alice Harriman of Mareeba, still has the pair of gloves he used while handling the "ribbons".

It was Minnie Wieland, mentioned in Chapter 11, who discovered the Crooked Creek silver lead deposit and showed it to Ted Torpy. He generously gave her a silk tie for her trouble, recalls her sister, Mrs. O'Leary of Mareeba.

In 1901, Torpy was also managing director of the Chillagoe–Ruddygore Mining Investment Company Ltd., and later he took over the mine on tribute. William Atherton was chairman of this company, and John Newell and D. C. MacDiarmid were directors. First known as The Consols, the mine was worked as an opencut, sixty feet deep and 130 feet long.

E. B. Torpy also had an hotel in Almaden, where there were five in 1904. As well as Torpy's and Wieland's, there was Markham's later run by Joe Peel, Maher's Railway Hotel, and another at the Eight Mile. Paddy Atherton had a butchery and general store. Jimmy Thompson was the baker. A well liked Chinese named Lum Wun had another store.

Almaden was a wild place during the Etheridge Railway construction. Hundreds of navvies painted the town red on pay nights. Next morning, dozens could be seen chained to logs and trees, like dogs, as there was no gaol.

Mr. McGregor of Mareeba remembers that John Candlish was a storekeeper who followed the railway constructions, building his bark-built stores as the lines progressed. A good all round athlete and axeman, Louis Plate, worked for Candlish. Mr. McGregor's father had a store at Einasleigh around 1908. The former recalls that the Einasleigh mine worked from 1897 to 1920, reopened once and then closed for good. There used to be two ore trains a day to the Chillagoe smelters. It made Almaden quite a busy railway junction.

CHAPTER 14

LAND OF MINERALS

Koorboora — The Tate — Mt. Garnet — The Smelters and Camels — Mt. Garnet Railway — Tin Dredge — Nymbool — Gurrumbah — Brownville — Gold at Mt. Luxton — Wadetown — Bamford.

Not many people today know where Koorboora is. It is situated between Dimbulah and Almaden, six miles west of Lappa Lappa which was once the junction of the Mt. Garnet branch line, pulled up over ten years ago.

There are only two or three miners' camps on this old field now, but it once possessed the richest wolfram mine in the world — the Neville — and many rich tin mines. Coal was also found there. The mining writer, William Lees, came up from Brisbane in 1907 and described Koorboora in these words: "Koorboora railway station is at an elevation of 1613 feet above sea level and the principal mines, mostly owned by the Irvinebank Mining Company, lie at varying distances within a radius of some three miles. The township, the usual single street, with galvanised iron and wooden structures, is about a mile to the north-west, and a short distance away is the Company's battery, the well known Shakespeare tin mine, and the residence of the manager, Mr. W. A. Waddell, one time general manager of the old Muldiva silver mines, and one of the most helpful mining men among the large number I had the pleasure of meeting . . . . " The mill manager at that time was D. Henderson.

Tony Linedale was on his way to Chillagoe on horseback in 1888, and camping on the later site of Koorboora, discovered the Shakespeare mine. He then prospected the area for John Moffat and the latter was granted a forty acre reward claim. Linedale encouraged the Munro Bros. and Alex Munro found the Fairplay. Other miners soon came, and mines like the Bismarck, Alexander, Shylock, Iolanthe, Rosalind, Iago, Ironbark,

Falstaff, and others were discovered, but were not worked seriously.

Specimen tin was so rich and plentiful that it could be picked up on the surface and sent to the Irvinebank smelters without having to be crushed or dressed. The Chillagoe Railway provided the access from 1900 onwards, and from 1899 the Irvinebank Company provided the incentive and assistance necessary. A ten-head battery was built; 2160 tons of tin metal was produced in seven years.

Veteran miners, William Neville and "Russian Jack" opened the Neville mine, but development did not come until 1903. By 1907, some 500 tons of wolfram had been produced; today it would be worth over a million dollars. Jack and Billy Little were among the pioneers of Koorboora. Billy Little was, of course, on the Hodgkinson and was a leading man in Thornborough being elected to Parliament as M.L.A. for Woothakata in the early 'Eighties. As well as mining he also dabbled in butchering and hotelkeeping. One of the streets of Thornborough and a Hodgkinson tributary stream were named after him. He and his brother opened the Southwick tin mine at Koorboora and sold out to the Irvinebank Company. They were working the Iago in 1907.

Koorboora was known for its variety of metals: the Telegraph was a tin and wolfram mine combined, and the Railway produced both silver-lead and copper. Tin, zinc, silver, and lead were all found at the 100 ft. level in the Tennyson. "Treatment problems have to be met with every day at Koorboora," Lees wrote.

As with the early quartz-crushing batteries, they were often erected in one place after being hauled many miles from Port Douglas or Mareeba railhead, used for a year or two and then transported somewhere else, all by bullock teams over tracks that could not be called roads. The Koorboora mill had seen service at Glenlinedale for a few years up to 1890; it was then taken to California Creek, and finally to Koorboora over a

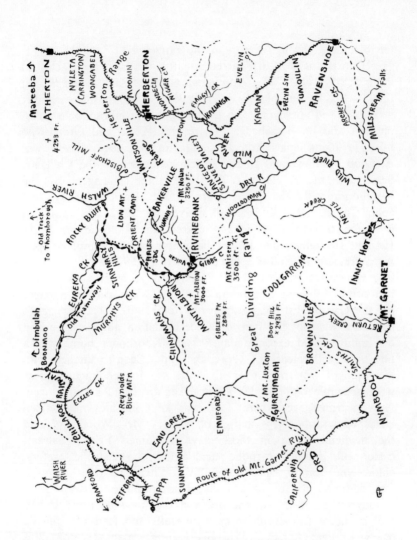

terrible track through a gap in the ranges.

Koorboora is in dry barren country, the hard ridges clothed in ironbark trees. The Aboriginal name is said to mean just that — "a barren place". Credit should go to the early-day geologists and surveyors who worked in these inhospitable areas, on foot and on horseback. There was White and Grant who filled in blank spaces on the maps of the day. There was A. Gibb Maitland and Ned Wheeler, geologists on the Chillagoe field, and many others. The first three managers of the Koorboora mill were Selby Burrell Ord, David Mackay, and John Coxall. W. A. Waddell arrived in 1902 and remained until the Irvinebank Company ceased operations about 1920. He had the unenviable job of liquidator of the company upon his retirement to Cairns. He died there in 1934.

His daughter, Mrs. O. H. Woodward, recorded some of her memories of life at Koorboora from 1902 onwards in a paper for the Cairns Historical Society in June 1960. The manager's residence was not the type of accommodation an executive and his family would expect today. Their Koorboora home was a tin shack with plenty of verandahs and a lean-to kitchen with a couple of iron bars over an open fire for cooking; utensils were a couple of billycans, an iron cauldron and a camp oven. Ants swarmed everywhere; food was kept in safes made from boxes with sapling legs in tins of water. Mrs. Woodward said the medicine chest in those days contained Friar's balsam, castor oil, iodine, carbolic acid, Hearns' headache wafers, chlorodyne, and a snakebite outfit. When the rains came it was common to see snakes coiled around the rafters. Mrs. Woodward recalled that the ore and the firewood came to the mill by horse teams and there were stalls and feed-lofts for 72 heavy draught horses. Whereas a mine manager nowadays would have the latest model car, Mr. Waddell kept two smart hacks.

Despite the rough conditions, gentility was preserved. Mrs. Woodward wrote: "A school room was built in the garden and we were taught by a series of governesses who thought poetry, music, and painting more important (for girls) than mathematics. Father was extremely musical, playing flute and violin, and we had many a concert party around the Lippe piano. Mother read to us daily in our teens, Shakespeare's plays (with coarse words omitted), all Dickens, Scott, and Thackeray, while we embroidered cloths. All our toys, with the exception of china-face dolls, were made by our parents . . . . " Every two years they went on a holiday to Sydney, travelling by ship from Cairns and staying with "Grandmother Absell." Trips by buggy to Port Douglas and Irvinebank were special treats.

Jack and Newell were the main storekeepers in Koorboora, the branch being managed by John Newell's nephew, Jack. The two hotels were kept by Coghlan and O'Brien, Lewis had a soft drink factory and refreshment room, and Hughes was the butcher. Bread came by train from Templeton's bakery in Chillagoe. Sandy Lemmon was a Company blacksmith and Denny Gordon the Company's saddler. Nat Absell and E. R. Absell were in the Company's office. Other employees one old timer recalled were Dan Mackie, Tom McBride, Alf Jones, B. Fabian, J. H. Curtis, and Willie Arbouin was another associated with old time Koorboora.

W. A. Waddell came to Koorboora from the Tate after being at Muldiva earlier. The Tate tin mines were more isolated and an even rougher place than Koorboora, being far off the beaten track in hot, lonely country. Tin had been found there in 1879 as has been mentioned, and there is still tin there. The late Ernest White who lived in Cairns when he retired and who arrived in Herberton in 1880, was manager at the Tate for the Irvinebank Company early this century. The official name for the place was Fischerton, but it did not stick. The locality is still known as "The Tate". Six thousand tons of high grade alluvial tin was won here up to early in World War II. The oldest mining centre between Herberton and Georgetown, it has had many ups and downs, and could live again.

A lot could be written about the Tate if space permitted. There was not only tin, but gold as well. The latter gave rise to another mushroom township around 1901, called Williamstown after the discoverer.

*   *   *   *

The railway to Mt. Garnet from Lappa was the first branch built from the Chillagoe Line. The discovery of copper at Mt. Garnet actually predates Chillagoe by five or six years, but it was not worked until 1898 and again it was John Moffat and his Irvinebank Mining Company which brought it about.

The actual discoverer was Albert Vollenwider, a Swiss, who came to Queensland in 1871. He landed in Cardwell from the steamer Tinonee and carried his swag over the range to Georgetown and mined for gold with varying success. He went to the Palmer in 1875 and joined in the rush to the Hodgkinson the following year.

He arrived in Herberton in 1881 and in September 1882, prospecting far to the south-west, he discovered copper at Mt. Garnet. Like similar finds in other out-of-the-way places it was then of no value, but Vollenwider had unbounded faith in it and refused to part with his lease. Mt. Garnet's mushroom-like boom began in 1896.

The Mt. Garnet area was then on part of Mullabulla Station, run by R. Perrott of Evelyn. Grant Bros. bought Woodleigh from the founder, O. C. Garbutt, in the late 'eighties. F. S. Grant took up Mandalee in 1896. Ned Campbell was the original owner of Strathvale, later well known as a Lucey family property.

The late A. F. Waddell, Irvinebank's historian, remembered Vollenwider as a big bearded man wearing a long coat with a wide belt, a broad-brimmed hat, and always carrying a whip — like a picture of a Boer farmer in South Africa at the time, he said.

The Irvinebank Mining Company started work on the cap

of the copper lode in 1896, with George Waddell in charge of a party of miners including Bill Lewis, (an early Watsonville miner) Jack Pollard (one of the discoverers of Irvinebank), Ted Angel (from Montalbion), and Andrew Henderson (one of the early miners on the Hodgkinson). Return Creek at Mt. Garnet is shown on some old maps as Nanyeta. This was the Aboriginal name meaning "come back", or "return" — hence Return Creek.

In 1899, the Mt. Garnet Freehold Copper and Mining Company was floated with a capital of £200,000, with C. W. Chapman chairman, and John Moffat managing director. All the machinery was hauled by teams eighty miles over the ranges from Mareeba railhead, through Herberton and Silver Valley. "Proved" ore reserves were 209,000 tons. A. L. Mills was the metallurgist. By March 1900, there were 160 men employed. A smelter with two waterjacket furnaces was under construction.

In January, 1901, the smelters were "blown in", and operations commenced. The tall smokestack was a landmark for many miles. About 440 men were employed. In November, 1900, the first land sale was held, and the town grew rapidly; it was soon a very lively centre.

To bring in coke for the smelters and take out the bagged matte, camel teams came to North Queensland in charge of Abdul Wade, who had the Bourke Carrying Company in New South Wales. It was a strange sight to see the long line of camels swaying along the stony track over the hills and through the bush, on their way to the railway at Lappa Lappa. With the building of the railway the camels were withdrawn and used between O.K. and Mungana as previously mentioned. The general manager of the Mt. Garnet Company reported on December 31, 1901 that "The Bourke Carrying Company have carried out their contract in a most satisfactory manner, and there has been no trouble in getting goods forward or product away." Apparently the cost of camel cartage was about 12 shillings per ton. The branch railway reached California Creek on 16 November 1901, and Mt. Garnet in April 1902.

James Allison who had opened branches of the Q. N. Bank in Thornborough, Watsonville, Montalbion, and Herberton, did likewise at Mt. Garnet. It has had its hospital from about 1901. Doctors recalled are Drs. Wallace, Thomas, and Perkins. Dr. Thomas was also at Irvinebank and Chillagoe, and Dr. Perkins in Mareeba later. Miss Nott (later Mrs. A. M. Waddell) was matron at one time. Mr. Martin was the schoolmaster for some years.

There were six hotels in Mt. Garnet at that time — the Mt. Garnet (D. Lucey); Federal (J. Coplin); Imperial (J. Noonan); Royal (R. Lillicrapp), Railway (Mrs. Wall); Miners' Arms (McCormick). Storekeepers were Jack and Newell — who functioned there until a few years ago — Armstrong, Ledlie, and Stillman, and A. Thompson. Butchers were Banks and Todd, Earl and Co., and Dubbo and Co. Blacksmiths were Fraser and Co. and L. Hanson. Bob McKinnon and H. Reid were bakers.

An old timer recalls the names of some of those attached to the stores, such as Mr. Stillman of A. L. and S., and also Fred Bimrose, Sandy Anderson, A. M. Waddell, Tom O'Connor, and Jack Newell, of J. and N. Mining agents, secretaries, etc. recalled were also active in other mining towns in the Cairns Hinterland long ago, such as "Big Ernie" Hunter, John Cairns, J. M. Hollway, J. H. Brownlee, W. K. Donald, and John Coxall. Randolph Bedford, a mining speculator, is the only one who recorded anything of this for posterity, and that in a very rare book entitled "Nought to 33."

In 1902 the smelters treated 43,994 tons of ore for a return of 3154 tons of matte containing 473,548 ozs. of silver and 2088 tons of copper. There were enormous piles of charcoal on hand, testifying to the hard work of charcoal burners.

But in March, 1903, Warden Haldane from Herberton reported: "Mt. Garnet is apparently almost crippled through financial difficulties . . . ." In June: "As the township is dependent on mining, the place is partially deserted, and the dismantling of buildings is taking place in all directions." On November 6, 1903: "The mines are closed down for want of capital." About £250,000 worth of copper had been produced, and the warden still called Mt. Garnet "a valuable mine".

Thus collapsed the brief boom days of Mt. Garnet as a copper and silver smelting centre, but years later it was to get a new lease of life as a rich tin dredging area and as such is still the largest active mining centre in the Cairns Hinterland.

However, when the smelters closed, it was not the end of Mt. Garnet, as Smith's Creek (Nymbool) came to the rescue. Donohue and Foulkes were the discoverers of the alluvial tin, in 1902. In 1905, over 400 tin miners were active in this area and at California Creek where the township of Ord sprang up. Emmersons had had a coach change thereabouts in the days of the Port Douglas-Georgetown Road which passed close by. Armstrong, Ledlie, and Stillman were storekeepers at Nymbool in the boom days.

The discoverers won two and a half tons of tin in a short time. A mate named Smith took up an adjoining lease and also obtained over two tons of tin. A syndicate was formed and J. M. Potter left the Mt. Garnet Company to manage it. Over £41,000 worth of black tin, or 585 tons, was obtained before granite was struck and the mine closed. Scores of other "small" miners did well at Nymbool for years. The place had three hotels — Keen's, Wall's and Anderson's, in 1907.

Bill Peterson remembers veritable fortunes were won by some lucky alluvial tin miners at Nymbool early this century even when tin was no more than £150 per ton. The unlucky worked like slaves for a pittance. Clyde Sinns was one who kept the field going for years. The area's lode tin makes it attractive today.

In 1907, Jim Dalziell and sons Jim and Harry found the very rich Boulder Mine. (Harry won the V.C. in World War I. later on). About this time George Gilmore found the even richer Gilmore Mine. In each case, fortune had smiled when the discoverers had almost given up hope. The tenacity of those old time prospectors is to be much admired. Up to 1914, the Gilmore produced £71,362 worth of tin, and some of the ore was as high as 50 p.c. metal. Ernie Hunter, then in Mt. Garnet, floated it into a company which paid handsomely. The nearby Tommy Burns Mine, found by Cardwell Peters and Fred Roos, led to the founding of Sunnymount township on the Mt. Garnet line in 1908. It flourished for a year or two. Rankin was the surveyor.

When Mt. Garnet closed in 1903, George Waddell was appointed receiver for the company and also controlled the railway. The line was taken over by the Queensland Government in 1915. Incidentally, the contractors who built it were Willcocks and Overend, and the 33 mile branch line cost £100,000. As the trains climbed the range between Ord and Nymbool, there was a splendid view looking back towards Lappa: range upon range of rounded mountains, flat-tops, and peaks stretching away to the Tate. Old miners have said recently that if the line had not been closed prematurely in 1963, it could have been extended south to the present Greenvale nickel mine for a fraction of the cost of the new line from Townsville.*

Enginedrivers remembered on the Mt. Garnet line early this century were Billy Garthwaite, Sam Cameron, and Billy Woods (son of Mick, the M.L.A.) Firemen were Bill Cahill, Charlie Diplock, and guards were Bill Nields, Doug Armstrong, and A.W.N. Waddell. The latter became well known in Mareeba as Woothakata Shire Clerk until his death. The Garnet line served Smith's Creek, Ord, and Gurrumbah. George Waddell retired to Mareeba where he died in 1932. Bill Cahill

---

* Comments railway historian, John Kerr: The maximum trainload on the Mt. Garnet line was 240 tons, using two engines. By comparison, trains of 4000 tons run to Greenvale, with four diesels. I doubt if the nickel mine could have ever made a profit on haulage restrictions necessary over the Cairns railway.

was killed in World War I.

The Mt. Garnet Annual Races are a social occasion looked forward to by station folk and others in the district, and the meetings go back a long way. One is recorded in the "Walsh and Tinaroo Miner" dated 6th. September 1911. A.M. Waddell was the secretary of the race club, J. Williams, president, and E. C. Crooks was judge. There were seven races including one for blackboys. In the Coolgarra Handicap, Mento, carrying 14 stone, and ridden by Tom Kerr, won all the way, the paper reported. The race ball afterwards was attended by eighty people. In the earlier boom times, Mt. Garnet had two famous football teams, the Rovers and Wanderers.

Tin dredging commenced at Return Creek in 1928. This was the first tin dredge in Queensland, if not Australia. A dam was built and the pontoons were launched on 25th. February. Poole and Steel of Melbourne were the builders. This dredge, like a floating factory, was a source of wonder and pride to Mt. Garnet residents from then on, but the vexed question of pollution of the Herbert River was a hot point a few years ago. When the flats of Return Creek had yielded their alluvial tin to this mechanical monster, it was moved to Smith's Creek where it still operates. The operators, Tableland Tin, have employed around a hundred men for years, and keep Mt. Garnet a small but prosperous community. The Ravenshoe Tin Dredging Company began similar operations at Battle Creek in 1952. Thousands of acres of good agricultural land exist in the Mt. Garnet district and some day this asset may be used to replace mining which has been the mainstay of the place for almost eighty years.

The township of Gurrumbah was busy early this century. A.T. Linedale and S.B. Ord were associated with the mill there which also had a fine dam for water storage. It was, naturally, another of John Moffat's enterprises, and dated from 1906 being situated on the head of California Creek, a particularly rich tin region.

(225)

In 1907, Ted Arbouin was in charge of the mill, L. G. Fitzmaurice was engineer and Oscar Bell and William Disher were tin dressers. Douglas Dunn was paymaster and book-keeper. Charlie Denford was a well known ore buyer in this area in early times.

R. H. Bimrose, and Armstrong, Ledlie, and Stillman were storekeepers. There were three hotels — Mining Exchange (D. P. Barry), Pioneer (A. E. Abrahams); and Carriers' Arms (J. Hughes). The township of Ord then consisted of Mrs. McNamara's hotel and Whereat and Co.'s general store.

Mike O'Callaghan of Cairns tells a macabre story — but rather humorous now after so many years — of a happening in Gurrumbah seventy years ago. A man opened a bakery with the assistance of the merchant firm of Cummins and Campbell. One Saturday night he put the batch of dough in the oven and headed for the pub, intending to return in time to draw the fire and take out the bread. However, he got into a poker game, lost all his money, and imbibed too freely.

On Monday morning a crowd was at the bakehouse waiting for bread. They could smell the bread burning but there was no sign of the baker. A small boy who had climbed up and looked into the bakehouse breathlessly reported he could see what appeared to be the body of the baker dangling from a rafter. Douglas Dunn, J.P., was the only representative of the law within twenty miles. There was a telephone to Mt. Garnet so he rang the police who told him what to do. He and an assistant broke into the bakery and drew the overcooked bread from the oven. To do so they had to push the swinging body of the baker aside.

Said Dunn later, in his broad Scots accent: "We couldna do nought else, ye ken. The pleece told us not to touch the biddy but to get the bread oot. We had to, too, for there was the multitude waiting to be fed." Some wag in Gurrumbah sent a telegram to Cummins and Campbell: "Baker hanged himself, send another."

Fingertown and Brownville are two other little mining townships lost in the passing years. One or two prospectors still cling to the area, and at Brownville the Watson family have endeavoured to cash in on the tourist boom and have a nice establishment, but the isolation could be a drawback. If the battery was still working it would be more of an attraction to visitors.

North of Gurrumbah, tin mining began on Emu Creek after Mulligan's discovery in 1881 and it loomed large in the brief boom period around 1907. About this time the Emu Creek Tin Mining Co. brought a battery from Mt. Usher near Rockhampton and re-erected it at the junction of Emu and Reid's Creeks. The company directors were D. Fraser (chairman), Harry Wade, E. B. Torpy, W. J. Munro, and C. F. Franklin. C. F. Valentine was a tin buyer here and had a store at Emuford. Jack Green ran the battery here for many years, and it is still known as "Green's battery". The Royal Standard was a very rich mine here some seventy years ago. It was found by Watson and Dougherty who had earlier struck it rich at Watsonville.

There was a copper mine in this vicinity long ago, at Mt. Babinda. The place was also called Copper Hill, Copperfield, and Moorefield — the latter for Billy Moore, a well known mining boss at Montalbion eighty-five years ago.

There was also gold. A sensation was caused early in 1895 upon the discovery of gold on a ridge east of Mt. Luxton on Wet Creek, not far from Cobb and Co.'s stables on the coach road to Georgetown. One assay was 150 ozs. to the ton. But it was only a small isolated reef and it faded out, as did the coach change.

Wadetown was a wayside settlement near where Petford is today. The former received its name from Harry Wade who had an hotel there before the Chillagoe Railway. For some reason, Petford replaced Wadetown when the railway came, and Petford was the jumping off place for the Bamford wolfram

(227)

and molybdenite mines, three miles away.

There were dozens of mines grouped in a small area, mostly on Bamford Hill — an important landmark. Some of the mines may still pay to work; the little field held its own until about 1923. Old timers say, however, it was a bad place for "the dust" — silicosis, or dust on the lungs. Many of the old time miners died of this terrible complaint — they coughed their lives away. It was the price paid by many of the Bamford miners. Their only defence against it while at work was to wear handkerchief masks or grow "tea-strainer" moustaches, but neither precautions helped much.

Among the Bamford pioneers were Freeman, Rollinson, and Jensen. The latter opened the Comstock silver-lead mine. Warden Jimmy Williams of Thornborough visited Bamford in January 1904 and reserved an area for a township site, naming it after F. W. Bamford, M.P.

In 1903, the price of wolfram was considered high at £101 per ton — it reached £1500 fifty years later.

Mrs. Alf de Jarlais kept a restaurant in Bamford long ago; George Woodhouse was the butcher, and Arthur Mackie was the publican. A man named Olsen, later a well known Southern journalist, spent his youth in Bamford, and in his old age he still thinks of it with nostalgia.

It is just another of the lost — but not quite forgotten — mining townships of many decades ago where men and women worked hard and long, and where children played — most of them nameless now — in this Pioneers' Country over the ranges behind Cairns: a veritable land of minerals.

CHAPTER 15

TRAGEDY AND PROSPERITY

Dimbulah — Wolfram Camp — Mt. Mulligan township — when Seventy-five Died — Pat Molloy — Mt. Molloy and its Smelters.

Dimbulah township grew up at the 26 Mile Peg on the Chillagoe Line as a watering place for locomotives. Mick Murray was the first stationmaster. The name is Aboriginal, meaning "long waterhole", referring to a reach in the nearby Walsh River which, before the advent of the Collins Weir, was dry for long stretches every dry season. It is now transformed into a beautiful running river.

Long before tobacco growing made Dimbulah famous as producing the world's best leaf, the Wolfram Camp mines and the building of the Mt. Mulligan Railway aided development.

Gordon Hay who has lived in Dimbulah almost 70 years, says there was only four humpies and a hotel there in 1912. Bill Johnson ran the hotel which he had built. He also had a butcher's shop and a bakery; the baker was named Coleman. His right hand man was Bill Hambling who left his old home on Leadingham Creek to live at the new township. He assisted Johnson with his cattle and horses. Johnson also ran mail coaches three times a week to Wolfram Camp and Thornborough. Unfortunately Johnson died when still a young man.

Around Christmas, 1912, the Hay family packed all their household possessions on their wagon and with enough corrugated iron to build a humpy, they left Mungana for Dimbulah. Jock Hay had a contract to cart bridge timber for the Mt. Mulligan Railway, then under construction.

One of the horses in the team of twenty-three was a jet black brumby that Jock Hay had had given him just before he left Mungana. The brumby was given the same treatment as a colt, though he was about fourteen years old; he had only been yarded once, as a foal. He was the wildest horse young Gordon Hay had ever seen.

(229)

Jock would yoke the team up, two abreast, open them up to form a "V", drive the new horse in between the two lines and bring them together again. The horse already had a headrope on him, and the big grey leader was hooked on to the rope. That old leader knew all about training a colt, just as his boss did. If the new horse fell down and the leader was hanging on too hard at a yell of "Ease up!" he would immediately slacken off.

The brumby had this treatment for four days; usually one day was sufficient. Eventually he was yoked up and he pulled so hard that his head had to be tied back, but he still fought, using up all his energy.

After a couple of days, and thirty miles on the way, the Hays pulled up to boil the billy at Eccles Creek, twelve miles from Dimbulah. The team was left standing in the road in some shade, and the brumby dropped dead. Gordon remembers his mother crying — she loved horses, and she liked that brumby because he put up such a great fight every day.

With commencement of construction of the Mt. Mulligan branch railway, Dimbulah grew quickly. But there was no post office; instead, there was a "travelling post office" on the mail train which ran three times a week from Cairns to Mungana. The postmaster was named Dean. Later, the stationmasters ran the post office as well. There was no public telephone until after tobacco growing started. Anyone had to ride fifteen miles to Wolfram Camp to telephone; it was served by a line from Thornborough run from tree to tree. All groceries came by train from John Walsh or Jack and Newell in Mareeba.

Gordon Hay attended Dimbulah's first school. He remembers his father yoked his team and went into the bush and cut forked saplings and bushes to build a bough shed and that was the school for some time, with an attendance of twenty. It ended abruptly when the teacher went on a prolonged "bender". In August 1914, a small school building twenty feet by eight feet was brought from Boonmoo, and it was the first official

(230)

school. Gordon Hay was the first pupil enrolled. The building was ceiled with calico but was a real "sweat box", he says. The first teacher was Miss Miriam Jacobs. Gordon recalls a humorous incident involving one teacher, Miss Clem Knox, but it was not so funny for her. She was chased by a billygoat that used to drink beer and had a set on women, and as she was wearing the hobble skirt fashionable at the time, she could not put on any speed and had to be rescued.

The Dimbulah school was enlarged with the addition of the old school brought from Kingsborough in 1925. Now the school has fifteen classrooms with some 270 pupils, primary and secondary. The town also has a Convent school with 150 pupils. Seven miles away the Mutchilba school has 100 pupils. Large buses bring the children in from the farms daily.

*   *   *   *

Wolfram Camp had its periods of great prosperity and depression. Discovered in 1891, E.C.J. Hunter shipped some of the first wolfram overseas but prices were then too low to make it a payable venture. The Irvinebank Mining Company with John Moffat always expanding his interests, erected a mill and reduction plant at Wolfram Camp in 1903. For the next ten years, German buyers were active and £95 per ton was paid on the field. Wolfram was a metal vital to Kaiser Germany arming for war.

John James was Wolfram's earliest prospector. Prominent pioneers were J. T. Nicholls, J. Tate, A. Baker, Walsh, Williams Gilmore, and Pearsall. Mrs. Blakeney was one of those who remained faithful to the field for close on fifty years.

At the height of its prosperity, Wolfram had a population of about 700 and like all the old mining towns was a wild place on occasions. As Bill Petersen said recently, "You had to be a well trained flying tackler to hold your own in a place like that." He worked at the German Bill mine and played a piano while his mate, Jack Lester, played a violin to entertain the miners of an evening in Mrs. Healy's restaurant. It was

(231)

not without risk for the premises were more than once wrecked by terrific fist fights among the clientele.

Hotelkeepers were Jim Fallon, Tom Killen, and Dan Blakeney. Storekeepers were Markham and Simpson, and Larry Comerford; the latter was also an ore buyer. Eddie Gilder also had an hotel there at one time; he later went to Atherton and opened a picture theatre which was subsequently destroyed by fire. As well as Mrs. Healy, Frank Vogler also had a restaurant. Joe Strange drove the four-horse coach from Dimbulah. It was a rough and difficult track, especially when the Walsh River was in flood.

When World War I. broke out and the demand for wolfram increased, Wolfram Camp boomed, and to cope with the output of ore, an English concern, the Thermo Company erected a forty head battery in 1915. They also built a fine dam. Most of the machinery came direct from England. Jack Hay of Dimbulah secured the contract to cart all 2000 tons of machinery and cement with his horse team. He took in Harry Rolls and Fred Wieland as partners in this. There were two $13\frac{1}{2}$ ton boilers, seven-ton diesel engines, and other plant. A hundred head of horses were needed in the teams on the Wolfram Road. Teamsters on the road at that time were the Rolls Bros. (Bill, Abe, and Glanville) from Kingsborough, Bill Lynch, Jim Bethel, Jack Swan, Stewart Bolton, Phil, Jerry, and Bill Healy and Friday Butcher. The boilers came from a gold mine at Charters Towers and after doing service at Wolfram were carted back to Dimbulah in 1922 by Walter Bird and Paddy Cahill. Bird had a fine team of thirty horses but nevertheless his wagon capsized nine times and he was stuck in the Walsh River for three weeks. The boilers were bought by a Cairns brewery.

Gordon Hay remembers the coach drivers on the Wolfram road in World War I. period were Mick and Terry Carr, Bill Newman, Bill Wall, and Bill Hambling. The latter was still the Wolfram mailman, then using a truck, in the late 1940's.

Famous mines at Wolfram in the boom times were Murphy

(232)

and Geaney, German Bill, Larkin, Forget-me-not, Victory, Lissner, Star, Harp of Erin, and Mulligan (the latter was named after the explorer). The German Bill produced £24,000 worth of wolfram in six months; the owners were Bill Croft and Tom Debell. The Murphy and Geaney was also very rich; Andy Murphy was the owner, and the manager was Jim James. The Thermo Company bought most of these mines and a group, called the Lissner Block, were connected up to the Forget-me-not tunnel with an aerial ropeway about one mile long. The company's manager was a well known Charters Towers mining man, Mr. Millican. Other staff men were Miles and Bowater, and Jim Thomason is the engineer remembered who spliced the endless rope — a 68 ft. splice — that carried the ore to the battery.

Wolfram Camp held its own as a mining centre until about 1921 when with the return of peace, the demand for wolfram eased. But the place was never totally deserted and when wolfram prices rose during World War II, the old mines were gone over again and a lot of wolfram was won. Irrigated tobacco farms, tractors, and fast cars, and not the plodding horse teams of a mining field, are now features of the Wolfram road.

Harry, Bill, Abe, and Glanville Rolls had teams on the road from Dimbulah to Wolfram Camp in 1916 when great amounts of machinery, building materials, and stores were being carted for the Thermo Company.

The Rolls family bred fine team horses at their farm on Caledonia Creek four miles from Kingsborough, on the old road over the Granite Range. When Harry Rolls yoked a new team of colts, just broken-in, to his wagon they were so well trained that they went into their collars and walked away with it like veterans.

Later, Harry Rolls was timber carting at Kairi on the Atherton Tableland, and Alex Thompson was ore carting at Chillagoe. He died "in harness", so to speak; he was out mustering his team one day, sat down under a tree and died there. Harry Rolls is also remembered as a fine man without an enemy in the world.

In 1921, horse teams were still holding their own in the mining country and in the scrublands inland from Cairns. That year, Gordon took over his father's team to cart flourspar ore from Emuford to the rail trucks at Petford. Harry Rolls was also carting with a 14 horse team. Alex Thompson had a team of nine in a heavy dray; seven of the horses were magnificent greys bred on Leadingham Creek by the pioneer Jackson family.

Alex Thompson had come to the North in the early days of the Port Douglas Road; he had swum his horses ashore at Port Douglas; he had nine Clydesdales. Half a mile from ship to shore was a long way to swim heavy draught horses.

There were three nine-horse teams carting ore to the battery at Wolfram Camp. The Irvinebank Company had a ten-head battery managed by Carl Jacobsen, and had a fine team of heavy draughts driven by Bill Healy. Herb Fryer had his own team. Each had a tip-dray carrying three tons, and the teams were stable fed.

Fred Fryer carted wood for the steam boilers, Walter Bird and Harry Smith, for the battery, and "Chummy" Martin carted it for the mines. It was a terrible climb up the hill to the Tully mine.

Gordon Hay remembers: "Alex Thompson had a mishap with the brake coming down the Tully Hill with three tons on his dray, and his shafter held it which was quite a feat. Everyone admired old Paddy, the shafter. A dray shafter had to give with each bump or rut, otherwise he got thrown off his feet and really got knocked about. Old Paddy knew all the ruts and bumps on that road, and was admired and spoken of by everyone interested in horses, even years after he had died.

"Alex got another shafter, and when I said that he was not like old Paddy, Alex said, 'No, and he never will be,' and

(234)

Irvinebank Mining Company's mule team carrying tin ore to the Gurrumbah battery, about 1906.

I saw him wipe away the tears with his sweat-rag. How he loved old Paddy.

"The whip horses were good to watch, and cunning. These were harnessed with special harness. They pulled the bucket up the shaft from behind and let it down from the front. The rope was taken from one end and put on the other end to raise or lower the bucket.

"The horse got used to going out a certain distance for months, and then when the shaft was sunk a bit deeper it was quite a job to get him to go past his old mark. Usually the driver was a lad called a whip-boy.

"When the knocker line or signal from below was given, some of the horses I saw got around into place to hook on to the bucket of their own accord. These horses had to be very reliable, as when a lot of dynamite charges were lit down in the mine and the knocker line was pulled, the miner had to get up fast." It was a case of a man's life depending upon the sagacity of his horse.

"Billy Rolls sank a shaft for Bill Kraft and Jack Taylor who had the Enterprise Mine on tribute. He had just lit a dozen fuses, got in the bucket after pulling the knocker, and the horse jibbed. Bill Rolls pulled nearly all the fuses out except four or five that had burnt down into the holes. They went off and Bill never got a scratch.

"He had just sold the jib horse to Kraft and Taylor. He was a beautiful roan but was 'broken-step', and no good for team work. If you had other horses working behind a broken-stepped horse, they also broke their step. This means they took three or four steps pulling and then let go and repeated it.

"I saw a nine-horse team with eight of them broken-stepped. When the team was sold when the owner went to the 1914-18 War, my Dad bought the one that wasn't broken-stepped."

*　　*　　*　　*

The thousands of gold seekers and others who swarmed along the Hodgkinson in the 'Seventies — over a century ago — were unaware that the imposing rampart that is Mt. Mulligan hid wealth of a different kind and which would be of great benefit for the North. This was coal, discovered in 1907 by W. Harris. Billy Richards and Robert Gibbons were also linked with the discovery. Warden J. Williams of Thornborough, and mining inspector Horsley reported on it, and John Moffat's Irvinebank Company took up a hundred acres. The coal was tested in the small tramway locomotives between Irvinebank and Stannary Hills.

Mt. Mulligan was hailed as the saviour of the mining concerns, as all coal and coke had had to be imported from the South by ship, and wood was burned as much as possible. The Chillagoe Company bought out the Irvinebank Company's interests. The first machinery to be installed was hauled from Dimbulah over very rough country by Louis Petersen and Bill Ward's horse teams, of Mareeba, in 1910.

In May 1913, the Governor of Queensland, Sir William McGregor, turned the first sod for the construction of the railway

(236)

from Dimbulah to Mt. Mulligan. W. A. Hannam was the engineer. Work proceeded rapidly and the line was completed late in 1914 at a cost of approximately £95,000. Hundreds of cuttings, built-up banks, and bridges and approaches were put in — all by pick and shovel and horse dray — within eighteen months. It was another private line built by the Chillagoe Company under Government supervision, and was taken over in 1919.

A big construction camp sprang up at Dimbulah; as a railway junction, the town's future was assured. Hundreds of men were employed at nine shillings per day. When the line reached the 18 miles peg the navvies struck for an extra shilling per day, and got it. Each man had to buy his own pick and shovel and when he left he sold them to his replacement. This was usual on railway constructions in those days. Gordon Hay can tell some good stories about the Mulligan railway work. There were many Kellys at work, mostly fighting Irishmen, and to distinguish them he says they were given prefixes such as Kelly the Rake, Crooked Kelly, Kelly the Rager, Broken-Nose Kelly, One-punch Kelly etc. Likewise there were many men named Bill Brown so they were variously named Singing Billy, Croydon Billy, Battery Billy, O. K. Billy, etc.

We will let Gordon Hay tell this story:

"In 1915, my father secured a contract to cart a Cornish boiler, weighing thirteen and a half tons from the siding at Thornborough on the then new Mt. Mulligan railway, to the Tyrconnell mine. He got his old mate, Abe Rolls, to go with him; between them they had two box wagons and 28 horses. A timber wagon was hired from Ward and Petersen of Mareeba. These wagons had a pole from the front carriage to the rear, and the wheelbase could be altered to short or long as required. It was the middle of the wet season, and the teams had to be taken sixteen miles to Thornborough to start work.

"I went as 'spare boy.' Anyone who helped a teamster was called a 'spare boy' — irrespective of age — and not an 'offsider', as some writers have it.

"The Walsh River was a swim. The wagons went right under the flood and the horses had to swim a few strokes. Abe couldn't swim but hung on to the wagon and came up like a drowned rat. Dad hung on to the near-side pin-horses' hames.

"We soon struck the boggy country. The horses went right down to their bellies and the wagons to their axles. We were from 8 a.m. to 4 p.m. digging and hauling ourselves out. The timber wagon was snigged through with a 300 ft. wire rope attached to the horses on firmer ground."

When they camped a bit further on, they were until after dark soaking the horses' tails to get the concrete-like mud off them. Arrived at the siding, twenty men came from the Tyrconnell Mine to assist. The boiler had a big dome on top and it was hard to balance.

Heavy ropes were attached, and where the rough road sloped around the sides of the stony hills, the wheels of the wagon lifted several times and would have capsized but for the men pulling on the ropes.

Gordon remembers: "We had all 28 horses yoked to the wagon, and I often think of how many would have been killed and what a mess there would have been had the wagon gone down over the side of one of those hills.

"In yoking the team, the horses nearest the wagon had heavy chains and the ones nearer the lead had light chains. You bought them by the pound weight. The heavy ones were 28 lbs. and the light ones 24 lbs. You couldn't hook another team in front of your leaders as the chains wouldn't hold, so the two teams we had were all mixed up. We always carried spare split-links to repair chains."

Gordon Hay recalls that there was a man in Thornborough "long years ago" who was a blacksmith and jeweller; a strange combination, but tradesmen were versatile in the frontier communities, and many were very clever men, and ingenious, too. Bill Bock could make a ring-pin for your watch or make something in the forge.

The axles on the coaches had to be changed often because of the abrasive granite sand. They used to come in cases, in half-dozen lots. Gordon says that one lot had a right-hand thread but no left-hand one, so Bock cut the left-hand thread with a diamond-pointed chisel.

The axles came in two pieces and had to be welded in the middle by a blacksmith, and this was no trouble to Bock.

*   *   *   *

Today, Mt. Mulligan township is a place of ghosts: rows of house blocks, remains of buildings, and the debris of the colliery poke out from a wilderness of rubber vines and yellow oleander bushes, the tall chimney stack and a few steel power poles landmarks, with the great wall of the mountain brooding over all. The bush is gradually reclaiming this town that was abandoned in 1957. Some say it was needlessly abandoned for Mt. Mulligan still had reserves of a hundred million tons of high grade coal. But it was a question of economics and Collinsville could produce it more cheaply. All the people who wanted to, were moved away to that town. Perhaps with a growing fuel shortage, coal will again be mined at Mt. Mulligan, perhaps for export.

All the buildings that were movable were dismantled and taken out on the last train from this town that lived just fifty years. The hospital was bought by Tom Volkman, a Dimbulah grazier, and is now the homestead of Mt. Mulligan cattle station belonging to Gordon Morrow.

The mountain dominates everything — brooding, silent, waiting . . . . It casts early evening shadows and at sunrise its cliffs are rose and blue in the sun's early rays. Springs well out in several places, including from the mine tunnel and from the mountain's summit.

The dam on Harris Creek on the summit once provided reticulated water for the town and its construction by the miners over sixty years ago was quite a feat. Blocks of sandstone were quarried on the spot to make the dam wall, and cement and tools were packed on mules from the more accessible western side of the mountain. To make mortar, sandstone was crushed to powder, probably in dolly-pots, as there was no sand available.

A great steel power pole with its cross-arm stands in bold relief over the desolation of this dead town. It is like a huge Cross, as if in requiem for those who perished here. Seventy-five men were cut down in the prime of life at 9.30 a.m. on September 19, 1921, when the Mt. Mulligan colliery exploded. It was the worst disaster in Queensland's history. Fourteen miles away at the Tyrconnell on the Hodgkinson the smoke cloud was seen, and at Mt. Molloy to the east and Silver Valley to the south-east, the boom of the explosion was heard echoing across the mountains.

Help came from everywhere. A special train was rushed from Mareeba with Dr. Perkins and Matron McCarthy, but there was only the recovering of lifeless bodies to do. It was a month before the last was taken out of the bowels of the earth beneath that sinister brooding monster of a mountain. No wonder the Aborigines of old believed it to be the home of a "debbil-debbil" or "Icu". Perhaps he was resenting the white man's intrusion — who know? In the mountain's forbidding shadow they now lie sleeping, all but forgotten in the abandoned graveyard of a vanished town. Perhaps some day a monument will be raised upon which the names of the dead will be recorded in stone.

On August 1, 1971, a thousand people gathered to attend a memorial service and reunion on the site of the township, just fifty years after the tragedy.

Among those present was Mrs. Wardle, daughter of W.J.C. (Billy) Richards, who had managed the coal mine for John Moffat in 1907. At the time of the disaster, Mrs. Wardle was Mrs. Frank Grant, and her husband was one of the victims. Memorial services were held by the Bishop of North Queensland, Bishop John Lewis, and a visiting Catholic priest, Rev. Fr.

(240)

O'Connor. Five explosions were set off to simulate the disaster as everyone recited the Lord's Prayer. The then chairman of Mareeba Shire, Mr. Mick Borzi, read out the names of the miners who lost their lives. The ceremony attracted the biggest crowd ever seen at Mt. Mulligan, even during its heyday.

*   *   *   *

Copper was discovered by the veteran teamster, Pat Molloy, at a spot only half a mile off the Port Douglas Road, in 1885. Naturally the hill, and the mine that came later, was called Mt. Molloy.

Molloy had two bullock teams on the Port Douglas-Herberton road. One trip, when camped at Granite Creek with a character known only as "Tom the Club" the driver of the second team, some of the bullocks strayed. Tom saw their tracks headed north towards the Mitchell. Molloy rode after them and tracked them for twenty miles. Cutting across country near Rifle Creek he rode up on the slopes of a prominent hill and suddenly came upon an outcrop of greenish rock — a rich copper lode. Molloy found his bullocks and pegged the ground; he worked it for a while simply by carting the richest surface ore to Port Douglas and shipping it to England and Germany. Due to this expense and resulting low profit, Molloy abandoned the prospect and concentrated on his cattle property, Rocky Plains.

He had built his homestead near Rocky Creek — the building still stands as a farm shed surrounded by huge mango trees. His grazing land stretched from Rocky Creek north-westward across Granite Creek to Cattle Creek and included the Paddy's Green tobacco growing area of later date. The latter name is said to have been derived when Pat Molloy sighting a locality covered in grasstrees, he mistook it at a distance for green grass.

As one can guess, Pat Molloy was an Irishman; he landed in Brisbane in 1863, a raw new chum with only a few shillings in his pocket. He worked on the first railway in Queensland,

(241)

from Ipswich to Grandchester, in 1867, then as a shepherd on the Dawson River, a miner at Calliope, and a timbergetter at Maryborough.

His first carrying job was when he was engaged to drive a wagon-load of stores from Rockhampton to a pioneer station on the Barkly Tableland in the Northern Territory — an 800 mile trip that took over a year. Returning on horseback to civilisation he reached a station on the Leichhardt River just in time to help defend it against a war party of Aborigines. He joined the party of pioneers who rode the vengeance trail. While he was in the Gulf Country, Molloy had several narrow escapes from death at the hands of marauding natives. He was now no longer a new chum, but a tough man of the frontier.

In 1870, he struck it rich on the Etheridge Goldfield. He married in Rockhampton, worked around Bowen and Townsville, and when the Hodgkinson gold rush began and Port Douglas was opened, he bought a bullock team and started carrying on his own account. Soon he had two teams on the road. The Molloy family's first home in North Queensland was on top of the range on The Bump Road.

The blacks were a serious menace to settlers and travellers. Eight of Molloy's horses were speared. He and other pioneers like Clarke, Fearon, and Groves, accompanied Sub-Inspector Douglas in a punitive expedition. They caught up with the tribesmen on Black Mountain, north-west from Kuranda, and effectively "dispersed" them with their Snider rifles in the custom of the times. Pat Molloy moved to Rocky Creek in 1880 or 1881. He died at Mareeba in 1923.

His copper discovery at Mt. Molloy was taken up again in 1893, this time by J. V. Mulligan and James Forsyth. The latter had been a manager for Burns, Philp at Normanton in 1880 and later he became well known as a mine owner and investor on the Croydon Goldfield; he was M.L.A. for Carpentaria from 1899 to 1907.

Forsyth and Mulligan are said to have made a profit of

£3000 and then sold it to a Melbourne company for £6000. This was big money back in the "Hungry 'Nineties" and it was no doubt the best "rise" Mulligan had made since the Hodgkinson. The Melbourne company did little work and failed to recognise the mine's possibilities. Forsyth again came into possession and with Buchanan and party won ore containing 30 p.c. copper.

John Moffat then came on the scene. He subsequently bought the property and organised further development. Mt. Molloy Ltd. was floated, and a smelter was erected at Smelter Town, two miles from the mine, connected by a tramline. Blister copper of 90 p.c. purity was produced. Over 250 men were employed at the mine and smelters in 1907. The mine appeared to be rich, with copper lodes 12 ft. wide.

Tony Linedale was manager of Mt. Molloy Ltd. before Jim Horsburgh took over. The mine and smelter manager was J. R. Raleigh, formerly at Mt. Garnet. The underground manager was Dick Rolfe. Others were Ron Ashcroft, accountant; Nat Absell, paymaster; Alex Harper, metallurgist; Bill Morrow, foreman; Evan Thomas, engineer; also Bill Webster, Bill Stovell, Frank Knox, Roland Matthews, and many more, such as Alex Harper and Bill Santowski who had been at Chillagoe in the Moffat days.

A dam was constructed, and the smelters were "blown in" on November 25, 1904. Flux for smelting was obtained from a low ironstone outcrop at Mt. Cardwell near Ord Siding on the Mt. Garnet line. It was railed to Biboohra and carted from there to Molloy by horse teams. However, in 1908 the branch railway from Biboohra to Molloy was completed. The line was constructed by the Mt. Molloy Company who financed it by selling £27,000 worth of shares held in reserve. The engineer in charge was C. E. Highfields who built the Irvinebank tramline for John Moffat. Arthur Garbutt conducted a coach line from Biboohra to Mt. Molloy before the railway was built. A photo exists of him sitting on the box seat of a former Cobb and Co. coach, "ribbons" in hand.

(243)

A story is told of a rival coach service whose owner-driver was proud to be carrying the mails and emblazoned the words "Royal Mail" on his vehicle. This also secured him the largest number of passengers. When he lost the mail contract he simply altered the last letter in the word "Mail" and carried on, still getting most of the passengers, who thought they were getting the best travel service in a coach called "Royal Maid".

It seems strange that with the Mt. Molloy mine so apparently rich it should have been abandoned and the smelters closed within months after the arrival of the railway. As with Mt. Garnet, financial shortage or want of capital, must have been the reason for the collapse of copper mining at Mt. Molloy. The copper must still be there. The timely granting by the Government, in 1908, of big timber concessions, together with the throwing open of blocks to settlers for dairying in the scrub country to the north-east, alone saved the new railway and Mt. Molloy township. It is a pity that the railway has now gone the way of other pioneer railways in the North: the rails were pulled up in 1961 even though the line was still serving timber-getting and dairying interests in the Julatten area. Again it was a case of economics.

It was in 1913 that J. M. Johnston and a man named Polenz opened sawmills at Mt. Molloy, bringing new life to the place that started as a copper mine.

The famous James Venture Mulligan made Mt. Molloy his home. His friend, James Forsyth built an hotel there and Mulligan and his wife (he had married Fanny Maria Buls in 1905) may have run it for Forsyth. (It was situated near where the Mt. Molloy cemetery is today, the first site chosen for the town being along what is now the road from the highway to the cemetery.) In any event, it was in this hotel in August 1907 that Mulligan met his death. It has been said he intervened to break up a brawl and falling — perhaps from a blow — he injured his head; however, his death was attributed to pneumonia, and Mike Rimmer, a writer who has studied details of Mulligan's career, has stated that a punctured lung from a broken rib may have been the cause. So died Far North Queensland's greatest prospector and explorer.

When J. M. Johnston's timber mill opened, a man named Gray bought Forsyth's hotel and converted it into a private residence. It was badly damaged in the 1920 cyclone and later it was removed. The Smelters Hotel in Mt. Molloy, was run by the Nissans for years. Syd Harris bought it and converted it into a residence, and the Grays lived there for many years; part of it still stands next door to the present post office.

When the railway arrived, there were many small mines, mostly worked by two or three men, in the forest and mountains north and west of Mt. Molloy. Copper, tin, and wolfram were being won. Six miles out, twelve men were working the Sweet William and Gladstone Syndicate mines under Charlie Sandilands. At Mt. Spurgeon, up in the ranges, stream-tinners were reaping a harvest of alluvial tin from Sandy and O'Shannassy Creeks and other mountain streams. At tremendous labour, a 450 ft. tunnel was dug by hand through a hill to divert a creek. At the time of his death, Mulligan had plans for the erection of a big tin sluicing plant.

This was a pleasant locality, heavily timbered and cool at over 3000 feet above sea level, but accessible only by pack teams. Packers charged £5 per ton to pack from Mt. Molloy to Mt. Spurgeon, a distance of 25 miles. The last eight miles was a sheer climb up the scrub-covered range, and it was worse coming down. The story goes that the Mt. Spurgeon tinfield was named after a dog — not after the famous British evangelist of last century. The aptly named Mt. Perseverance Wolfram field, situated high up on the divide between the Mitchell and Mossman watersheds, was discovered in 1917.

CHAPTER 16

WOLFRAM AND TIN

Mt. Carbine — Boonmoo — Stannary Hills and Irvinebank Tramway, Stannary Hills township and Rocky Bluffs.

Who discovered wolfram — at first thought to be manganese — at Mt. Carbine is not clear. It has been lost in the mist of the years.

But it is known that J. V. Mulligan and his prospecting mates were on the headwaters of the Mitchell, discovering the McLeod River, in 1874. Mulligan was back in this area with James Newell and W.B. Stenhouse in 1883. Mulligan seems to have been credited with naming Manganese Creek which runs through Mt. Carbine township. An 1881 report from the Mines Department mentions the discovery of manganese in this locality, and a 60 acre lease was applied for by Daly, Lord, and party. Matt Petersen has also been mentioned as a discoverer of Mt. Carbine.

In 1895, Samuel and Joseph Baird definitely found wolfram in Manganese Creek. Other miners came, and it was about this time that the field was named — suggested, it has been said, by Carroll Walsh, a miner who may have had a win on the great horse, Carbine, who won the Melbourne Cup in 1890. At that time, wolfram was worth only $16.00 per ton. In 1898, it was $80.00. on the field.

No claims were registered until 1904, as it was a long ride to Herberton, and therefore no records exist of early mining. Joe Baird was too late in registering; he was beaten to his ground by Kilpatrick and Grogan who are recorded as registering the first claim on the field, originally worked by the Bairds, and quite rich.

Sam Baird, however, benefited in other ways. He opened the first hotel, the Miners' Arms, in 1904. In 1896 he had married Margaret Keating in Mareeba and they had a family of four. Sam died in Mt. Molloy hospital in 1910, and his wife later became Mrs. W. Carr. She ran the hotel for many years. Today, the main street of Mt. Carbine is named Baird Street.

Alluvial wolfram was "banjoed", sluiced, or "jigged" by hand in Manganese Creek when there was sufficient water. Carbine Hill became honey-combed with two and three man "shows" such as the Caledonia, Hit or Miss, Johnson's, Anderson's Edith, Hurry Up, Dead Finish, True Blue, Triangle, X-Ray, Welbeck Abbey, White Elephant, and others.

In 1906, the Irvinebank Company became interested in Mt. Carbine and bought out or took up all available leases on the hill. The battery the company erected began continuous crushing on 30 May, 1911, at the rate of fifty tons of ore per day. It was considered a modern plant in its day; it had ten head of stamps. The company employed 100 men in the mill and in its mines. Fifty other miners were working their own shows or were working alluvial.

This provided for quite a thriving township at the end of the first decade of this century. The company mine manager was F. C. West. Neil Campbell snr. and Bill Harris were shift bosses. Leading men at the battery were Joe Fisher, Gus Mulligan, Bill Evans, and Bill White. Ore dresser was Jack Tait. In the office was Fred Sundet, Douglas Dunn, and J. White. Other employees were Bill Alexander, Doug Kelly, Chris Bottrell, Arthur Shanahan, Joe Jones, and "Nugget" Paton.

Miners of Mt. Carbine around 1910 had been on other fields earlier, so some of the names are familiar: Bill and Matt Petersen, Ralph Young, Martin Trahey, Joe Barry, Bob Clark, Harry Rosser, J. Rolls, August Johnson, Tom Brown, George Sutherland, Jim Claussen, W. Meldrum, A. Munden, J. Flynn, D. Byrnes, J. Blunt, A. Smith, J. T. Martin, Robert Sefton, Jack Stack, Louis Burrows, Jack Watson, C. Samundsett, also Fitzgerald, Rhodes, Beadle, Rolfe, Anderson, Simpson, Kershaw, Williams, Cassell, Hartley, Keating, Clark, Walsh, McDonald, Sorenson, Perrett, Kiddy, White, and others.

About seventy of the wages men had their meals at the

(247)

Miners' Arms where Mrs. Carr provided good food, including vegetables, fruit, milk, and home made butter from the Carrs' farm, Acacia Vale on Holmes Creek. The miners who had their own shows lived mostly in humpies along Manganese Creek or at their mines. Corned beef and damper was their staple diet with an occasional bandicoot, possum, or wallaby for "beef".

Lola O'Brien, now of Gordonvale, was a child, Lola Pickering, in Mt. Carbine around 1912-16, and has many pleasant memories of it. She recalls that the stores were Bottrell's, Jebreen's, Rolls', and Walsh's. There were three hotels in the boom period just before World War I. — the Wolfram (which still functions), with the National opposite (run by William Cassells and later William Lovell). Nearer the creek was Carr's Miners' Arms. Peter Nissen then had the Wolfram Hotel (now Bethel's). George Hill was the butcher at one time, later Brian Grogan. In the 'thirties, Paul Hawkins of Brooklyn Station delivered beef to the door for threepence per pound.

The first school was a "tutorial" one, built of calico, hessian, and corrugated iron by the towns-people. A Mr. Augustine was in charge. The first Government school opened on 16 March 1908, and the first teacher was George T. White. In 1912, there were 57 pupils, and Flo Montgomery was an assistant teacher. Later she married Dr. Grakovich, a Russian who was the second doctor at the hospital. The first was Dr. Lampe. Matron Cook was in charge for many years assisted by nurses Gertie and Annie Groves. Before the hospital was opened, Mrs. Baird (later Carr) gave first aid and was a midwife.

Mr. J. Pedrazzini was a popular teacher. The school closed in 1927 but re-opened in a new building in 1938 and it lasted until 1957. Now a school bus conveys children to Mt. Molloy over a good bitumen road, which is part of the Mulligan Highway to Cooktown. Jack Sorensen, W. Carr, and J. Edwards had horse teams on this road seventy-odd years ago. Edwards delivered the huge boiler for the Irvinebank Company's mill in

1910. Simpson was the town blacksmith.

Police remembered are Sergeant Tom Mullins, Constables George Selby and Crimmins, and a blacktracker named Larry. Mt. Carbine also had a racecourse, a tennis court, and a rifle club. Other entertainments were held in the School of Arts, and there were picnics to waterfalls and to the Mitchell River. Householders had to buy their water for two shillings per 100 gallons from Tony Durston who carted it in a tank on his dray. Old timers remember the "big wet" of 1911 when Manganese Creek flooded and the township was battered by a cyclone which badly damaged Port Douglas.

In 1917, the Irvinebank Company sold out to the Thermo-Electric Ore Reduction Co. which also had mills at Bamford and Wolfram Camp. In 1918, wolfram reached a record high of £170.12.6 per ton ($341.25). But when World War I. ended, wolfram became almost unsaleable. Mt. Carbine's boom years were over.

With Europe again arming for war in 1937, wolfram mining again became profitable, and there were said to be 200 men doing surface "scratching" and going over the old workings. There were 40 men there in 1944 and Norris' "V" battery was in production.

After the war there was another lowering of wolfram prices, but the Korean War soon caused another boom, and now machinery, such as bulldozers came into use in mining. Wolfram reached $3000 per ton in 1951. Ross and Bradley opened the Popeye battery with three stamps, and Smith had a ten-head battery on the Mitchell River.

In August 1969, Roche Bros. from Melbourne came on the scene, taking up a lease of the whole of Carbine Hill and the old workings. The result has been spectacular — the rise of the biggest open-cut wolfram producer in Australia with one of the world's most modern plants. Today's high wolfram price, around $7000 per ton, has given incentive to this remarkable development by a private enterprise. As Ken Roche commented to the writer, "I am sure old John Moffat would approve if he could but see it."

A company township with all modern amenities, has been built. The pioneer miners of Mt. Carbine would not be able to believe their eyes any more than would John Moffat.

It is the day of the big mining companies; Mt. Carbine is an example of how the use of modern methods and machinery pays dividends. Fields that were once thought worked out can now be made payable; massive mechanical loaders can move more dirt than a miner's shovel. But it is the huge areas that become tied up under prospecting authorities that come in for criticism.

The hardy individual prospector opened up the old mines in the Cairns Hinterland, but such men are rare today. This area has the greatest variety of minerals in Australia.

*   *   *   *

Boonmoo, overshadowed by the Boonmoo Pinnacle, is but a name today, but it was once quite a busy township, first as the nearest railway station to Irvinebank and then as an important junction. Bob Brennan and Arthur Hastie were the first stationmasters. There were two hotels — Dillon's and Bill Jackson's, and the latter family were residents for many years.

Boonmoo Pinnacle is a very impressive landmark, especially from the eastern approach. It can be clearly seen a dozen miles away before one reaches Dimbulah, if motoring from Mareeba on the fine bitumen road. Irrigated tobacco fields now run almost to its foothills. William Lees, a journalist who visited the district seventy-odd years ago refers to the mountain as "Mt. Moffat", but it always seems to have been known as Boonmoo Pinnacle as far as I can gather. J. V. Mulligan has a great natural monument in Mt. Mulligan. Why shouldn't another great man of the pioneer mining days be honored in like manner by officially renaming Boonmoo Pinnacle — a not very imaginative name — "Mt. Moffat." Such an outstanding landmark not far from the site of his labors would be a

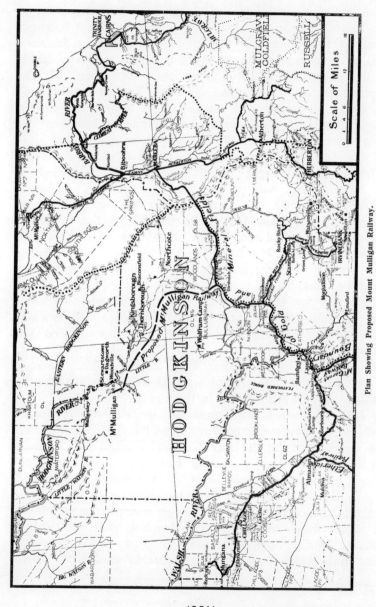

Plan Showing Proposed Mount Mulligan Railway.

THE FIRST SOD OF THE LINE WAS TURNED BY HIS EXCELLENCY THE GOVERNOR ON 11TH MAY, 1913.

(Reprinted from "Qld.Govt.Mining Journal")

uniquely fitting memorial to good old John Moffat.

In 1901-02 the Stannary Hills Company built a 2 ft. gauge tramline from Boonmoo up the Eureka Creek Gorge to Stannary Hills, a distance of about 14 miles, and then to Rocky Bluffs on the Walsh River, about seven miles further on. T. G. Stephens was the surveyor and engineer. The construction was an engineering triumph. In one section the line climbed 350 ft. in four miles. The cost was £2000 per mile. There were 31 bridges, the Eureka Creek bridge being of ten spans.

For four years Stannary Hills was the nearest rail station to Irvinebank and wagons and drays brought all the output of the batteries and smelters to Stannary Hills for despatch. Passengers and mail also came that way by coach. Then in September 1906, John Moffat authorised construction of a line to Irvinebank from. a spot on the Stannary Hills-Rocky Bluffs tramline. Surveyor Mineham, H. T. Smith, and Robert Frew were engaged in supervising this, and William Highfield was resident engineer.

The tramline reached to within a couple of miles of Irvinebank by March 1907. Large quantities of goods and firewood needed for the smelters was hauled there — it was called All But — by the tiny locomotive, "Betty", and on April 21st. it made a trial run to Boonmoo through Stannary Hills. Finally, on the 24th., two trainloads of firewood were brought over the new line to the Loudoun Mill in Irvinebank.

On 29th. June a grand picnic was given by Mr. and Mrs. Moffat to celebrate the entry of the "Iron Pony" into Irvinebank. This was held at All But and there was a grand feast, sports, and train rides, with everything free, and a day such as no one who was there ever forgot. It was indeed a great day for old time Irvinebank and the commencement of seven great years of prosperity. From then on all transport to and from the outside world came by the tramline from Boonmoo on the Chillagoe Line. For many years the little 14-ton wood-burning locos. hauling long lines of miniature trucks around the sharp bends and cuttings were part of the life of this mining field. The Irvinebank and Stannary Hills tramways were purchased by the Queensland Government in 1919. Trains ran irregularly until 1938 and in 1941 the tramlines were pulled up. The little locos. ended their days on cane lines at Innisfail and Ingham.

William Lees described the Irvinebank and Stannary Hills tramlines in his "Copper Mines and Mineral Fields of Queensland" published as a newspaper supplement in Brisbane, in December 1907, as follows:

"The two feet line, the 'Betty' and 'Baby' Krauss engines, the carriages used from Irvinebank to Stannary and on down the cliffs to Boonmoo, are all of such dwarf type that one wonders how all the passengers and loading will get into the cars and arrive at their destination. But the 'Baby' or 'Betty' puffs and struggles along by gully side and open granite country, through avenues of firewood stacked for the smelters and thousands of tall ant-hills; by ridges where one overlooks a vast extent of undulating country, broken in the middle distance by the blue hills of Montalbion silver field, and then winding down the head of the Eureka Creek, passes unconcernedly by huge cliff or deep gorge, or mining camps, to the busy, also dwarf-like, railway station of Stannary Hills."

Lees described the Stannary Hills-Boonmoo section "one of the most wildly picturesque lengths of line in Queensland." Hauled by a little "Brush" engine with what Lees called a "Spitzkatzen smokestack", the little train "jiggled along quite happily on the 3 ft. step in the cliffs." This was in the Eureka Creek Gorge.

"A precipice keeps affectionately at our right hand for miles; eternity at close range is on our left in the shape of huge cliffs . . . . as the rock face hurries by. You look ahead over the trucks to the engine and see apparently the end of everything. Sky seems to meet cliff, railway line and gorge edge, and one commences pretty rapidly to try to remember his prayers, for to all appearance we are going over into the gorge below, this

(253)

3 ft. wide cliff-edge platform seeming to end a few dozen yards ahead. This kind of fright is apparently included with the ticket (3s. 6d.), for it happens two or three times. If one looks to the cliffs above, there poised in mid-air is a fifty-ton boulder held there by goodness knows what . . . . It is a very interesting piece of engineering work for those who like that kind of thing . . . ."

A trip on this unique tramway with thrills like this would be a great tourist attraction today if the line and its little locomotives was still in existence as it very well could have been. It is another part of our national heritage that has been lost to the wreckers and scrap-iron merchants because nobody cared or had any sense of history.

The discovery of tin in 1884 at Stannary Hills was part of the westward spread of prospecting that commenced at Herberton in 1880. The Stannary Hills mines were developed first by John Moffat and others, later by the Stannary Hills Mines and Tramway Company, and John Darling and Sons. Both firms were based in Adelaide. The former company invested £200,000 of South Australian capital in this enterprise of a mill, mines, and tramway.

Back in 1884, when Stannary Hills was known as Eureka Creek, Warden William M. Mowbray of Herberton reported: "The area of proved payable lode tin country is being extended to the westward beyond Irvinebank and Eureka Creek, ore being now frequently packed on mules for distances of 25 miles and over to the Western Company's mill." This mill was at Watsonville.

The late A. F. Waddell wrote in 1949: "From these early times we find up to the year 1899 that various mines were being developed and opened up in which W. Vandeleur, John Moffat and others appear to have had a hand, and the Adelaide concern calling itself the North Queensland Tin Mining Corporation was interested in the area together with such men as Samuel Dixon, H. R. Dixon, F. H. Snow, J. F. Cudmore, and

Map of the Herberton Shire

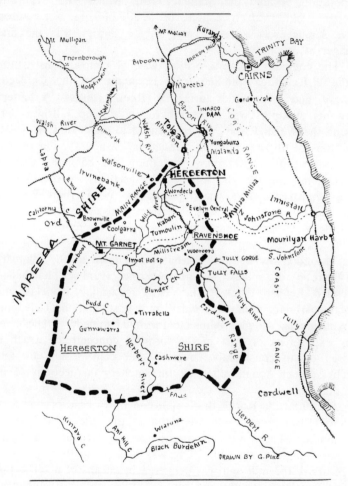

DRAWN BY G. PIKE

D. Lindsay." About the end of 1900, the abovementioned Corporation became the Stannary Hills Mines and Tramway Company Ltd. with a capital of £600,000 in £1 shares. J. K. Samuel was secretary and Sabine Paisley was the first manager at Stannary Hills.

The company's biggest project was, of course, construction of the 2 ft. gauge tramline from Boonmoo on the Chillagoe Railway, and seven miles further to Rocky Bluffs. A battery of twenty stampers was erected here on a steep hillside over-looking the Walsh River. It commenced to crush in June 1903. Sixty tons of tin ore could be crushed in 24 hours. Tin returns were not up to expectations, but upon the company seeking John Moffat's advice who supplied finer screens for the battery, yields improved. This was reported by W. Herbert Phillips, then chairman of directors. Sabine Paisley resigned, and F. G. de V. Gipps became general manager. He retired in 1906, and C. E. Nicholas took over.

The company controlled what was known as the Stannary Hills group of mines — notably the Ivanhoe, Kitchener, Extended, Eclipse, Black Rock, Young Australian, Ironclad, and also the Arbouin mines five miles south-east, and the Caledonia at Watsonville. Pugh's Almanac for 1907 stated: "The company exports its product in the form of concentrates which is dressed up to considerably over 70 per cent of fine tin and which is much sought after by tin smelters on account of its fine quality."

By 1906, the Rocky Bluffs mill had thirty head of stampers, each of 1360 pounds and were run at the rate of 102 drops per minute. There was a constant flow of miniature ore trains on the tramline to the mill. Ore was brought to the top of the gorge above the mill and was delivered by means of a self-acting incline tramline into the ore bins. Fifty men were employed. The Stannary Hills Company claimed that their Rocky Bluffs mill was one of the finest in Queensland; 2500 tons of stone was being treated each month for an average return of eighty tons of tin.

The two hundred residents of Rocky Bluffs township, their houses perched on a rocky hillside, enjoyed what was then considered a great luxury which towns of ten times the population did not have — electric light and reticulated water supplied from the crushing mill.

Mining was booming seventy years ago, yet metal prices were very low compared with today. For instance, sixteen tons of black tin from the Tommy Burns mine realised only £1160. Eight tons from the Gilmore returned £543. Fifteen tons of wolfram was worth a total of £969. But in those days when the average wage was £3 ($6.00) per week, that was big money.

Stannary Hills township was a busy place, and work was plentiful. There were five hotels — the Stannary Hills, kept by Mrs. F. Adams; Eureka Creek, D. J. Kelly; Federal, S. F. Rundle; Commercial, P. L. Harcus; and George Bardon's hotel. The latter spent his retirement in Mareeba and passed away at well over ninety years of age. He told many stories of the boom days on the tinfields in that country of pioneers.

The late Jimmie Brown, chairman of Mareeba Shire in the late Nineteen-forties and early 'fifties, was the last hotelkeeper in Stannary Hills and one of the town's last inhabitants. Another of these who stuck to the place to the last was Billy O'Neill the storekeeper.

There is nothing left at Stannary Hills today but a few heaps of rubbish; one can follow the old tramway formation to Rocky Bluffs and marvel at the tenacity and workmanship of the old timers. It is hard to believe that from October 1908 to July 1909, the Boonmoo-Stannary Hills tramline carried 11,260 tons of goods and 3807 passengers. Stannary Hills township had a population of at least 1000. It had a brass band composed of very gifted musicians like George Hume (cornet), Jim Kirkman (tenor horn), and Gilbert Petter (euphonium). Jenny Clark was a fine pianiste. Such people never had a chance to capitalise on their talents.

(257)

There was a hospital with resident doctor. Two that an old resident remembers are Dr. Sapsford and a lady, Dr. Rose Benham.

Eighty children attended the Provisional School where J. H. Holloway was head teacher. There were five stores, the leading one being the ubiquitous Jack and Newell. The others were kept by James Donaldson, George Lisha, George Tomkins, and Yee Hop. E. H. Hatrick was the butcher. J. A. Sheehan was postmaster and the law was represented by First-class Constable Pat Welch. The big mines had their managers: Lass O'Gowrie managed by John Donohue; the Dead Finish, A. Wishart; Great Eastern, W. Vandeleur; and the Gladstone, H. Reid.

But the Stannary Hills Company was not getting sufficient returns for its enormous outlay, and during 1908 the concern was reconstructed. Its first report dated "Adelaide, 26 April, 1909" was not cheerful. This was the period of the big industrial strikes on the mining fields when trade unionism began to assert its power. The company's mines were idle during most of the wet season; water rose 296 ft. in the Ivanhoe mine. Nevertheless, Mr. Nicholas concluded his report confidently: "Dividends are absolutely assured in the future". It was a vain hope.

In October 1911 after a further re-organisation, a loss of £2,738/4/3 was reported by the chairman of directors, John Darling. The new general manager, John H. Stockdale, reported that the mill crushed nearly 17,000 tons of ore for a return of only 142 tons of tin concentrates. At this time, the Cairns Hinterland was cut off from the coast except by pack-teams, because of the collapse of No. 10. Tunnel on the Cairns Range railway.

In April 1912, the tramline was reported to be very busy, with four trains to and from Irvinebank and Boonmoo daily, and two to Rocky Bluffs. A lot of Mt. Mulligan coal was being hauled to Irvinebank. In June that year, Mr. Stockdale sailed for the south on the Wyandra and the Stannary Hills mines closed down. In October, John Darling and Son took over. The writing was already on the wall, and the outbreak of World War I. was the final blow. The John Darling Company, with V. Martin, manager, was merely to preside over the demise of Stannary Hills. The Rocky Bluffs battery and the tramline were the first to go, and in 1919, the Boonmoo-Stannary Hills line was taken over by the Queensland Government, as previously mentioned.

As with the other ghost towns, folk who helped pioneer the place and lived in the days of hard toil and few comforts, sleep on the site of their hopes and labors in the lonely little cemetery at Stannary Hills. Only three graves have head-stones — those of J. F. Dillon, Thomas Dillon, and Bertha Hodges — while at least twenty others are unmarked and the occupants are unknown. They are just some more of the forgotten pioneers of Far North Queensland.

Mrs. N.M. Kelly of Ravenshoe has recorded some of the story of the old pioneer, Daniel Joseph Kelly of Stannary Hills, and I am grateful to her for this information.

Earlier, the name of D. J. Kelly appears as the proprietor of the Eureka Creek Hotel in Stannary Hills. The Kellys came from Brisbane north to Charters Towers, and then to Mt. Garnet and Stannary Hills in 1902. D. J. (Joe, or "Sandy"), had two hotels and a butchery in this mining town during the first decade, assisted by his sons. He bred some fine horses in the 1910-20 period, sold for remounts for the Indian Army, and also ran cattle. The brand, KD4, was well known.

At Christmas, Joe kept open house, and would collect all the old miners in his spring cart and bring them in for a free Christmas dinner. One of the miners who boarded at the Kellys' hotel was E. G. Theodore who later became Premier of Queensland.

The Kellys hung on at Stannary Hills until it became a ghost town, in 1935. Mrs. N. M. Kelly recalls that one of the mine manager's houses situated on the hill behind the town had a billiard room with huge plate glass doors. The home stood abandoned and in perfect condition until destroyed in a bushfire. Mrs. N. M. Kelly wrote: "Throughout the North are men and women who look back with affection on the days of Stannary Hills and the colourful characters it held, not the least of which was D. J. Kelly."

MINING BONANZA?

The following report appeared in the "Tablelands Advertiser", the weekly newspaper published in Mareeba, on January 30, 1980. It shows that in the centenary year of the discovery of tin at Herberton, there have been significant mineral discoveries which, with present day high prices, may create a boom that may dwarf those of pioneer days. It also proves that the old fields have certainly not been "worked out". The old timers only scratched the surface, as it were, with pick and shovel. Modern machinery could reveal riches untold.

"The new operation in the Herberton/Baal Gammon/Irvinebank area is a joint venture of Great Northern Mining N.L., Newmont Pty. Ltd., and ICI Australia. Great Northern announced the discovery of a major body of mineralisation on the field 11 km. from Herberton covering an area 350 m. wide and 500 m. long containing ore which at current prices would be worth about $750 million. Mr. A. Hay of Oakbridge Ltd., Great Northern's parent company, said: 'This development will put Herberton on the map.' He forecast that Herberton's Centenary will be marked by a mining boom similar to the one that founded the town 100 years ago."

The Queensland Minister for Mines, Mr. R. Camm, was reported in the Queensland press as saying that tin was now (1980) worth $15,364 per tonne. This compares with £35 or $70 per ton one hundred years ago.

CHAPTER 17

"GOD BLESS JOHN MOFFAT"

Irvinebank in the Days of John Moffat — the Mighty Vulcan Mine — Tolga, "Edge of the Scrub" — the Railway reaches Herberton at last — On to Ravenshoe.

The full story of Irvinebank is a long and colorful one, and impossible to tell in this book; it would fill a large volume by itself.

The shadow of John Moffat looms large over Irvinebank. In fact, he *was* Irvinebank, and when he retired and handed over to others, his beloved Irvinebank gradually faded away. He was regarded more like a friend than an employer. When the Town Dam burst in the 1893 floods, the majority of his employees gave their labour free to repair the damage and get tin stone turned into metal for the markets. It was a period of severe financial depression. When better times came they were fully rewarded. John Moffat never forgot their fine gesture. There was never any industrial trouble until the Southern based unions and radicalism intruded into the Northern mining fields in 1909. A few years earlier, the union organisers, E. G. Theodore and W. McCormack, both of whom were to become leading Labor parliamentarians, worked as miners at Irvinebank.

The whole of the Cairns Hinterland benefited by John Moffat's energy and enterprise. As an old timer has said, "for every bob John Moffat made, he put ninepence back." He married Margaret Linedale, sister of A. T. (Tony) Linedale, Moffat's right-hand man in early times.

Moffat was generous to a fault, and highly respected by all. It has been said that even the children of Irvinebank ended their prayers with "God bless Mummy and Daddy, and Mr. Moffat." To the whole town he was a father-figure, and with six hundred men on his payroll at the height of Irvinebank's prosperity he was one of the biggest private enterprise employers in Queensland.

His retirement in 1912 and the outbreak of World War I in 1914 causing closure of the metal markets, was Irvinebank's death blow, as it was to all the other once prosperous mining towns. Moffat died at Toowoomba on June 28, 1918 aged 77 years. Thus passed one of the North's greatest pioneers, and one of the finest men who ever lived.*

Following his death, the old Irvinebank Mining Company was taken over by the Queensland Government. The smelters closed in 1920 and machinery and buildings were dismantled. However, during the 'thirties, the whole of the crushing plant was reorganised and renovated and it became the State Treatment Works crushing ore brought in by miners with small "shows" in the area. Lachlan (Lock) Kirkman was manager for a great many years, and his sister Dot was the town's postmistress until recent years. Charlie Wyatt was chief battery-man for a long period. In 1975-76, the works were again renovated and modernised. With only some 150 inhabitants today, Irvinebank is a sad ghost of former days. The Loloma Company caused some activity recently when it built a mill on Jumna Creek, near the site of Hardman's Mill of 70 years ago.

Irvinebank was described by a newspaper writer in September 1907 as being one of the most solid and progressive townships in North Queensland. William Lees wrote in a "Queensland Country Life" supplement:

"Irvinebank is situated at the confluence of McDonald and Gibbs Creeks . . . . where the big dam of the Irvinebank Mining Company, twelve and a half acres in extent, is located . . . . High hills surround the township, rising abruptly up from the main street which runs along the bank of McDonald Creek . . . . Below the mill dam, the creek again narrows to a steep

* The life and times of John Moffat are such a big subject they can only be briefly touched on here, in particular Moffat himself. For the full story of this remarkable man, read "John Moffat's Empire" by Ruth S. Kerr, published to coincide with the Centenary of Herberton in 1980.

valley between the hills, on the left side of which winds, for a considerable distance, the narrow tramline which goes to Stannary Hills and eventually joins the Chillagoe Line at Boonmoo, 27 miles distant . . . .

"The Irvinebank Company's works overlook the dam from above the junction of the two creeks. Upon the northern side of the dam are several stores and hotels, while on the hill above stands the hospital . . . . and nearby, the school and the new post office. The principal business portion is at the south side of McDonald Creek, and the street running at right angles thereto, up the steep hill, by which for twenty years all the stone from the mines went to the mill by horse teams. This section of the town is the chief meeting place of the miners and residents.

"Under Wade's verandah where the acetylene gas burns, men talk mining and development business, and adjourn to the bar to fix the matter. Here are the chief stores, Jack and Newell, and Armstrong, Ledlie, and Stillman, whose names are household words throughout the Walsh and Tinaroo; the two banks, the fine brick building of the Q.N. Bank and the Bank of New South Wales. Near the former is the reading room of the School of Arts, well stocked with newspapers and journals, and containing a fine collection of the minerals of the district.

"Adjacent to this building are the offices of Messrs. Brownlee, Donald, and Co. Ltd., sharebrokers etc. who are, by their list, apparently the secretaries of everything in the district, from the Walsh Shire Council and the hospital to the Walsh and Tinaroo Newspaper Co. Ltd. Next to this is the old Post and Telegraph office . . . . now occupied by the Bank of N.S.W., and opposite is the fine School of Arts Hall.

"Scattered about the steep hillsides are the residences, four, six, and eight rooms, with their stony surroundings, usually set off by our friend, the goat, with an ever accompanying school of kids — the chief livestock of this country from Mareeba to O.K. The building trade is very good at present, and shows

(263)

the faith and confidence possessed by the inhabitants in this, one of the most solid and progressive townships in North Queensland."

Of all the tin mines in North Queensland, the mightiest of them all was the Vulcan Mine at Irvinebank. At fifteen hundred feet it was the deepest in Australia. In the days when tin prices fluctuated between £30 and £100 per ton, it is said to have produced ·£750,000 worth of high grade metal during its thirty-odd years of life. What the same production would be worth today, defies the imagination.

Assistant Government Geologist, S.B.J. Skertchly, reported in 1895: "The mine was discovered about the year 1883, and up to 1887, 12,000 tons of ore had been raised . . . . said to have yielded 1500 tons of black tin and 900 tons of metallic tin . . . . It has twice been abandoned, and the present proprietors (the third set) have taken out nearly £66,000 worth of tin and have received over £28,000 in dividends in five years."

The Vulcan lode was discovered by Italian woodcutters who soon sold their claims to a syndicate of local miners for £2000 and went home to Italy for a holiday. All early records of crushings date from October 1890. Two years later the Vulcan Tin Mining Company was formed, and the names of shareholders is like a roll call of Irvinebank's pioneers: R. M. Bradby was chairman of directors, H. J. Armstrong, secretary, A Robb and G. C. Young, auditors. Some of the applicants for shares were Robert Wyatt, George Richardson, William Dougherty, John McAllan, Michael Dunne, James Brown, William Speirs, Alex Robson, Harry Bradshaw, Louis Lewis, John Sanders, George Bradbury, W. Clark, B. Donovan, R. McLean, C. H. Barrett, Thomas Swan, Sydney Sheppherd, James Gibbs, Thomas Martin, Nicholas Hardman, and others. Some of the descendents of these people are with us still.

Up to February 1907, 88,096 tons of stone had yielded 8794 tons of black tin valued at £377,362, whilst the dividends totalled £162,030. From 1890 to August 1919 the great

Vulcan Mine is recorded as yielding 12,111 tons of tin valued then at £612,619. Shareholders had rceeived over £185,000 in dividends. Old timers remember that week in, week out, thirty head of stampers were employed at the Irvinebank mill pounding away on the very hard Vulcan stone. Mine managers they recall are Tom Swan, Dinny Lucey, Syd. Sheppherd, R. A. Rolfe, Jim Brodie, and Jim Dawson. Mick and Jim Sheehan, George Crook, Watty Ray, Jack Ramm, and Frank Gane, were well known drivers of the seven-horse drays which carted the ore and firewood. The Vulcan Company was renowned for its magnificent horses.

In 1913, however, the Vulcan Mine was linked to the crushing mill by an aerial ropeway across the valley. A similar ropeway was installed from the Governor Norman mine. It was an effort to cut costs as the ore became poorer. Sir William McGregor, the Queensland Governor, opened the latter ropeway at a formal ceremony when he visited Irvinebank.

In 1928, when the Whitworth Company took an option over the whole of the Irvinebank mining area, a lot of money was spent at the Vulcan in a seemingly unplanned and futile manner, and when the company faded out in 1930, the mine closed for good. Apparently it was impossible to dewater the mine in the manner then attempted. One may look up the steep gumtree covered hillside today without knowing that near its summit are the remains of the once mighty Vulcan and in earlier times, the Tornado.

If one climbed this hill 75 years ago one could have viewed the busy town of Irvinebank, seen the smoke from the ninety-foot high smokestack of the smelters, heard the forty stampers pounding away, the peculiar noise of the big Krupp ball mill, and the continuous blast of the tin smelters and calciners; heard the tinkling bells of the packteams and seen them winding around the mountainside; seen the clouds of dust in dry times raised by the plodding horse teams; and near at hand was the continuous "shoof, shoof" of the air compressor at the Vulcan itself. Today there is only silence and a scene of neglect and decay with a handful of rooftops of a township barely clinging to life.

Once it had many stores and business houses, a hospital, doctor, and two good brass bands. They welcomed at least three State Governors on the lawn in front of the School of Arts Hall which still stands. There were four hotels — Jim Bethel had the first, the Mining Exchange; then there was the Orient (S. Ramage); and the Cosmopolitan, first kept by Jimmy Gibbs. In 1901, Harry Wade erected the Royal on this spot. At the other end of the town was the Commercial (the Australian of today), first kept by "Red" Jim Tait from Montalbion. Next door was the Vulcan, built by W. Dougherty (one of the discoverers of Watsonville) and kept by Mrs. Abrahams during the boom years.

John Moffat's old home still stands on the hill overlooking the township and the dam. The town's water supply, the Ibis Dam, was constructed in 1906-07, and due to superb workmanship, is still in good repair. John Moffat's home, built of pitsawn cedar about 1883 and still containing the great man's massive office desk and chair, must be preserved for posterity at all costs. Irvinebank should be high on the list for the National Trust; the place is a vital part of our heritage.

In May 1950, a plaque in honor of John Moffat, on a memorial cairn, was unveiled in front of the School of Arts Hall. In October 1953, a second plaque was unveiled on the same cairn in memory of Irvinebank's historian, Augustus Frederick Waddell whose father, Allan Waddell, was manager of the Loudoun Mill for John Moffat from its inception. When the Moffat plaque was unveiled by the Royal Geographical Society of Australasia, the ceremony attracted about a thousand visitors, the greatest gathering seen at Irvinebank since the picnic at Allbut which John Moffat and his wife held to celebrate the completion of the tramway, in 1907.

The first vehicle to reach Irvinebank was a buckboard

driven more or less up the bed of Gibbs Creek by a hardy Scot, "Dad" Young, from Montalbion, reached by the main wagon road from Port Douglas.

Most of the other roads were made by driving a wagon and team straight up some impossible-looking spur to a mine. Ted Henry wrote in 1947 of incidents fifty years previously:

"The only flat place would be the ore paddock or under the hopper at the mine, and then the teamster would have to take the chain horses off and manoevre the shafter around, then pull the dray around, to be able to get near the place.

"Keeping the brakes on was an art, for if they were kept too tight the wheels would skid. The driver would be on the near side working the brake handle and stepping up and down in the wheel rut or on the bank. It is a wonder more drivers were not killed.

"Three who were crushed between their drays and cliff-faces at Irvinebank at different times were Jim Shay, Jack Leatham, and Charlie Bradley. Bill Tracy had a nasty experience on the Queen of the Ranges Hill at Irvinebank when something went wrong with the brake.

"He was on a steep grade six hundred feet above the level country and he kept the horses going at top speed with the whip and did not have time to turn to the left at the saddle of the hill about threequarters of the way down, but sent them thundering right down the spur and pulled up on the sportsground — the only flat country for miles around.

"On a Saturday afternoon, the carriers would shoe their brakes with the heels and soles of old leather boots. One new hand wanted to know where he could get the boots for them, thinking to be helpful. He was told he would find plenty under the beds in the rooms above the stables. So he went and got an armful, cut the tops off and nailed the rest to the brakes. Wasn't there an uproar when the drivers came home and found he had cut up all their 'Sunday boots! ' "

The late Ted Henry also wrote:

(267)

"The old road down the back of the Hospital Hill in Irvinebank was so steep that it was said if anyone tried to lead a goat down it, it would somersault, and do Catherine wheels all the way down to the creek below. About a dozen yards from the bottom there was a sharp bend in the road to connect with the main road going up past the dam.

"Phil Foxlee was coming down with a load of firewood one time; his chain horses could not have had a strain on the load for the dray went straight over, the load capsized, and the shafter was killed. The other horses escaped injury.

"Later on, the carriers put cocked shoes on the hind feet of the shafters so they could get a grip on the terribly steep mountain roads. Seven-horse teams in the drays were used for a long time, and when they got the twelve-horse wagon teams, the Irvinebank Mining Company had seven-eighths of an inch muffle chains around double spokes on the rear wheels as single spokes would break in some of the steep places.

"They had some very good draught horses in the drays and wagons in those days, and it used to be said one could sleep on the backs of the Vulcan Company's horses, they were so wide.

"Bill Rogers bought the horses for the Irvinebank Mining Company. One time he arrived back with thousands of pounds' worth of horses from Collaroy Station in the Mackay district. The company's drivers would come along to the horse yards and take their pick, the Vulcan drivers always taking the biggest and heaviest.

"Bill Bennett had a team of twelve greys, and they were a magnificent sight. Then there was Paddy Kirby who always took the culls that were left, and in no time he would have the best team of the lot. He always trained his horses well, and in a nasty corner they would, at a word from him, come down the chains like bullocks, and not a kick out of any of them . . . ."

George Crook, another of the Irvinebank teamsters, was a very strong man. He is credited with being able to lift a case of galvanized iron, weighing half a ton.

From all accounts there were indeed some mighty men and horses eighty years and more ago. We will never see their like again.

*   *   *   *

The railway that had been begun at Cairns in May 1886 as "the Herberton Railway" had reached Mareeba in August 1893 and rested there for ten years. Then in June, 1903, work commenced on the next stage, the twenty-one miles from Mareeba to Atherton, with engineer Archibald S. Frew the contractor. Though there was an upgrade of some eleven hundred feet, there were no engineering difficulties. The route followed the old Port Douglas Road southward, passing close to such old time stopping places as Rushworth's, Forrest's, and Barney Hayes'. Through Martintown which became Tolga, and so to the little township of Atherton surrounded then by dense rain forest.

It was a gala day when the first train steamed into Atherton. The late Charlie Wessells of Watsonville remembered it. The Watsonville brass band, one of the best in the Far North, played stirring music and hundreds of people were at the station which was decorated with arches of ferns, flowers, and maize plants. The ribbon was cut by the Premier, Sir Robert Philp.

With Atherton the terminus for the time being, the road to Mareeba, once busy with coaches, buggies, teams, and also traction engines, was deserted. No longer was it necessary to cart all Tableland produce and timber to Mareeba for railing to Cairns. Atherton grew in importance, and the hopes of the people of Tolga that their little town would become the "capital" of the Tableland, were dashed. The name, Tolga, is said to be an Aboriginal word meaning, "the edge of the scrub" and if so, it is a very apt naming.

Martin Bros.' sawmill had been the main factor in the creation of Tolga, and there was a rival sawmilling business run by the Morrow family. For many years George Martin was chairman of the Tinaroo Shire Council. Sawn timber, principally cedar, was sent to Mareeba by horse teams and traction engines before the railway was extended to Atherton.

The late J. J. McDonald whose father was not only one of the discoverers of Irvinebank but who was an early pioneer of maize growing at Spring Creek near Tolga, wrote in the "North Queensland Register" of February 6, 1971:

"The demand for the cabinet timbers of the Barron Valley, as the Atherton district was then known, brought a new type of businessman to this Pioneers' Country — the timber buyer. They seemed to be from every part of Australia, and soon they could be seen visiting the selector on his farm, inspecting his stands of timber and buying trees to fulfill Southern orders. The previously impoverished settler now had a ready market for the valuable timber that he would have previously burnt . . . . Having more money now, he could employ a timber cutter . . . . and another new type of man arrived on the Tableland. These skilled men came from Victoria and New South Wales, and what mighty axemen they were! . . . . He could now afford to buy sawn timber, galvanized iron, and wire, and the old slab hut was soon replaced by a comfortable dwelling, and he could marry and raise a family . . . . "

The Iron Horse had thus brought civilisation to the scrub-lands and the full richness of the beautiful Tableland country was revealed. The way was opened for it to become a rich dairying and mixed farming district with a permanency not known on the mining fields.

But Herberton still did not have its railway. Atherton was to be the railhead from 1903 to 1910. In 1887, Surveyor O. L. Amos had completed a survey line as far as Carrington at the foot of the Herberton Range which divides the Barron waters from those of the Herbert. In 1888, his survey reached Herberton. With the line still being constructed up the Cairns Range, no further attention was paid to the Herberton end until 1907 by which time the mining town had declined in importance.

The objective of a railway, from an official point of view, was not mining, but the timber resources of the Evelyn Tableland and Cedar Creek (Ravenshoe). Without these, Herberton may never have got its railway.

Surveyor Stringer made a new survey over the Herberton Range, and in 1908 the site for the Herberton railway station was selected. A start was made on clearing the scrub from Atherton to the foot of the range in August. The constructing engineer was Mr. Parkinson. With John Newell, John Ledlie, and others, the route was inspected. A main construction camp was establishd at Black Gully and numerous shanties and eating houses sprang up. Harry Chatfield made more money from his "Range Hotel" in a month than he could in six months of coach driving.

By the end of September, 300 men were at work, but in October a hundred men left for the Etheridge construction as they objected to wages of eight shillings and sixpence per day instead of the ruling nine shillings — sixpence being of some consequence in those times. In March 1909, the engineer reported progress as satisfactory but complained that the amount of drinking indulged in by the workers was retarding progress; there were eight hotels in six miles, besides grog shanties.

At the beginning of 1910, the tunnel at the top of the range was constructed, and the tunnellers, under Ganger Fitzgerald, were working on a large cutting in Grace Street, Herberton. The main construction camp had been moved from near Carrington to Nigger Creek (Wondecla) near the Herberton showgrounds, in January. In mid-March, the formation was completed and ready for the plate-layers. But the pay issue had not been settled and from May to July the men were on strike for their extra sixpence per day. The strikers were forced out and men were taken on who were prepared to work for 8/6 per day, and so construction got going again. By August 16th., the whistle of ballast trains was heard in Herberton. A month later the rails were laid through Herberton to the ballast pit at Nigger Creek.

The grand opening of the Cairns-Herberton Railway took place on Thursday, October 20, 1910. The first train arrived from Cairns at 12.30 p.m. The engine driver was Mick Woods, the former M.L.A. for Woothakata (he had lost his seat to Theodore in 1909). The ribbon was cut by the Acting Governor, Sir Arthur Morgan. The jubilant crowd of three thousand people roared its approval, and then poured out to Wondecla for a monster picnic at the showgrounds. Almost 200 sat down to the official luncheon in the Shire Hall. Sir Arthur was presented with a model locomotive, with the words "At Last" painted on it. Herberton had waited almost 25 years for this day, so the words were appropriate. In 1964, a framed picture depicting the engine that opened the line to Herberton was presented to the Shire Council.

In 1911, the railway went on south, from Nigger Creek to Tumoulin, 3162 ft. above sea level and the highest altitude railway station in Queensland. In 1916, a further short extension was made to Ravenshoe. No longer would Cobb and Co. coaches and laboring teams be climbing the range to Herberton. With the opening of the railway, an era ended.

CHAPTER 18

WHEN WAYS BEGAN TO CHANGE

The Call to Arms — Ravenshoe — Settlers of the Scrublands — Gillies Highway — E. W. Heale — Yungaburra and Kairi — Cyclones — Railwayman's Heroism — Mareeba in the Twenties — Last of the Teamsters.

August 4th. 1914 was a fatal day on the North Queensland mining fields as it was to the world — the outbreak of World War I. A wave of patriotism swept Australia, with closer ties to Britain than now. The proud Empire that girdled the world, and the Motherland in particular, was in mortal danger, and her sons, of British stock, responded nobly to the call to arms. None more so than the men of the Australian bush — the stockriders and the miners.

All ninety members of the Irvinebank Rifle Club and thirty or more from Watsonville — the finest sharpshooters in the North — reported at Cairns to bring the Kennedy Regiment up to full strength. Sixty Irvinebank-Watsonville men sailed from Cairns on the Kanowna for Thursday Island and New Guinea to meet any German threat, a large portion of New Guinea then being a German colony. Most of them, and other enlistments later, went on to the main theatre of war in Palestine, Gallipoli, and France. Many did not return. Irvinebank also gave a nurse to the Army Medical Corps.

There are two hundred names on the Roll of Honour on the Cenotaph in Herberton; 21 were killed in action and seven died of wounds; including "W. Perrott, (Aboriginal)."

Thus were the mining fields denuded of their manpower, and with the collapse of the overseas metal markets, the towns, and the companies that kept the towns going, could not survive. (The Queensland Government bought the whole of the Irvinebank Mining Company's assets — mills, smelters, buildings, machinery, tramlines, etc. for £22,500 in 1919).

The Roll of Honour on the Cenotaph in Arnold Park,

Mareeba — for half a century it stood at the intersection of Byrnes and Atherton Streets in the centre of town — bears the names of 110 Mareeba lads who answered the call; 47 were killed in action or otherwise died. Considering that Mareeba had a population of only about 1200 in 1914, it is a fine record.

The womenfolk in the bush also played their part. Old timers remember Mrs. Sonny Prior running concerts in Mungana to aid the war funds, and riding around on her pony to collect donations for the Red Cross. Further out, the wives of station owners and managers marshalled their kitchen "lubras" and produced hundreds of kerosene tins of beef extract, laboriously boiling down the meat over smoking open fires and furnace-hot stoves. The extract, in sealed tins, went to the front lines in France; many an Australian soldier would have had cause to bless some hard-working bushwoman for his cup of hot "beef tea".

A little known war memorial stands in a grassy paddock at Evelyn, east of Kaban, and carries the names of 42 men " . . . . from Evelyn Scrub who did their duty in the Great War". Ten of them paid the supreme sacrifice. These, too, were the sons of the pioneers of the Tablelands — men with names like Daniel, Kidner, Mazlin, Winkel, Grigg, Harte, Steele, Hull, and others.

Near here was Mrs. Hull's Cressbrook farm, Keough's Bellview, and an early sawmill erected by E. P. Williams, and another by Jim Newell, brother of John Newell. The latter mill used a waterwheel in Mill Creek for power. Hay and Haigh had a mill at Evelyn Central, and another early miller was George Pearson. This was when the settlers were selling their scrub trees so their blocks could be cleared. It has been said that timber fetched two shillings (20c) per 100 ft. in those days.

As far back as 1896, Evelyn Scrub had a school, Bill Harte ran a store and Mrs. Hull had a butcher's shop, later run by Ted Daniels. Before the railway came, the track from

Herberton to Ravenshoe, through Kaban and Tumoulin, was known as "the mailman's track", the mail being conveyed on horseback. Only the war memorial and a few graves now mark the site of the pioneer settlement of Evelyn Scrub.

It was the enterprise of none other than John Moffat which led to the founding of the town of Ravenshoe, for it was he who, in 1899, built a sawmill there; the area was then known as Cedar Creek. John Kidner and Jack Bailey brought the machinery from Mareeba on their bullock wagons — a two weeks' journey. The first timber produced from this mill in November, 1899, was loaded on wagons and taken to Mt. Garnet to build Denny Lucey's hotel — the first in that mining town. Watson was the first mill manager, assisted by Joe Mitchell and Irvine Thomas.

In 1909, John Moffat sold the mill to Fred Robinson of Wooroora Station and Robert Perrott of Evelyn. J. M. Johnston leased it in 1915. The next owner was William Mazlin Jnr. who moved it to the site later occupied by Rosenfeld and Sons' large modern mill which, in 1950, was producing two million feet of sawn timber annually. Timber and dairying has always been the lifeblood of Ravenshoe.

In 1907 the Government threw open 35,000 acres of scrublands east and south of Atherton for dairying. In the Ravenshoe area, surveyors Porter and Drew surveyed 300 blocks. Porter also surveyed the town of Ravenshoe, though the original site chosen was further east at Chilverton. In 1911, a tunnel-like track through the scrub was cut by George Rankine from Ravenshoe to Chilverton. In 1913, Jack Kidner cut a track to Vine Creek, and McMillan, Hastie, and Rankine cut the first track to the Tully Falls.

The dairying blocks were taken up by groups of settlers. They came north to the Tablelands with horse and bullock teams, and in buggies, in the biggest migration of pioneer families since the rush for pastoral land in the Eighteen-sixties. Most of the settlers came from northern New South Wales or from Charters Towers where gold mining had begun to wane. The latter arrived with horse teams in 1910 and 1911. George and Alec Rankine, Peter Strang, Charlie Kerr, and Bob Witherspoon arrived with the first mob of cattle and horses on September 10, 1910 and began clearing the scrub on their virgin blocks.

The Norman family arrived early in 1911 with fifty head of cattle for the Charters Towers No. 2 Group at Evelyn. The Bolton family arrived by horse team with a ton of roofing iron in October 1911. The Major family and Tom Merrin arrived the same year. They all endured great hardships — the land was clothed in almost impenetrable tropical jungle and the rain seemed to be almost continuous. Access to many blocks was on foot or bridle track cut through the scrub; settlers had to carry supplies for miles on their backs. Many are the stories told, or handed down, of those days. Some day a book will be written about the settlers in the Tableland scrublands sixty years ago.

A. Snellman opened the first store in Ravenshoe in 1907. Thomas Merrin, Snr., opened his store in 1911. Armstrong, Ledlie, and Stillman opened their branch store in 1918. The first hotel was the Club, built in 1912. A "Bachelors' Hall" was built by John Moffat's mill employees before Ravenshoe began, Moffat donating the timber. In it, the township's first school was opened with May Adair the teacher. In February 1912, a Provisional School was opened in Ted Mawby's house with Cecily Sollieux the first teacher. A State School was opened on March 3, 1914. The first white children born in Ravenshoe were Joe Malone and Rose Beh.

Bill Roberts whose father took up a selection on Blunder Creek, between Ravenshoe and Mt. Garnet in 1912, remembers his first experience with a bullock team:

"Dad purchased eight young bullocks from Paddy Beck, out Sundown way. He and my two elder brothers tried to 'gentle' those steers and coupled them in pairs with a rope collar on

(276)

each and a hobble chain between, but they soon found they were 'getting nowhere fast.' So Dad bought two old leaders from Bob Perrott of Evelyn Station, and Charlie Williams, a bullocky, brought them along. Jack and Ben were really well trained leaders and we soon had a bullock team.

"We needed the team to cart building material and supplies to our selection, and later to uproot huge gum trees with the use of block and tackle, to pull a three-disc plough, and to take farm produce to the railheads at Mt. Garnet and Tumoulin.

"We became very fond of these docile animals, and the team was later increased by the purchase of three steers from Denny McGrath of Biboohra, (DM3 brand), then two Herefords from Fred Christensen of Mt. Garnet; these latter were Lyndhurst bullocks ("shield" brand), and the team was named behind Jack and Ben, Spot and Nobby, Fred and Christmas, Denny and Mac, Jerry and Baldy, Paddy and Strawberry, and the polers were Murphy and Mick.

"When being yoked, first the offside leader would walk into place, be yoked, and the driver would hold the yoke aloft for the nearside bullock which would walk into place and be yoked also. Each bullock came up in his turn to be yoked. When we lost Baldy, Jerry with his wide set of horns would make a nuisance of himself trying to get a place in the team, and when hunted out, he would follow the team like a dog.

"At that time Ravenshoe was brand new, and a great number of bullock teams were engaged in hauling logs to mills at Ravenshoe and Tumoulin and to the railway to be despatched to the coast. 'Bullockies' I knew well were Charlie Beh, Jack Kidner, Tom Malone, Bob and Harry Witherspoon, and Harry Ernst. Jack and Ted Toohey, Wheeler Winkel, and others, had horse teams."

The Ravenshoe area owes much to one of its early champions — Francis Alfred Grigg, after whom the main street of the town is named.

About 1900, he opened a store at Wondecla when the

Deep Lead was producing vast quantities of alluvial tin, and when the railway was extended he opened another at Tumoulin. His Ravenshoe store began to function in 1914, and in it he was associated with W. G. Leal. He became chairman of the Herberton Shire Council in 1915 and was a member until 1936. W. R. Sollieux and Miss Marion Major were other well respected Ravenshoe citizens. The Herberton Shire Council provided timber free to build the School of Arts in 1912.

Two of Ravenshoe's churches — the Anglican and Roman Catholic — both came from Irvinebank, being removed when that town declined. The Methodist Church was erected in 1920. Today, Ravenshoe is well known for its boys' college, St. Barnabas, run by the Bush Brotherhood of the Church of England.

The scrub area at Evelyn was not settled until 1909 when blocks that had been resumed from Evelyn Station were occupied for dairying. The first settlers arrived by the Berrybank road and some of the stalwart families remembered were named Hughes, Hamilton, Pearson, Lavers, Bell, Minchin, Maconachie, Kennedy, Graham, Smith, Williams, McAuliffe, Brown, Maggs, Taylor, Ferguson, Haigh, White, and there were others. In the early days butter was made by hand on the farms and taken on horseback to Herberton. When the railway reached Tumoulin, it was collected by buggy and sent to Golden Grove factory, Atherton. The butter factory at Ravenshoe was opened in 1926.

Construction of fine bitumen roads from the 'thirties onwards, transformed the Tablelands. The Evelyn Highway was constructed by way of Longland's Gap in 1935. The Palmerston Highway was opened from Innisfail to Ravenshoe in 1936, and was later extended to Mt. Garnet via the Innot Hot Springs. This road follows a route in use since 1899.

The biggest road construction of all was, of course, the Gillies Highway which provided the whole of the Tablelands with its first trafficable road to Cairns — something for which the pioneers had begun searching in 1876.

The Gillies Highway, constructed in 1924-25, followed part of Robson's Track and the pack track used by the Herberton mule teams. It was a triumph in engineering and considering it was built without the earthmoving machinery we know today, it was also a triumph in construction.

For years the road had been the vision of a great Tableland pioneer, Edward W. Heale; his plan of the route the road should take was largely adopted by the engineers. He was supported by William Neal Gillies when M.L.A. for Eacham. He was briefly Premier of Queensland in 1925. The road was said to have 612 bends in twelve miles. Until improved in recent years it was for one-way traffic only.

A spectacular view of the Mulgrave Valley is obtained from Heale's Lookout where a vandal-desecrated memorial honours this pioneer who is little known outside the Tableland. It has been said, rightly, that "Teddy" Heale was "a man twenty years before his time; but he knew what was needed." He was the first to send frozen milk to the coastal towns — now one of the Tableland's most important exports.

E. W. Heale joined the firm of Morrow Bros. as a partner and in 1903 the firm sent the first consignment of sawn maple to the South from their mill at Tolga. Heale built a beautiful home, now in ruins, called Fleetwood House, and engaged in agriculture, stock raising, as well as being interested in timber and in anything that would advance the Tableland. He was chairman of the Eacham Shire for a period.

It was probably railways, now in the discard, which assisted the early settlers the most; the logs and sawn timber, cream, maize, and other produce could be got to market by rail, especially by the branch line that was eventually constructed to Millaa Millaa.

As has been mentioned previously, Tolga once aspired to be the Capital of the Tablelands, but was quickly overtaken by Atherton. Tolga boomed briefly around 1909-10 during the construction of the branch line to Kairi, Kulara, and so to

(279)

Alumbah Pocket which became Yungaburra, and then to Peeramon, Malanda, and Tarzali. Eleven years after construction began at Tolga, the rails reached Millaa Millaa in 1921.

Year by year the scrub was felled, the timber taken out on the trains as the rails advanced, the country gradually being changed to rolling grasslands with only charred stumps to show that a great forest had once existed; pockets of scrub along the creeks and on inaccessible hillsides, with always the cloud-covered backdrop of the Coastal Range with great Bartle Frere visible on clear days; rich volcanic soil and bountiful moisture — a paradise for dairying, a temperate highland country in the tropics within forty miles of the humid coast.

Today, milk from these dairy herds goes two thousand miles by road tankers to Darwin every few days; to Mount Isa, Alice Springs, and Townsville. Construction of a railway made butter factories possible at Malanda and Millaa Millaa. Table-land cheese is also much in demand. For years now, "Malanda Milk" has been a byword.

*   *   *   *

This book is mainly concerned with the Mareeba and Herberton Shires and the remainder of the Tableland that affected those areas (see map) and for reasons of space, the Yungaburra-Malanda-Millaa Millaa area can be dealt with only briefly. This area, with complete stories of the struggles of the pioneers — people like the English, Roseblade, and Winfield families and many others — deserves a separate book. The town of Malanda dates from 1908, and the Eacham Shire was constituted in 1911, when the railway came.

At Yungaburra, the first settler is said to have been George H. O'Donnell, and others were David McCroan and John Stewart. The latter grew arrowroot and manufactured it, his product being deemed "highly commended" at a World Exhibition in London. The nearby Boar Pocket, where McCroan kept an hotel, was a well known camping ground for the packers.

One of the best known pioneers of Yungaburra was Henry

(280)

Sydney Williams, founder of the grazing, butchering, and motor sales firm of Williams Estate. His name has been mentioned previously in this book; he formed Strathvale Station, Mt. Garnet, in 1888, moved to Carrington (Nyleta) in 1890, and started a butchering business, eventually making his headquarters at Yungaburra. Branches were opened at Malanda, Herberton, Peeramon, Tarzali, Atherton, and Cairns. Henry Williams died in 1905 but his descendents are carrying on motor and farm machinery sales businesses in North Queensland today. Henry Williams and his wife had seven boys and four girls. He had led an adventurous life, being born in Southampton, England, in 1840, and ran away to Australia as a boy. He arrived in Bowen in 1867, and settled for a while in Townsville from 1871, where he began his business career.

A man named Henderson was the first selector at Kairi, a few miles east of Tolga, and his farm is now part of the State Government Experiment Station. Other early settlers who went in for maize growing and mixed farming were John Alexander Irvine, G. B. Rankine the surveyor, Hans Sorensen, W. T. May, Frank Halfpapp, and others. Later came Walter Holman, Herman Schaffer, James Lipscombe, John Dowling, Patrick May, Peter Favier, and the Pasettis.

The late J. J. McDonald whose parents were early maize growers near Tolga, wrote some of his reminiscences in the "North Queensland Register" dated October 4, 1969; it illustrates the hazards of travel in the area in the pioneering days. "My mother took us for a visit to the Irvines of Kairi. We had two horses in the buckboard, one a grey and the other a brown. It took over three hours to get from Tolga to Kairi, about four miles of winding track through the dense scrub. On the return journey we left later than intended, and darkness overtook us. My mother could just make out the grey horse and we had to rely on them finding the road. Alas, one of the horses was stung by a stinging tree, and we had a hectic time trying to get the maddened animals unharnessed in the dark, leaving them to find their own way home, while we walked, in pitch blackness".

The McDonalds also visited friends at Carrington, but in that direction travel was even more risky if there was a sudden storm as the scrub road south of Tolga could become impassable very quickly. On one occasion, Scrubby Creek rose suddenly. Mr. McDonald and his young brother were washed out of the buckboard and only by good luck were they able to grasp a bush and haul themselves back into the half submerged vehicle through which the flood was racing. In the other direction, it took a whole day to drive from Tolga to Mareeba to do shopping, so it meant staying the night in Mareeba.

How the settlers would have blessed the coming of the railway, making travel so much easier! The advent of the Soldier Settlement Scheme for maize growing in the Tolga-Kulara area meant an upsurge in this industry. Gone were the Chinese and their hoes, and tanks on farms for storage of maize. By 1916 the Atherton Tableland was producing nearly one million bushels of maize or thirty per cent of the Queensland crop, per year. Establishment of a maizegrowers' co-operative led to the erection of grain silos at Tolga, Kairi, and Atherton, in the early 'twenties. When the men returned from World War I., many former miners and prospectors went on the land, and what was the mining fields' loss was the farming country's gain. On Tableland maize and dairy farms a more stable way of life was found. Atherton's early newspapers, "The Barron Valley Advocate" and "Tableland Examiner" championed the cause of the settlers whenever possible.

The last year of the First World War coincided with a cyclone disaster on the North Queensland coast. The 1918 cyclone is still remembered, especially at Innisfail where, on March 10, enormous damage was caused and seventeen lives were lost. The country inland did not escape; miles of scrub east of Ravenshoe was battered, trees blocked roads, and in Herberton many buildings were badly damaged. The little mining town of Coolgarra was almost demolished.

Less than two years later, in February 1920, another cyclone roared inland over Trinity Bay; Kuranda was severely damaged, stores and houses being unroofed or collapsed. There was also considerable damage at Mareeba and as far inland as Thornborough and Chillagoe. Mt. Molloy suffered the most; the school, Jack and Newell's store, the hospital, School of Arts and many houses were demolished. The bush was denuded and trees uprooted for miles. In the scrub, the havoc was tremendous.

The cyclone of 9th. February 1927 that caused great damage in and around Cairns, brought torrential rains to the Tablelands as well as the coast. The Herbert River headwaters around Herberton received such a deluge that a wall of water went downstream upon Ingham where twenty lives were lost in the flood. There was much damage to inland railways, the Etheridge Line being in such a state that it was considered safe for only railmotor traffic, steam trains never using it again.

This caused the final closure of the Einasleigh copper mine as the ore could no longer be railed to Chillagoe smelters. The latter were also forced to close for a time. The Etheridge Railway was out of action for months in 1927 as bridges were washed away. This meant that people living along it and all Georgetown and Etheridge district folk were completely cut off as there were no roads suited to the type of motor transport then in use and, of course, no aeroplanes. The Government was then so indifferent to the needs of Northerners that they had to get on as best they could, just as in earlier times.

They therefore returned to using the means that had never failed them in the past — horse teams. Even an old Cobb & Co. coach was again used on the old road between Almaden and Georgetown. Until the Etheridge line was repaired for railmotors months later, the old Georgetown Road again heard the rumble of coach and wagon wheels, vital supplies being carried by Furber's horse team from Almaden.

Cattle, and not minerals, saved the Etheridge Railway. For

some years, diesel locomotives have hauled cattle trains along it, to Mareeba and Cairns meatworks. The trucking yards at Mt. Surprise are particularly busy during the meatwork season. It is also only cattle trains that have kept the Almaden-Mungana line open.

A railway drama, enacted in 1922, is described by the late Hugh A. Borland in his book, "Roadway of Many Memories", (1951). The hero was young Denny McGrath of Mareeba.

"Climbing perilously, "S" wagon to "S" wagon, on a run-away train speeding backward down an 1100 ft. grade, a railwayman, Denny McGrath, on the night of September 12, 1922, averted a major disaster. The train, made up of empty timber wagons and a van, had left Mareeba around midnight, and during shunting operations at Tolga, wagons and van broke lose. McGrath, by a millionth chance, was a passenger, asleep in the van. First he knew was when he woke up to find the breakaway making back to Mareeba. In its path labored another Tolga-bound train, referred to as "32 Up". The Atherton Ambulance, police, and Mareeba doctor were warned of the impending impact. But Denny McGrath, in the darkness on the swaying train, had gone truck to truck handbreaking each in turn, bringing the runaway to a halt. There was just time for him to place detonators on the rails and so save a collision and inevitable loss of life . . . . ."

Denis McGrath saved the lives of the crew of "32 Up". For his brave deed he was awarded the Clarke Gold Medal and the Railway Department gave him £50. He passed away about ten years ago.

*   *   *   *

The mechanised era dawned in 1910 with the sudden appearance of an apparition in Mareeba's unmade streets — a snorting motor car, probably the first automobile in the Cairns district. It was owned by Dr. Savage, and strangely enough, an Aborigi al named Sandy was the driver. Thus we have an original Australian, then deemed a member of one of the most

(284)

primitive races in the world, as the first man in Mareeba to manipulate the world's newest transport invention!

Although horses continued to hold their own for many years the blacksmiths' shops of the early days were gradually replaced by garages in the 'twenties. Arthur Lane was the last of the old time smithies and coachbuilders to retire, about 1950. Stan Abrahams ran the first taxi in opposition to Fred Cruickshank's horse-cab service.

Agriculturally, Mareeba had little to offer. The dry bare landscape from May to November, and sometimes longer, deterred most farmers who preferred instead the greener Tablelands. Maize and vegetables and a few fruit trees seemed to be all that could be grown, and on a small scale. Cotton was successfully grown by Walter Hastie and others near Mareeba in 1922, but the industry did not become established.

James Dowie, headmaster at Mareeba State School for many years prior to 1926, and W. J. Harland, head teacher from 1926 to 1933, were the first to set an example of planting shade trees, and the Shire Council and Race Club soon followed suit. The weeping figs in Byrnes Street, many of them now having reached the end of their usefulness, were planted during the shire chairmanships of E. A. Atherton and G. H. O'Donnell.

The seats under those trees in Byrnes Street were the favourite meeting places of the old timers for more than forty years; there they could yarn about the long dead past — they made it come alive — with mates of other days. Now most of them have to use the seats placed under shop verandahs which are not so restful or secluded as the old ones under the trees. The weeping figs made Mareeba's main street one of the most pleasant in the State. They have not been retained without a fight for road-planners wanted to convert the nature strip into a highway. To do so would have ruined the character of Mareeba. Many of the pioneers of the Far North have made their homes in this town.

Back in 1922, Mareeba was lighted by benzine burning

lamps — W. G. Reynolds was the lamplighter — and it was July 1936 before the town was lighted with electricity from the Barron Falls. These hydro-electric works were begun in 1932 and the first stage completed in 1935. Extensions, including two dams, have been made since which, while increasing the output of power, have succeeded in spoiling what was once North Queensland's greatest tourist attraction next to the Great Barrier Reef — the Barron Falls. For most of the year they are now so dry that many tourists believe the name is correctly "barren falls". Water can, however, be released to flow on special occasions such as for the benefit of visiting V.I.P.'s. No doubt John Doyle would be aghast to see the price of progress!

Many ex-miners from Irvinebank worked on the construction of the hydro works and the construction camp had so many men from that centre that it was known as "Little Irvinebank". Under the direction of Jim Dawson, once underground boss at the Vulcan Mine, a 1200 ft. tunnel was driven for the turbines.

Erection of power lines with massive timber poles to Cairns and Mareeba around 1935 was no mean feat, and it is interesting to recall that in this work the bullock teams were invaluable; there were no bulldozers or four-wheel-drive vehicles at that time. Rod Veivers of Kuranda, with his bullock team, did most of this work. The power line was erected along part of the old wagon road down the range to near Smithfield, and Veivers' team would have been the first to use it since the late Eighteen-seventies.

Incidentally, Arthur Olive, later a Mareeba tobacco farmer, drove a four-cylinder one-ton Chevrolet truck up this incredibly steep track about 1928. It was probably the first and only motor to tackle this route, long before the present highway was built.

Bullock teams were in use hauling logs from the scrub in the Kuranda and Mt. Molloy areas until the early 'fifties, Charlie Morton, Percy Newman, and Pashen having some of the last teams before the bulldozers took over. Many parts of the Coastal Ranges and Tablelands were inaccessible for motor trucks, but on the roads they gradually ousted the bullock teams. Mechanical haulage to Lawsons' mill at Mareeba began around 1925 when Leyland and Mercedes "steam wagons" were used. One or two of the bullockies did not give up without a fight, however. The engine of one of the "steamers" was blown up with a stick of gelignite.

Many of the early day teamsters spent the close of their era timber-hauling on the Tableland and around Mt. Molloy in the 'twenties. Horse teams of sixteen or eighteen animals were used on the open road — it was a fine sight to see them bringing in logs to the mill at Ravenshoe as late as 1933 — while in the scrub, bullocks were preferred. Teams of up to 26 bullocks were used.

Some of these latter-day teamsters around Mt. Molloy in the 'twenties were Jim Edwards, Mick McNamara, Stafford Clacherty, Henry Gadd, Bill Kells, Jacky White, Joe Leber, Herb Chambers, Ted Strike, and Jim and Abe Rolls. Some, like the Rolls Bros., had been old Hodgkinson carriers.

One old timer tells of a man and wife team who worked a tin claim on Big Woolaman Creek, south-east from Herberton, at this same period. They carried their tin in bags on their backs twelve miles into Irvinebank, including two crossings of the 3000 ft. Mt. Misery range, and carried their supplies home the same way. The miners who hung on, after the good times were past and tin prices were so low they could barely survive, had the hearts of lions. Many lived to ripe old age, still working, like Jim Howarth of the Nettle Creek diggings who was still actively mining at the age of ninety-eight, and then lost his life in a car accident on the Mt. Garnet-Ravenshoe road.

In 1924, the struggling dairy farmers in the Julatten area just north of Mt. Molloy, formed a co-operative and built a butter factory at Bushy Creek, and it endured for forty years. In 1926, the Mt. Molloy railway was extended some miles northward to Rumula to tap timber and dairying lands. It is an interesting point that at one time this was the most northerly place in Australia to which one could travel by train from the Southern States.

Now there is very little dairying and no railway, the latter replaced by bitumen roads. With the decline in dairying and the recession in the beef industry, the economy of such areas as this is at a low ebb. Those who hang on need the tenacity of their forebears. This is still Pioneers' Country!

CHAPTER 19

DREAMS FULFILLED

The Great Depression — Latter Day Pioneers — Impact of World War II — Water Means Wealth — Prosperity Now, such as the Pioneers Dreamed About.

The Mareeba railway yards are quiet now.

Yet Mareeba was once a railway town with employment for a couple of hundred men. In the years between the World Wars, there was always the sound of trains, the whistles of locomotives, the noise of steam, the crash of buffers and couplings — Mareeba was a busy railway junction. During the Second World War with troop trains and supply trains taking men and the sinews of war to and from the training areas on the Tableland, the railway was at its busiest.

But with peace and the passing of steam, closure of the branch lines to Mt. Garnet, Mt. Molloy, Dimbulah-Mt. Mulligan, and the Tolga-Millaa Millaa line, the railway yards quietened, trains became less and less, until now the maze of tracks are almost deserted and it is a rarety to see a train shunting. Motor transport has almost ousted the Iron Horse.

With the passing of the steam trains, a lot of the old life went out of Mareeba, replaced by other sights and sounds common to progressive towns everywhere — speeding traffic, neon lights, and supermarkets.

The Foxwood timber mill — for long years it was "Lawson's" — and its smoking chimneys still dominates the main street; once on the outskirts it is now almost in the centre of town. In this pollution-conscious age, the mill may some day be forced to move, but meanwhile it remains as it has always been, a symbol of industry in Mareeba.

The town's next most important industrial project was the Bacon Factory, established in 1923. The late Hugh A. Borland declared that surely "Mareeba was the favourite of the gods for it was given a bacon factory in spite of the fact that not a pig is reared within tens of miles of the town." Well, very few, anyway.

The Floreat Bacon Factory was a co-operative concern like many other primary industry outlets on the Tableland and was due mainly to the efforts of W. C. Abbott, M. Lynch, and others. Mr. C. Dunlop was manager for many years. Only recently have smallgoods ceased to be manufactured; this was a blow to decentralisation and a loss in employment. It is ironical that it was found cheaper to bring smallgoods eleven hundred miles from Brisbane than to manufacture them locally. Combined with its cattle slaughtering section, the bacon factory has been a wonderful asset to Mareeba and district over the years.

In 1936 the present railway trucking yards were built. Highly successful cattle sales began in special yards nearby from May 1948, the prime mover being W. H. (Bert) Simms, a well known Mareeba stock and station agent for many years and now living in retirement in Bundaberg. Cattlemen like Ken Atkinson and his sons, the late Walter Lawrence, Paul Hawkins, and Maurice de Tournouer were associated with this enterprise, North Queensland Saleyards Ltd. In the years of high prices, cattle sales brought a million dollars a year to Mareeba. Some successful horse sales have been held there recently.

When the saleyards opened, large mobs of cattle were brought on the hoof, and later by road transport, from Peninsula stations. The Chillagoe and Etheridge railways were also busy with cattle traffic. Cattlemen and horsemen have always been attracted to Mareeba, and when an annual rodeo was commenced in the late 'forties, it drew them like a magnet. From small beginnings, the rodeo has grown to one of the biggest in Australia, with champion riders competing for thousands of dollars in prize money. The rodeo in July is always well supported by the public, and is increasing in popularity, crowds of up to 18,000 not being unusual.

The fortunes of Chillagoe have waxed and waned ever

(290)

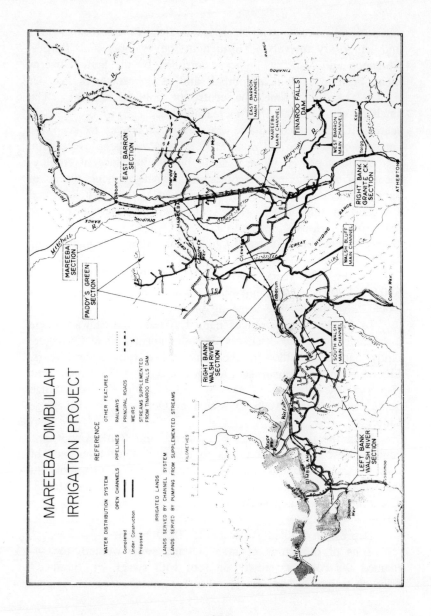

MAREEBA DIMBULAH
IRRIGATION PROJECT

REFERENCE

WATER DISTRIBUTION SYSTEM   OTHER FEATURES

OPEN CHANNELS   PIPELINES   RAILWAYS

Completed   PRINCIPAL ROADS
Under Construction   WEIRS
Proposed   STREAMS SUPPLEMENTED
                                         FROM TINAROO FALLS DAM

IRRIGATED LANDS

LANDS SERVED BY CHANNEL SYSTEM

LANDS SERVED BY PUMPING FROM SUPPLEMENTED STREAMS

KILOMETRES
2   0   2   4   6   8

EAST BARRON SECTION

MAREEBA SECTION

PADDY'S GREEN SECTION

EAST BARRON MAIN CHANNEL

MAREEBA MAIN CHANNEL

TINAROO FALLS DAM

WEST BARRON MAIN CHANNEL

RIGHT BANK GRANITE CK SECTION

WALSH BLUFF MAIN CHANNEL

RIGHT BANK WALSH RIVER SECTION

SOUTH WALSH MAIN CHANNEL

LEFT BANK WALSH RIVER SECTION

(291)

since its discovery, with temporary closures of the smelters and temporary revivals. Throughout the 'twenties and 'thirties, Chillagoe and Mungana mines, controlled by the State Government, became a political football and at one stage, in Premier E. G. Theodore's time, the centre of political scandal. The smelters were operated at increasing loss, and as ore became scarcer it was railed all the way from Cloncurry to keep the smelters open. The old mine at O.K. was also gone over again. The smelters proved to be a small but useful place of employment during the Great Depression. Finally, under threat of Japanese invasion and scarcity of manpower, the smelters closed for good in July, 1943. Ten years later they were dismantled and sold. Houses fetched £12 at auction. (Real estate advertisements in 1979 listed Chillagoe building allotments at up to $1500 each).

In the fifty years, 1909-59, the Chillagoe Field yielded $10,000,000 worth of minerals. The previous twenty years would have yielded the same again.

In 1923, two Aborigines named Archer and Stewart made a valuable silver-lead discovery 28 miles north-west of Chillagoe. Aptly named Nightflower, the mine lasted only a few years. Fluorspar mining began at Chillagoe around 1928 which year also saw the opening of the Mt. Garnet tin dredge. Huge quantities of lime have been mined at Ootan on the Etheridge Line.

With the tin dredges at Mt. Garnet and Battle Creek, the country west of Herberton was to again produce thousands of tons of tin, but it did not cause the boom and prosperity to the whole area as had tin mining in the days of John Moffat. The era of the independent prospector was ending.

*   *   *   *

Depression stalked Australia as 1930 began.

Tens of thousands of men — and some women, too — roamed the country, mostly on foot with swags, or "jumped" rides on trains, in hopeless searches for work.

(292)

But in the Far North, in the Mareeba district, there was optimism in a new industry: tobacco growing. Unfortunately, the depression caused many inexperienced people to jump at the chance of what they thought would be easy money by farming. It was not easy work and if one made good at it, it was like winning a lottery. All farming is a gamble and tobacco growing at that time proved to be the biggest gamble of all. It is different now, with irrigation and scientific know-how.

Tobacco growing is the basis of Mareeba's present prosperity — it brought $22,480,603 to the local growers in 1974-75. Six and a half million kilograms of leaf were sold. Other crops grown in the irrigation area were worth $342,400.

From early successes through the depths of tragedy to success again, the industry struggled through many discouraging years.

In 1928, the first tobacco trials were conducted by N. A. R. Pollock of the Queensland Department of Agriculture and Stock (now Primary Industry) and R. A. Howell, a Commonwealth officer. Results were so satisfactory that in 1929, the Bruce-Page Federal Government approved the Mareeba-Dimbulah area for tobacco growing, and early in 1930 the Moore State Government threw open large areas of this land for selection; portions of it were cleared with relief labour, but generally each selector had to do his own improvements, and often his own road to provide access. Sometimes it was a minor feat of bushmanship to find the block the eager selector had taken up on the map. Here was pioneering such as the folk of an earlier day faced.

Horses were still the main motive power. There were a few steel-wheel tractors and out on Cattle Creek one old traction engine (Penfold's), but most of the new settlers set to and grubbed out the tough old box and bloodwood trees by hand or with the help of a horse-powered tree-puller; they used axes and mattocks from daylight till dark, and then stacked fires to burn logs and stumps far into the night. Slowly a few acres were cleared on each selection, barns and kilns erected. Five hundred acres were planted in the 1930-31 season.

Despite scarcity of water on many blocks for watering out the young tobacco plants, crops were generally good and the weather kind that first season. The yield averaged 600 lbs. of leaf to the acre. The district crop was worth £38,000. That was big money in that depression time. Mareeba was a boom town. New shops were built, new businesses to serve the farmers were opened, new homes were erected as the population grew. There was jubilation on the hundred or more farms that had sprung up. Leaf prices averaged 30c per pound.

More farms were opened in 1931. Now there were farms in what had been the poor-class grazing country at Chewko, Paddy's Green, The Springs, Tinaroo Creek, Emerald Creek, Shanty Creek, along the Barron, the Clohesy, and on Lower Leadingham, Eureka Creek, and the Walsh around Dimbulah. Instead of being only a railway junction, Dimbulah became a thriving township. In 1931-32, four thousand acres of tobacco was planted.

Then came unfavourable tariff revisions imposed by the Lyons Government, coupled with unseasonal weather. There was too much rain or not enough, or rain at the wrong time. Leaf would not cure; 1932 was the "black year" when blue mould and other diseases swept the farms. Insect pests also appeared. With limited scientific knowledge available and few insecticides, the industry almost collapsed.

Hundreds of new-chum farmers, and brave souls who had risked their all, lost everything. From 1200 growers in 1932, numbers dropped to less than 600. The slump had bad repercussions on Mareeba business, and it was at least a decade before the district lived down an undeserved bad name. The scores of abandoned properties bore mute evidence of the tragedy.

Only the hardiest, the real farmers, and those possessed of the true pioneering spirit hung on and saved the industry. The most favoured were those whose farms were located on water. These battlers were Australians, Italians, Albanians, Yugoslavs, and a few Irish and Scots. Some were reduced to living on kangaroo-rats and wearing sugarbags, but they hung on. So they could stay on their farms — usually only by courtesy of the Bank — some grew vegetables, cowpeas, maize, peanuts, and millet. Gradually things improved.

Throughout the hard times, the pioneering spirit showed through. One battler who received a cheque for four shillings and sixpence (45c) for his entire crop after expenses were deducted, framed it.

From an all-time low price of 24c per pound in 1944-45, the price gradually climbed to 34c. in 1947-48, the last low price year, and with increased scientific assistance available and the introduction of DDT and other fumigants, tobacco growing was not such a risk as formerly.

In 1946 it was possible to buy a "dry" farm anywhere in the district for as low as £250; one with a lot of improvements such as good buildings may fetch £600, and one with irrigation available may realise £1500. One of these latter farms today, with machinery and improvements would be worth from $100,000 to $250,000 according to improvements and the size of the tobacco quota. Nowadays, instead of a shack or an enclosed verandah of a barn serving as living quarters, farmers have beautiful homes of brick or concrete with all city amenities.

Typical of the tobacco farm pioneers were Mr. and Mrs. Wally Reichardt. They retired in Mareeba in a lovely home after forty years tobacco growing on Leadingham Creek, six miles from Dimbulah. Wally died in 1978. The couple were an example of the tenacity and faith needed to make a success in this land that is still Pioneers' Country. Without it they would never have achieved the distinction, in 1954, of sceuring the then world record price of 210 pence (about one dollar) per pound for their superb quality lemon leaf. Mr. Ken Martin, then secretary of the Tobacco Leaf Marketing Board, stated this leaf was the finest quality in the world, and also the best on world grading standards. Mrs. Reichardt had done the grading herself.

The Reichardts' success was the result of twenty-three years' struggle. Time after time their crops had failed because of the weather or insects, but they never gave in, even though water had to be carted in a 300 gallon tank on a vintage-model truck from the Walsh River three miles away to water the crop — four truckloads to the acre, carting and watering by hand every day, gambling that the rains would come at the right time after the many rainless months of the dry season. There were some eight thousand plants to the acre, each placed there by hand and each with a paper cover to protect it from the sun in its early stages; eight to sixteen acres were grown every year. The ground would have been laboriously prepared with a single-disc plough or a disc cultivator drawn by a horse and a mule. It was years before Wally Reichardt could afford the luxury of a tractor. If the crop failed because of rain at the wrong time, hail, drought, or blue mould, Wally would grow cowpeas or maize or cut timber for the Mt. Mulligan mines, but he still planted out his tobacco when the season came around again.

He and his brave wife reared their family in a lonely cottage of bush timber and corrugated iron without the benefit of electricity or even a kerosene refrigerator. Mrs. Reichardt cooked on a wood stove and washed in kerosene tins. It was typical of farm homes in the 'thirties and 'forties. The children rode ponies six miles to school each day and in the wet season the Walsh River would be in flood, often too dangerous to be forded.

The Reichardts, like scores of other farmers, would never have eventually achieved prosperity without irrigation.

Only since about 1947 has the need been fully realised, though there were a few voices crying in the wilderness long before then. For years, irrigation was the dream of Mr. Edgar Short, a Dimbulah farmer and chartered accountant, who visualised a huge irrigation scheme utilising Walsh River water in floodtime with a series of weirs to conserve it with pipes or channels to take it to the lower lands around Dimbulah.

His fieldwork and exertions through the North Queensland Tobacco Growers' Co-operative Association, and then the Tobacco Leaf Marketing Board — which created orderly marketing and realistic prices — influenced parliamentarians like Harold Collins, M.L.A., and finally the Queensland Government to embark upon the even more imaginative Mareeba-Dimbulah Irrigation Scheme using the Barron River and then estimated to cost between £19 million and £22 million, in 1952. The work of Mr. Short was recognised by the Queen who bestowed on him the O.B.E.

Pioneers of tobacco growers' organisation were, as well as Edgar Short, Ernie de Lacey, William Henderson, Tom Gilmore, Ralph Leinster, Norman Studt. OBE., and Messrs. Mesh, Walker, Veness, Faichney, Henson, and others. For a while "N.Q." brand cigarettes and loose tobacco were manufactured in Mareeba and successfully marketed. In Dimbulah, the "F.H.V." brand was produced in the mid-fifties by Messrs. Faichney, Henson, and Veness in their own factory.

A big programme of weir construction, begun in 1946, was the forerunner of full scale irrigation. The first weir was on Emerald Creek with a modest capacity of 44 acre feet, followed by a weir on Granite Creek holding 198 acre feet in 1948. The latter was the first mass-concrete construction. The following year, the largest weir, the Bruce on the Walsh River, with 790 acre feet capacity, was completed. Another Walsh River weir, the Leafgold, finished in 1952, and one on Eureka Creek, provided irrigation for farms west of Dimbulah. Upstream, the Collins Weir was opened in 1953. These weirs enabled tobacco growing to expand to about 2200 acres by 1953 and the crop brought in over £2 million ($4 million) for the first time.

The stage was then set for the construction of the great Tinaroo Dam, the key to the whole scheme, and completed in

1958. The first large dam to be built in Queensland for irrigation, it filled on 31st. March 1963. It holds 330,000 acre feet of water and the resulting lake, covering about 8300 acres, is one of the prime tourist and sporting attractions in the Far North. It is ideal for boating, water-skiing, and the like.

For the first time, water that Nature destined for the Pacific Ocean was diverted by means of 200 miles of pipes and concrete channels to irrigate farmland and to flow into Western or Gulf Waters. With Tinaroo storage on the Barron River being over a thousand feet higher than the Mareeba-Dimbulah lands, it was estimated at the time that 78,000 acres could be irrigated, providing for 1400 farms, all by gravitation without pumping. (In 1952, only 2000 acres could be irrigated). Dry creekbeds were turned into permanently running streams with water from Tinaroo channels. The scheme is still by no means complete.

In 1975, the total area under irrigation in the Mareeba-Dimbulah area was 5370 hectares on 567 farms.

There is still plenty of scope for expansion with irrigated pastures and crops other than tobacco. In fact, it is a pity that a district such as this should have tobacco, a recognised enemy to health, as its main source of wealth. Food producing crops should be found to replace tobacco in the area's economy. It has been proved that a great variety of crops can be grown. Rice growing, now being tried on the Arriga lands, could usher in another valuable crop for this district. However, full use of the Tinaroo Dam water cannot be made while a portion of its output is needed for hydro-electric power at the Barron Falls. Legumes, pastures and pasture seeds, vegetables, maize, and citrus grow well in the area. Two large Research Stations are carrying out vital work with a variety of crop trials.

Irrigation has created one of Australia's most prosperous regions. The dreams of the pioneers are being fulfilled. If irrigation could also come to the area between Ravenshoe and Mt. Garnet, from the Herbert River, another good farming region could be established. Tobacco has been grown on a small scale at Innot Hot Springs for years with varying success. It has also been grown at Watsonville and Chillagoe. A successful group of farms exists on the Mary River between Mt. Molloy and Mt. Carbine; tobacco has been grown there since 1957.

*   *   *   *

World War II was an interlude which, although causing setbacks in production, helped with development such as bitumen roads, and the tens of thousands of servicemen who were stationed at Mareeba and at Rocky Creek, Wondecla, and Ravenshoe, returned to their home areas keen ambassadors for this beautiful corner of North Queensland; many returned to take up residence after the war.

One of the biggest wartime air bases was situated at Mareeba. The huge airfield was carved out of bush and farmland on the Atherton road in 1942 when Japanese invasion threatened. From it, United States "Flying Fortresses" flew on nightly bombing missions against the Japanese in New Guinea, the Solomons, and other Pacific islands.

Mareeba was an important bastion in the defence of Australia, and its airfield definitely helped to stem the southward push of the enemy. Today, part of the wartime airstrip provides the only sealed strip in use in the Cairns Hinterland, but it is not a licensed aerodrome. It is controlled by the Mareeba Shire Council and is used by charter operators, private aircraft, and for aerial spraying.

When Mareeba and the Tablelands were "invaded" by American and Australian troops, local residents did a magnificent job in entertaining and assisting the sick and wounded. Many men today remember the big Army hospital at Rocky Creek. The "igloo" picture theatre building still stands there, in the bush, and is now a private residence. The free-spending Americans, thinking nothing of paying the then unheard of price of £1 ($2.00) for a watermelon, were the delight of Mareeba farmers and shopkeepers.

George Bryden, writing in "Far North Focus" on September 8, 1975, recalled that the girls of the Tableland towns had to have especial stamina when attending dances. At one dance in Herberton there were twenty girls and two thousand soldiers! Good Tableland vegetables and dairy produce, and the bracing climate, did much to refit the men of the Sixth, Seventh, and Ninth Australian Divisions for further battles in the islands to the north. Wrote Bryden:

"Thousands of these young Australians did not return from these Island battlefields. Those that did will always remember the Atherton Tableland. Many return to visit but all that remains to show that an army once camped there are stone fireplaces and crumbling training trenches."

Another big development scheme for the Tableland country and affecting a larger area, was the Tully Falls hydro-electric scheme involving harnessing the falls and building the 150 ft. high Koombaloomba Dam impounding an area of four thousand acres of water. In 1952 it was described as "the most ambitious scheme of its kind yet undertaken in North Queensland." It was designed to produce 73,800 k.w. of power, and the first became available in 1955. The cost was around £12 million. Tully Falls are now an integral part of the North Queensland electric power system.

In 1955, Herberton celebrated the 75th. anniversary of its foundation. A tablet was unveiled by Hon. H. Collins M.L.A. on a stone cairn near the post office to commemorate the fact, and also to honour Newell, Jack, Brandon, Brown, and party who discovered the Great Northern tin lode in 1880.

Celebrating its centenary in 1980, Herberton remains, dreaming of the past with many of its buildings — that is, those which have escaped the wreckers' hammer — redolent of the boom days of mining. Though it may never see such prosperous times again, the town is solidly established, and new sources of wealth may well unfold. Tin is still its wealth, however. The reconstructed Great Northern battery (now a modern "metal concentrator") processes $2 million worth of tin per annum from various mines.

Its climate, 2893 feet above sea level makes Herberton one of the healthiest places in Australia, and this alone is a great asset. So too is its old-world peace and charm, its flowers of a temperate climate, the violet haze of jacaranda blooms in spring, and its setting among age-old mountains. Although within the tropical zone and only eighty miles from Cairns, the climate is such that grapes, apples, peaches, and all kinds of vegetables flourish. Even wheat has been grown on the fringe of the dairy lands. The vineyards at Kalunga produce excellent grapes and this industry could expand.

The Herberton Shire covers 2480 square miles, and the town has a population of about one thousand. The present Shire grew out of the Tinaroo Divisional Board of 1880 which originally included the old Walsh Shire and the Eacham and Atherton Shires. The latter was separated in 1896.

What is now the Mareeba Shire was at one time part of three Divisional Boards as they were called before Federation. These were Barron, Woothakata, and Walsh, with headquarters at Cairns, Thornborough, and Montalbion respectively. The Woothakata Divisional Board with an area of 24,870 square miles was constituted on 11th. November 1879, at Thornborough, as previously mentioned.

The Walsh Divisional Board with an area of 4110 square miles was constituted on 18th. May 1889. It was created from part of the Tinaroo Board, then at Herberton. The Walsh headquarters were subsequently moved from Montalbion to Irvinebank.

The Barron Divisional Board was created on 20th. December 1890, and until 1919 it included the town of Mareeba, but met in Cairns. On 1st. January 1909, the Chillagoe Shire came into existence from part of the Woothakata and Walsh Shires, but its life was comparatively short. W. Chandler was the first chairman.

Finally, in 1919, local agitation brought about Mareeba's transfer from the Barron Shire to the Woothakata Shire with Mareeba its headquarters instead of Thornborough which was almost a ghost town.

On 15th. April 1932, both the Chillagoe and Walsh Shires were abolished and included in Woothakata. This meant that Chillagoe and Irvinebank ceased to be Shire "capitals". On 20th. December 1947, the name was changed to Mareeba Shire. Its area is 20,430 square miles. This is almost twice the size of the Kingdom of Belgium. But whereas Belgium has almost as many people as the whole of Australia, the Mareeba Shire has a population of about 13,000, almost half of whom live in the town of Mareeba.

*   *   *   *

In this story of the development of a vast region inland — "over the range" — from Cairns and the coastal fringe, the reader will probably be struck by the successes of private enterprise over the years; and especially how the hard work of individuals — miners, graziers, farmers, and others — contributed to progress.

In private enterprise there was first of all, John Moffat and his associated companies, their production value running into millions of pounds — in the days before the dollar. The Chillagoe Company which, like John Moffat, built railways, opened mines, and caused towns to rise. And lastly the Dairy Co-operatives, the Maizegrowers' Co-operative, the Bacon Factory Co-operative, the Tobacco Growers' Co-operative, and other similar organisations. They have all been of immense developmental value to this part of Australia. Only private enterprise in the hands of far-seeing men could have brought it about.

Such is the story of a picturesque region of North Queensland, rich in history and of the courage of the pioneers. Their story is but briefly told here — there is enough to fill a much larger volume, but much also has been lost in the mists of one hundred years; names, too, of many worthy folk will have

(302)

been omitted.

To these people — the Unknown Pioneers — this book is dedicated.

THE   END

APPENDIX

Here are the names of some of the great many carriers (horse and bullock teamsters) and packers (horses and mules) who played a vital role in opening up this Pioneers' Country behind Cairns from 1877 to the coming of first the railway, then motor transport. Between 1877 and 1893, there were thirty horse teams with wagons, forty-four bullock teams, and thirty pack teams operating on the old Port Douglas Road. Some may be missed out, or lost in the passing years; but a number of the descendants of these pioneers are with us still. These men were packers:

Rudolf Berzinski, Emil Berzinski, George Young, Barney Hines, Charlie Muller, John Marnane, Bill Marnane, Harry Corbett, Hugh Bradford, Jack Cairns, Bill Griffin, Christie Thygesen, W. Ardah, Charlie O'Brien, John McDonnell, Jim McNamara, Dick Donelly, Tom Meredith, Joe Mascal, Jack McCabe, Tom Totten, Jim Sorensen, Gabriel Sorensen, Harry Fischer, "Sergeant" Hill, Tom Harvey, Will Atherton, "Tom the Greek", "Peter the Greek", "George the Greek", "Sam the Roman", Harry Dick, Borghero Bros., and others.

Horse and bullock teamsters on the Port Douglas Road included: Bill Patterson, Ted Palmer, Billy Tucker, Christie Keys, Tom Beataib, Joe Coffil, Jack Trezise, Bill Logue, Bill Bussey, Jack O'Brien, Bill Cleland, Bill Wieland, Hans Wieland, Alec Stewart, Alex Thompson, Peter Peterson, — Keating, Charlie Logue, Tim Martin, Jack Orchard, Jim Murphy, Jacob Althus, Bob Gordon, Louis Peterson, Harry Smithson, John Lovell, Mick Boland, Bill Fitzgerald, Jack Bailey, Jack Mullavey, Ted Gane, Malachi McGrath, Dick Lloyd, Joe Eccles, Mick Tyrell, Bill Graham, John Alexander, Joe Hines, George Jackson, Archie Gibson, Jack O'Neal, Jack Holmes, Jack White, Dick Ryan, Jack Langtree, Con Behan, George Greenwood, Alex Hemmings, Mick Bannon, Tom Thompson, Jim Reynolds, "Parson" Wade, Ted Troughton, George Bell, Harry Gliddon, Bill Levis, Dick Cuddy, Frank McGrath, Tom Ellem, Pat Molloy,

Fred Holmes, Charlie Emmerson, John Hambling, George Kidner, Bill Clarke, Ted Malone, Phil Garland, Bill Louden, George McLeod, Ben Pierce, Tom Horan, Tom Quinn, John Ford, Jim Tait.

Most of the above names were supplied by the late Walter Trezise, a Port Douglas pioneer. A memorial to the teamsters and packers has been erected on the site of Craiglie, a carriers' township on the old road, four miles out of Port Douglas.

There were other teamsters on the roads through the Mareeba and Herberton districts and the following are remembered, but some will have been missed: Bill Lewis, J. Leidingham, Paddy Macnamara, C. Standen, T. Hallam, Tom Moody, Martin Willies, T. Prior, Stewart Bolton, Jack O'Neil, Jack Cahill, Bill Tucker, Jim Sloan, J. O'Brien, Keron Glendon, Paddy Tracy, Dan Gallant, Jack Hales, Jack Casey, Friday Butcher, Healy Bros., Rolls Bros., Jock Hay.

Some of the carriers were packers also at one time or another. Here are some of the carriers who drove for the Irvinebank Company: Jim Donovan (his team appears in a photo of Irvinebank dated 1884), Alex McLennan, Bill Dougherty, Bert Royes, Dan Culhane, George Crook, Jack Ramm, Sandy Gollan, Jim Best, Jack Stern, Tom Mills, Bill Sheppard, Bill McCormick (later Premier of Queensland), Jack O'Keefe (later MLA for Cairns), Bill Bennett (he had a team of 14 dapple-greys), Tom McBride, Jim Bohan, Alf Burnell, Charlie Flannigan, George Rose, Bill Prouse, Geo. Conway, Geo. Fallon, Charlie Green, Sheehan Bros., Geo. Creighton, Jack McAllister, Wat Ray, Jack Tunnie, Tom and Jack Hooper, Tom Donnelly, Charlie Hansen, Ted Rouse, Bob Kerridge, Bill Johnston, Geo. Gane, Dave Wilson.

BIBLIOGRAPHY

Pioneer Pageant, by Glenville Pike (1952).

In the Path of the Pioneers, by Glenville Pike (Herberton Shire Council, 1952).

The Men Who Blazed the Track, by Glenville Pike (Mulgrave Shire Council, 1956).

John Atherton, by Glenville Pike (Mareeba Shire Council, 1957).

Cairns Historical Society Bulletins, Numbers 24, 29, 106, 140, 142, 143, 158, 163, 194.

From Wilderness to Wealth, by Hugh A. Borland, 1940.

Mareeba, by Hugh A. Borland, 1946.

Roadway of Many Memories, by Hugh A. Borland, 1951.

"Hodgkinson Mining News" files, 1876-77 (Parl. Library, Brisbane).

"Cummins and Campbell's Monthly Magazine", Townsville, 1937-57.

So Passes Glory, by Ellen E. Arnold (Aust. Agricultural Co., 1973).

History of Cairns, by J. W. Collinson (5 vols. 1939).

"Queenslander" files, 1905.

"Cairns Post", cuttings.

Copper Mines and Mineral Fields of Q'land, by Wm. Lees.

Articles by "The Drifter", W. H. Peterson, "Rusty Spurs", "Timber", "Molloyite", and others, in "N.Q. Register" 1969-76. Also by T. Crowe, 1951.

A Flower Hunter in Queensland, by Mrs. Ellis Rowan (Angus & Robertson, 1898).

Lectures on North Queensland History, Second Series 1975 (James Cook University).

Pugh's Almanac, 1907.

"Wild River Times" Magazine, Herberton, files 1974-75.

"Far North Focus", Cairns, Sept. 8. 1975.

Northmost Australia, vol. ii., by Dr. Robert Logan Jack (Simpkin, London, 1921).

Roads of Yesterday, by Glenville Pike (1977).

Veins of Carbine Hill, by R. Rudd and G. Pike (Qld. Wolfram, 1978).

PICTORIAL HISTORY

James Venture Mulligan, one of North Queensland's greatest prospectors and explorers. 1837-1907.

(307)

A typical prospector at work in the days of the gold rushes to the Palmer and Hodgkinson.

View of rugged country looking towards Kingsborough from the Tyrconnell Mine, today. Lonely and silent now, this area was a hive of activity a century ago.

—*Author*

This boiler, lying rusting on a mountain-top at the deserted General Grant Mine at Kingsborough, may have been the one that carrier Ted Troughton hauled over The Bump from Port Douglas in 1878 with 48 bullocks yoked four abreast. It weighed nearly ten tons.

(309)   —*Author*

The burial of William Fanning, the first of many to die in the early days of the Hodgkinson gold rush; probably on the site of Kingsborough, and Gold Commissioner Howard St. George is presiding.

(By courtesy Oxley Library).

Pioneers George Jackson and his wife sleep on the site of their labors, among the trees they planted on Leadingham Creek.
—Author

Once the Main Road from Port Douglas to the Hodgkinson, where it crossed Leadingham Creek. Wheel ruts and ancient blazed trees clearly mark parts of this road the Pioneers knew.
—Author

The Tyrconnell gold mine in its heyday, when it was the greatest on the Hodgkinson.

Trail riders pause at the old Tyrconnell mine. Part of the Cairns Centenary celebrations was a journey by horsemen from Thornborough to Cairns to re-enact the pioneers' trek to the coast in September 1876.

Cairns Centenary Comtee photo.

The rough crossing of Explorer Creek below the Tyrconnell. Near here is Glen Mowbray, a valley in the ranges where hundreds of miners gathered threatening to lynch Mulligan in mid-1876. The area is now quite deserted.

—Author

The steepness of the rough Rob Roy Hill on the washed-out track to Kingsborough tests the strength of a modern Toyota (arrowed), but the old time teamsters hauled wagons loaded with up to 13 tons of mining machinery up grades like this, with 36 horses.

—Author

(314)

This was how roads were built in 1877: Remains of the main coach and wagon road between Thornborough and the coast where it crossed Caledonia (also called Butcher's) Creek between Thornborough and Kingsborough. — Ron Burnett, photo.

There are only two houses in Thornborough today. In foreground is the boiler from Martin's crushing battery, one of the earliest on the Hodgkinson. — R. Burnett, photo.

(1) *A home in Thornborough in 1887, that of I. Williams.*
(2) *Carl Alex Egerstrom in his garden about 1887. He carved his own tombstone from a nearby rock and was buried here in 1900. Poinciana trees still bloom over it.*
(3) *Martins' home in Thornborough, 1887.*

"Carinya" in Thornborough, the home of John Rank. It was moved to Mareeba about 1920 and still stands in Walsh Street.
—D. Webb, photo.

1 2 3 4

5 6 7 8

MEN OF THE HODGKINSON SEVENTY-FIVE YEARS AGO

1. Mr. Collins, battery manager. 2. E. Rawson, assayer. 3. Frank Grainer, storekeeper. 4. J. Rank, commission agent and later Woothakata shire clerk. 5. N. Knudstrup, battery manager and engineer. 6. J. Harris, mine manager. 7. Gielis, hotel-keeper. 8. E. Leisner, miner.

GEORGE J. EVANDEN

Pioneer building constractor at Thornborough and member of Woothakata Divisional Board (Shire) for 22 years, being Chairman several times. This photo was taken in 1906, a year before his death. Both he and his wife were born in Rochester, England. Their children were George, Will, Louisa, Edward, Frederick, Jonathan, and Isabella Matilda (Bell).

—D. Webb, photo.

Mathewson,   Brisbane.

Mrs. Emma Evanden, wife of George Evanden, who died at Thornborough in July 1888. With her is her youngest daughter, Louisa, who married John Rank of Thornborough. She was born in Brisbane and came to Thornborough when two years of age, being carried up The Bump Road from Port Douglas by Bill Louden in 1877. She died at 91 years of age.

—D. Webb, photo.

Some of the ladies of Thornborough, and Freeman's Hotel, about 1890.

Remnants of the Hodgkinson region's Aboriginal tribes gather at the Court House, Thornborough, about 1890 for annual hand-out of blankets and clothes by the police. Note many are carrying spears.

This is the way little girls looked in their "Sunday best" back in 1908. Gladys Rank, of Thornborough, aged nine years. The photo was taken on September 1, 1908, by H. P. Brims' "Britannia Studio" at Mareeba.

—Photo from D. Webb.

THORNBOROUGH, N.Q., A ONE-TIME RICH GOLDFIELD

1.—*Old Police Station.*
3.—*The Township.*

2.—*Court House.*
4.—*What remains of the Old Assay Office and smelters.*

A THORNBOROUGH WEDDING, FEBRUARY 1903

Centre, Standing: Mr. W. A. Pepper, bridegroom; Miss E. A. Williams, bride.

Rear, standing, l. to r.: A. Carson, best man; Lily Williams, bridesmaid; J. Williams, brother of bride; and Susie Williams (right) bridesmaid.

Seated: Rev. Mr. Barton; Mr. James Williams, Gold Warden and Acting Police Magistrate of the Hodgkinson; Mrs. A. Williams, wife of J. Williams and mother of the bride.

—Photo from G. Dakin, Brisbane.

JOHN ATHERTON

The founder of Mareeba. He and his family settled at Emerald End on the Barron River in 1877. He died in 1913. This photo was taken about 1870.

(Loaned by Mrs. J. Atherton, Brisbane).

A Memorial to John Atherton, the founder of Mareeba, was unveiled on the bank of Granite Creek, in August 1957. Among those present were (L. to R.) Mr. E. Atherton, Glenville Pike (representing the Royal Geographical Soc. of Aus.) Mr. Ralph Leinster, Mrs. E. A. Atherton, Cr. C. Davies, (Chairman, Mareeba Shire Council).

ATHERTON FAMILY, EMERALD END, 1883

L. to R.: Ernest (first white child born at Mareeba), Mrs. Catherine (Kate) Atherton, Poll, Lucy, Esther and the Governess.

In Front: John Atherton, Kate and Jack. Eldest sons William and Edmund, absent

A Memorial to John Atherton, the founder of Mareeba, was unveiled on the bank of Granite Creek, in August 1957.

Memorial near Mareeba to J.V. Mulligan, unveiled May 1954. (L. to R.): The late D. A. O'Brien Sec. Royal Geo. Soc., Cr. Davies, G. Pike.

A genuine Cobb & Co. coach participated in an historical cavalcade through Mareeba on June 12, 1977, to mark the town's Centenary. Passengers in the coach were descendants of the founder of Mareeba, John Atherton, the pioneer.

—Tableland Advertiser, photo.

JOHN DOYLE 1842-1932
Explorer and bushman, discoverer of the Barron Falls, 1876.

CHRISTIE PALMERSTON
The celebrated explorer of the North Queensland rain forests.
A man of mystery, he is now almost a legendary figure.
(Photo from J. W. Collinson Collection)

(329)

Native Mounted Police troopers and horses paraded for the officer in charge, Sub-Insp. R. W. Garraway (far right). At Barron River Police Camp, 1888.

—Photo supplied by E. Stephens.

One of the few photos of Cobb & Co. on the Port Douglas Road. The coach has stopped to leave mail for the Barron River Police Camp one day in 1887, and Rod McCrae is the driver.

Rookwood Station near Chillagoe in the late 'Eighties. It was taken up by Thomas Stewart, a little remembered pioneer who was also an explorer with William Hann in 1872 and Bill Smith in 1876.

Heavy wheels and massive iron tyres that, derelict, have defied the years: Remains of a heavy horse-drawn dray used by the pioneer, John Doyle, lying in Arthur Best's garden in Mareeba.

—*Author*

Cobb and Co's coach leaving Port Douglas for Granite Creek and Herberton by way of the Bump Road, 1883.

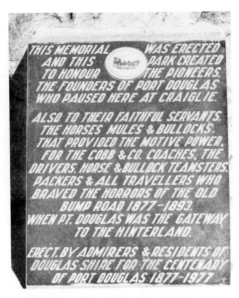

*The inscription on the Memorial to the
Teamsters and old time travellers on the
Port Douglas Road, at Craiglie.*
—Tableland Advertiser, photo.

*The road from Port Douglas to the Hodgkinson crossed the
Granite Range by Dora Gap. Some of the handiwork of the pioneer
roadbuilders of 1879 still remains in this stone-pitched embankment.*
—Author

The buckboard was the "unmechanised jeep" of the past and was in popular use in this Pioneers' Country for it could go almost anywhere. This is Jim Grant crossing the Upper Herbert River outside Mt. Garnet.

This was the address presented to James Robson at Redbank, near Cairns, January 1, 1884, in recognition of his feat in opening the pack track to Herberton a year or two earlier. It appears in "More About Cairns — the Second Decade", by the late J. W. Collinson, 1942.

Cairns pioneers of the time when James Robson blazed the pack track from Herberton, grouped at a re-union on New Years' Day, 1900. Standing: Aboriginals 1 and 2; Capt. Innes, W. P. Reddan, W. Pryn. Sitting, l. to r.: C. Leavis, E. Roberts, J. Robson (who blazed the track), T. Thomas, Con. O'Brien, I. Hartill, W. H. Collinson, Frank Brown, G. H. J. Wreide, A. Keeble, J. Miller.
(Photo from J. W. Collinson Collection)

Packhorses were the surest means of transport in the pioneering days, linking Cairns with its hinterland before the railway.
—Photo from G. Peters.

(336)

Split slab and shingle-roofed, this typical wayside hotel was a welcome stop for packers and travellers at Boar Pocket, on the packtrack over the range from Herberton to the Mulgrave and Cairns.

Pack teams such as this kept Herberton supplied with all necessities by means of Robson's pack track. The later Gillies Highway followed part of this route.

(337)

Scrubby Creek (Carrington) in the 'Eighties — a welcome stop for all travellers on the Port Douglas to Herberton Road.

Tom Purcell's Junction Hotel just south of Atherton where the so-called "Cairns Road" (the pack-track) turned off. The wagon teams would be going down to Port Douglas.
—Cairns Historical Society photo.

SORENSEN FAMILY

This photo was taken at the Big Mitchell in the 'Nineties. The Sorensens were well known settlers on the old Port Douglas Road.

Back row, l. to r.: Alick Sorensen, Christina, Gabriel jnr.

Front row, l. to r.: Dora (Doretta), Gabriel Sorensen snr. Mrs. Sorensen (nee Zigenbine), and Frederick.

—*Photo from D. Webb.*

About 200 horsemen and women rode from Thornborough to Cairns in 1976 to re-enact the opening of the first track with the hinterland, following the original route blazed by Bill Smith and Inspector Douglas in 1876.

— Markey Photo.

CAIRNS IN 1878 — TWO YEARS OLD

Abbott Street on right.

Some of its early citizens: Back row, left to right: Hartley, Warner, Scales, Spence, Pritchard, and Smart. In Front: Smith, Tomlins, and Stow.

The Main Street of Herberton in 1883.

Cobb & Co. coach, Robert Croft driving, about to leave Herberton for Port Douglas, about 1885. The coach carries a sign "To Geraldton" pointing backwards. This was no doubt placed there by supporters of those who wanted a railway built from Geraldton (Innisfail) to Herberton instead of from Cairns or Port Douglas.

*Bank officers celebrating Christmas, 1888, at Herberton.
L. to R. at back: Arthur Zillman, Jack Green, Paul Elwood, C. T.
Emslie, James Allison (Q.N. Bank manager, Montalbion, Watson-
ville, Mt. Garnet, Herberton, in turn), Fred Tricks. In front:
V. W. Boyle. T. C. Coomber.*

Tableland Aborigines just after contact with white settlers.

The Great Northern Mine, 1880.

Herberton in 1890.—Photo by A. Atkinson.

John Newell, one of the founders of Herberton.
—Oxley Library, photo.

Wondecla Sports Ground, where the Herberton Shows were held. Part of the annual Tin Festival is held here. It will be remembered by ex-soldiers as an Army camp in World War II.

—Author

WILLIAM (WILLIE) JACK
1834 – 1910. With John Newell, was one of the discoverers of tin at Herberton and helped establish the town in 1880. A pioneer storekeeper.

—*Oxley Library, photo.*

Finegan, the horse that won the Boldy-Finegan match race for £4000, also the Cadda-Finegan match for £500. Owners, Smith and Maines. Herberton, 1888.

—A. Atkinson, photo.

Show Committee, Herberton, 1910.

—Cairns His. Soc.

The Great Northern Battery at Herberton, on the Wild River, 1906.
—A. Atkinson

The Cenotaph near the Herberton post office looks out over the little mountain town.
—Author

Jack & Newell's general store, with the staff, at Herberton, about seventy years ago. It functioned for ninety-eight years. The building has been restored.

Cobb & Co's coach at Atherton, 1895.

Horse team hauling logs into Atherton, about 1903.
—Oxley Library, photo.

How a log was loaded on to a wagon by the "cross hand" method when no ramp was available. Team horses had to be staunch, reliable, and intelligent.

MONTALBION SCHOOL, 1898
(SEE CAPTION OPPOSITE)
— *M. O'Callaghan, photo.*

Brumbies now come to drink at Montalbion Dam which once supplied a thriving town.

—Author

Coolgarra in 1900.—Qld. Govt. Mining Journal.

MONTALBION STATE SCHOOL 1898.

Schoolmaster.   **W. T. Atthow. (D)**

Row No. 1.

Eileen O'Callaghan (D)., Ruby Mihr, (Mrs. F. S. Andrews). (D). Josephine Langtree (Mrs. Sam. Costigan), Norah Cummings (Mrs. Tom Murdoch) (D)., Monica O'Callaghan (Mrs. W. A. Collins) (D)., Lena Dowdell (Mrs. Arthur Rogers), (Lena was the youngest daughter of Jimmy Dowdell, a member of J. V. Mulligan's Party, who found the Palmer Goldfield in 1873) (?)., May Johnston, (?)., Isabella Johnston, (Mrs. Alex. Sparkes) (D)., Margaret Murphy (D).

Row No. 2.

Jack Barnes (D)., killed in 1914-1918 War, Ernest Still (D)., Patrick Murphy, (D)., Frank Gane (D)., Billy Still, (D)., Albion Murphy, (first white child born in Montalbion,) (D)., Patrick Cummings, (D)., James Barnes (D)., Jack Tait, (D)., Alf. Gane (D)., Dick Langtree, (D).

Row No. 3.

Jim Tait (D)., Frank Cummings (D), George Blackley, (D)., Jack McCarthy, (D) Jimmy Gane (D)., Bill Barry (D)., Norman Still, (D)., George Langtree, Mike O'Callaghan, Mick Cummings, (D), died from illness in England, whilst with the A. I. F. in 1914-1918 War), Arthur Mihr, (D).

Row No. 4.

Albert Pollard (?), Dan Barry, (D)., killed in action in France, 1914-1918 War, Jack Johnston, (?), Sarah Tait, (Mrs. Jack Molloy) (D)., Isabel Blackley (?), Jessie Blackley, (Mrs. W. Kilner), (?), Janet Blackley, (?)., Catherine O'Callaghan, Ivy Still, (?), Mary McCarthy, (D), Mary was Matron of the Townsville District Hospital for over 20 years, but died about 6 years ago), Jack Langtree, Bill Tait, (D), killed in 1914-1918 War.

    "D". denotes — Deceased.   **"?". denotes — Uncertain.**

Township of Montalbion, about 1889.

The author examining the present site of Montalbion; few traces remain.

(354)

The conquest of the mountain barrier. The Cairns Range railway under construction, around the Barron Gorge, 1889.

—Photo by A. Atkinson.

Herberton in 1909, before the railway. The railway cutting was made where arrowed. The two-storey building was the Cosmopolitan Hotel.

(356)

The cyclone of 1918 which devastated Innisfail was also a calamity for Herberton. This was the Cosmopolitan Hotel built by John Hogsflisch in 1880. The site is now occupied by Mr. Berry's house.

Shops in Grace Street, Herberton, hit by 1918 cyclone.

One of many wrecked homes in Herberton: McBride's house. (March 11, 1918)

The first Progress Association formed at Coolgarra, between
Herberton and Mt. Garnet, in 1884: Back row, l. to r.: D. McGregor,
A. Wilson, J. Reid, and P. Armagnacq. Sitting, l. to r.: J. Cross,
F. Muir, and S. J. Delaney.

Packhorse mailman ready to leave Herberton for Mt. Garnet,
probably about 1900.

—A. Atkinson, photo.

(358)

A family travelling by covered wagon, Mareeba District, probably in the nineties.

—Photo by courtesy Cairns Historical Society.

Paskins Family, Mareeba: W. Paskins (second from left) conducted Terminus Hotel at Granite Creek from 1898 to 1925. Built by Mick Fitzgerald who sold to Paskins, the Terminus was the second hotel to be built in Mareeba, apart from Freeman's on the north side of Granite Creek, which was burnt down. Left: Ann (Mrs. Hiram Jubb); Mr. Paskins; Dell; Mrs. Elizabeth Mary Paskins.

—Photo from Mareeba Shire Council.

(359)

1 2 3 4

5 6 7 8

SOME OF THE EARLY CITIZENS OF MAREEBA
1. L. Courtney, stationmaster (the first at Mareeba); 2. Rudolph Hampe, cordial manufacturer; 3. Charlie Arbouin, ore buyer; 4. Dr. Savage (who owned the first motor car in Mareeba in 1910, driven by an Aboriginal chauffeur, Sandy); 5. F. Cruickshank, auctioneer; 6. D. Earl, insurance agent etc.; 7. T. Hallam, ore buyer; 8. Geo. H. O'Donnell, printer.

—By Courtesy Mareeba Shire Council.

Boiler being transported by wagon for the new battery on Mareeba Goldfield, 1909. L. to R.: Howard Ward, Bill Ward, and Mr. Gordon.

—Mareeba Shire Council, photo.

The Queen Constance Mine Mareeba Goldfield.

(361)

Opening of crushing battery, Mareeba Goldfield, 1909.

Mareeba Town Band outside Exchange Hotel with Carriers' Arms
(on site of present Hotel Marsterson) on near left (about 1903).
          —Mareeba Shire Council, photo.

MAREEBA TOWN BAND, 1910.

First commemoration of Anzac Day in Mareeba, about 1919.

(363)

MAREEBA SHOW COMMITTEE, c.1909

*Back row, l. to r.: W. J. Smallwood, C. H. Strattmann, Andy
Dunlop, T. R. Kelley, R. Hampe, Geo. H. O'Donnell, G. Donald.
Second row, l. to r.: Douglas Earl, C. Cruickshank, John Atherton,
Robert Love, W. J. Bailey, Andy Whittacker. Front row, l. to r.:
J. A. Costin, John Ryan, George Robins.*

—Mareeba Shire Council, photo.

*The late J. J. Meehan, a well known horseman in his day,
competing at the Mareeba Show in July 1913, riding Abbott's
"Romeo" to win the Figure-of-Eight.*

(364)

Byrnes Street, Mareeba, about 1910, looking south. Royal Hotel, Federal Hotel, and Railway Hotel (now the Grahame) on left.

An advertisement in Pugh's Almanac for the year 1907. This hotel, a Mareeba landmark for sixty years, was destroyed by fire in 1952.

Officials of the Mareeba Turf Club in 1905. Back row, L. to R.: T. Ure, M. J. Geaney, W. J. Bailey, R. Hampe, G. Donald. Front row, L. to R.: J. McElhinney, T. R. Kelly, C. H. Strattmann, John Atherton (with walking stick), J. Carthew, W. J. Smallwood.
—Photo by courtesy John McElhinney.

Byrnes Street, Mareeba, in 1916, showing Jack & Newell's store (now Budget Supermarkets Pty. Ltd.) Q. N. Bank, and Dunlop's Hotel.
—Photo by courtesy R. Newell.

The historic Atherton homestead, Emerald End, in 1916. Built of pitsawn cedar, it was burned down in 1961.

(367)

Members and staff, Mareeba Shire Council, 1924. It was then the Woothakata Shire, and did not include the Irvinebank or Chillagoe areas. The name was changed to Mareeba Shire on December 20, 1947. It has an area of 20,430 square miles. Back row, l. to r.: Councillors Albert Veivers, William Gardner, Frank Crowley. Second row: R. Hampe, H. Geraghty, R. Clacherty, M. Mathieson, A. Tudehope. Front row: Gladys Rank, typiste; John Rank, Shire Clerk; and E. A. ("Paddy") Atherton, Chairman, later M.L.A. and Minister for Mines.

—*Mareeba Shire Council, photo.*

Veivers' bullock team crossing the Barron River near Kuranda with a massive kauri log. Horse team at rear, buggy in foreground.
—*A. Atkinson, photo.*

Alfred Street's coffee plantation, "Fernhill", near Kuranda, in the 'Nineties. Mountain Grove orange orchard is now on this site.

—A. Atkinson, photo.

Kuranda about seventy years ago, showing Remilton's Hotel (now Kuranda Hotel site) and before present railway station was built. Early-day tourists are being rowed across the Barron River to "The Maze", later called "Paradise", owned by Mr. Duggan.

(Photo from Mr. Starcke, Kuranda).

JOHN MOFFAT, 1883
Orig. by Elliott & Fry Baker St. London.
—Isobel Debenham.

John Moffat's house, Irvinebank, 1886.

—Isobel Debenham.

Irvinebank Dam, May 1884. John Moffat's camp, bottom right. Battery under construction, bottom left. Hill on right is behind present hotel.

—Isobel Debenham.

John Moffat's dam and battery, 1884. Broken in the 1893 flood, it was rebuilt with logs and concrete in its present form.

The Irvinebank Company's complex (guided by John Moffat) at Irvinebank at the height of its prosperity in 1907. Note the horses in use — the stables in the foreground.

(Cairns Historical Society Photo).

(373)

Irvinebank from the school, in 1907. The long tramway station building, middle left, had just been erected. The School of Arts (right) has recently been restored. The present huge fig-trees in front had just been planted. None of the shops remain.

—Cairns Historical Soc. photo.

The famous Vulcan Mine from the Tornado, 1907.

The Great Southern Mine at Irvinebank seventy years ago. Discovered in 1882, it is still producing tin.

Some leading men in Irvinebank about 1909. 1. W. Rogers;
2. Harry Wade, hotelkeeper. (Ten years earlier, he had a hotel on
the Chillagoe Road near the later site of Pe.ford). 3. T. M. Deluger,
store manager; 4. W. Donald; 5. H. J. Armstrong, merchant;
6. S. L. Ramage, hotelkeeper; 7. N. Barnett, jeweller. 8. James
Tunnie, assayer. — Mareeba Shire Council, photo.

A wagon and team near the tramway station, Irvinebank, about
1908. The team belonged to either George or Matt Ross (Matt
standing by shafts), Charlie Blyde, stationmaster, in white helmet.
—Photo, Cairns Hist. Society.

The glory that was Irvinebank: The smelters, crushing mill of forty stampers (right), the dam, and town (left) from Hospital Hill, in 1907. Photo by a photographer named Livesey.

When twelve horsepower meant a team like this of twelve gallant animals pulling their hearts out on some of the roughest tracks in Australia: near Montalbion early this century.

—Qld. Government Mining Journal.

One of the Irvinebank Mining Company's tram locos on the Stannary Hills-Irvinebank line, late in 1907.

"She's coming round the mountain" on the old Boonmoo to
Stannary Hills tramline up the Eureka Creek Gorge.

Bill Hudson, loco driver. Bob Bliss. Jack Donaldson. Jim Cifuentes. Maybe Harry Wiseman.

Arrival of Chillagoe train at Boonmoo, c.1910.

A busy day at Stannary Hills tramway station in 1907, with two Lilliputian-type trains at once.
—From "Copper Mines and Mineral Fields" by Wm. Lees.

Stannary Hills in 1907.

(380)

Stannary Hills, 1907. — A. Atkinson, photo.

The township of Watsonville seventy-five years ago.

(381)

PICNIC PARTY ON IRVINEBANK TRAMWAY c. 1909
*In carriage, from left: Unknown; Gus Waddell, John Moffat
(obscured).   Standing in front, from left: First two unknown,
number 3 is Willie Waddell; Mrs. W.E. Stovell; W. E. Stovell; Miss
Nora Stevens; Mrs. G. C. Young; Mr. Farquhar, mgr. NSW Bank;
Marion Young.*

—*Cairns Historical Society photo.*

*IRVINEBANK COMPANY'S MULE TEAM.
Carrying Ore, Reid's Creek District.*

OUTSIDE ASSAY OFFICE, IRVINEBANK, 1906

L. to R.: Lionel Lampard (d), worked in the Irvinebank Co. store, near Smelters. Alf Jones (d). Jeff Wasteneys, assayer, died from fever in West Africa. Jack H. Curtis (d), assayer. A. G. ("Buff") Oxley (d), nephew of Sir Samuel Griffiths, premier of Qld. and Chief Justice. Jim Tunnie, (d), chief assayer.

Two men sitting on steps: George Mihr, son of hotelkeeper, Montalbion. Harold C. Kingsbury, son of the then Crown Prosecutor of Qld.

Sitting in front: J. J. Hyde, a travelling tin buyer.

—*Cairns Hist. Soc.*

Rocky Bluffs Battery on the Walsh River, and the "gravitation tramway" down the 400ft. hillside. It was connected to Stannary Hills by a seven mile tramline.

(384)

North Australian Mine at Watsonville

Rainbow Tin Mine, Irvinebank, many years ago. It is still producing.

—Cairns Historical Soc. photo.

Dry-blowing for tin seventy years ago.

IRVINEBANK RIFLE CLUB, 1911

Back row,, l. to r.: W. H. Kernan (d). Bob Donald (d) George Peters (d). Richard Gipps (d). George Speed (d). F.G.D.V. Gipps, (d), manager Stannary Hills Company, 1905-06. Alf Linde, killed in France, 1914-18 War.

Second row, l. to r.: W. P. Collins (d). T. J. Moran (d) Irvine bank storekeeper. George Henderson (d). Alec Henderson (d). Jim Guilfoyle (d). G. F. Hewitt (d). W. T. Waddell, killed on Gallipoli, 1915. Oliver Woodward, in charge of blowing up Hill 60 in France in World War I. Became Gen. Mgr. Broken Hill Nth (d). Fred Wilkinson (d).

Third row, l. to r.: Jack Murrane, killed in W.W.I. Syd Ramage (d), built present hotel in Irvinebank, The Aus'ralia, 1904-05. H. J. Armstrong (d), won King's Prize in Townsville when 18 yrs. old, 1907. Jack Guilfoyle (d). George Kerr (d), bootmaker in Irvine bank, shop burned down, Dec. 1908. Bill Stewart (d) —Syd Ramage's partner, former carrier at Winton, came to Irvinebank in 1902. Charlie King (d). Jim Dawson, cap ain Irvinebank Football Team. Manager of the Vulcan in 'twenties. In charge of some work on Barron Falls Hydro Construction, 1932. Wounded in W.W.I. (d).

Front row, l. to r.: Joe Murrane (d). Percy Fitzmaurice (d). Mike O'Callaghan. Frank Rogers (d), a barber, had shop in the block burnt down in 1908.

(387)

PICNIC GROUP AT IRVINEBANK, c1911

(original photo by J. Vallance, from Cairns His. Society)
Standing, l. to r.: J. Farquhar, mgr. Q.N. Bank; Dr. McFarlane;
William Gunn; Willie Newell; C. Howitt; Godfrey Stevenson; Bishop
Feetham; William Stovell Mrs. Stovell (nee Effie Stevens); George
Robb; Mrs. Allan Waddell; Russel Pearce; Norah Stevens; Isabella
Waddell; D. McAuliffe (Bank N.S.W.); Miss Fairley.

Seated, l. to r.: Isabel Moffat; Bessie Moffat; Maidie Linedale;
Isabel Newell; Mrs. Godfrey Stevenson (nee Nellie Lamport, played
Hilda in ABC serial, Blue Hills, in 1950-60.) Elsie Stevens; Onie
Stevens, Jean Waddell; Willie Waddell; Gus Waddell.

In front, l. to r.: O. H. Woodward; Lucy Waddell; Rev. J. C.
Milliken (Presbyterian).

(388)

KOORBOORA RIFLE CLUB

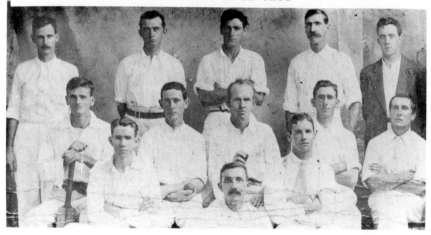

IRVINEBANK CRICKET TEAM, Easter 1920
*Standing: P. Murphy, V. G. Martin, W. Speirs, E. Arbouin,
F. Jones (scorer). Centre row: J. Speirs, W. Hoult, F. J. Robinson
(captain), Mike O'Callaghan, S. J. Bavinton. Three in front, l. to r.:
V. Henry, A. S. Lloyd, W. Robertson.*

(389)

The Great Southern Mine in its heyday.

Irvinebank Mill and Smelters, 1908.

Showing Carrier passing a Trestle.
Aerial Tramway, Governor Norman Mine, Irvinebank

John Holmes Reid, 1849-1929. He was John Moffat's successor up to the demise of the Irvinebank Company and its handover to the Queensland Government in 1919.

The Vulcan, deepest and richest tin mine in Australia.

Hundreds of visitors assembled in front of the old School of Arts, Irvinebank, for the unveiling of the memorial cairn and plaque to John Moffat, May 24, 1950.

—Author

The famous Chillagoe Smelters, 1909.
—Qld. Govt. Mining Journal, photo.

Chillagoe township in 1907, with the smelters in full blast.
—Photo from "Copper Mines & Mineral Fields" by Wm. Lees.

(393)

IN THE CHILLAGOE SMELTERS, ABOUT 1909

CHILLAGOE RAILWAY & MINES STAFF
Back row, l. to r.: A. George, J. Stark, W. Roggencamp, Arthur
Lloyd. Second row, l. to r.: —Campbell, F. Germaine, P. McDermott,
C. Wallace, J. Edgar. In front: W. Millar.

(394)

One of the old Chillagoe Company locomotives, once a familiar sight in Mareeba. This was a B15 type built by Walker's Maryborough, in 1899 and in use until 1967. The photo was taken at Mareeba in the early 1900's. — From Aust. Rly. Historical Society's Bulletin No. 473., being part of the G. E. Bond Collection.

Township of O.K. early this century. It lasted for about ten years while the mine and smelters were working.

—Cairns Historical Society photo.

Mungana, about 1905.

Traction engine hauling ore from O.K. to Mungana, a distance of over fifty miles.
—From "Copper Mines & Mineral Fields of Q." by Wm. Lees.

Zillmanton mine, the forerunner of Chillagoe as a copper producer.

CARDROSS SMELTERS.
1911
CHIEFTAIN MINE IN BACKGROUND.

Mammoth Company's Traction Engines at Mungana.

Camel pack team and Afghan drivers, taking copper ore from Mt. Garnet to Lappa, 1901.

Early days of Mt. Garnet: Camel Team—unloading coke and tools.

Mt. Garnet Smelters, 1902.

Charcoal Burning for the Smelters.

Some of staff of the Mt. Garnet Freehold Copper and Silver Mining Company, November 1902:

Front Row (left to right): Roland Ashcroft, A. M. Waddell, Stuart Robertson, (clerk). Middle Row, L. to R.: F. E. Connah (chief assayer); George Waddell (former general manager); John F. Way (assist. g.m. and accountant); J. W. Ashcroft (g.m. and metallurgist); Peter Brander (mine mgr.); —Davies (smelters); E. E. Morey (clerk). Back row, L. to R.: J. L. Purves (assayer); R. L. B. Walker (surveyor); —McLennan, (clerk); J. R. Raleigh (assayer); —Ross, (storeman).

The main street of Mt. Garnet, November, 1902.

NYMBOOL FOOTBALL TEAM, 1903
*Bill McCormack, later Premier of Qld. is moustached man in
front, with arms folded.*

—*Cairns Hist. Soc.*

Main street of Wolfram Camp about 1915.
—*Photo from Gordon Hay.*

A NICE WOLFRAM SHOW AT BAMFORD.

Koorboora Smelters, 1906.

(402)

Almaden in 1907. Torpy Hotel (left) and Peel's Royal Hotel (right).

Carriers' Arms Hotel in Almaden. This photo was taken in 1949
                                        —Author

Mining the old way: Bob Spurrier at the windlass of his Golden Drop gold mine, Pennyweight Creek, Mitchell River, fifty years ago.
—Photo from F. R. Spurrier.

Mt. Molloy township from the copper smelters, 1904.

MT. MOLLOY RACE COMMITTEE, 1928

Henry Gadd, Jack Pedracini, Jack Edwards, George Petersen, George Crowley, Jack Keedie, S. F. Harris, William Boyd, Darby McNamara, Chas Vains, Walter Tighe, Jack Woodhouse, and William Hanna.

—Photo from Mareeba Shire Council.

(404)

Logs brought into Molloy by Joe Leber, teamster, in August 1929, contained 4323 super feet of timber.

1928: MALANDA

Mt. Carbine battery, 1913, when owned and operated by the Irvinebank Mining Co. The administrative buildings of R. B. Mining, now working the wolfram lode, are on this site.

(405)

MT. CARBINE, 1911
WASHING ALLUVIAL WOLFRAM IN MANGANESE CREEK
BATTERY IN BACKGROUND.

A fine old pioneer — Eric Baker (1889-
1979), nephew of John Fraser, at official open-
ing of the new Mt. Carbine mine, May 1978.
—Author.

(406)

A early day wedding in Mt. Carbine. L. to R.: Neil Campbell, Mrs. Bolton, Molly Campbell (known as the "Belle of Mt. Carbine"), Billy West (groom), Isabell Campbell (bride), Alma Bolton, Joe West, Mrs. Campbell, Mr. Campbell. The groom's brother, Fred, was mine manager for the Irvinebank Company, and the bride's father was shift boss.

(Photo by courtesy Lola O'Brien).

MT. CARBINE STATE SCHOOL, 1915
(See Caption on opposite page)

The Head Teacher is Mr. J. Pedrazzini (left, back row). Miss Flo Montgomery, Assistant Teacher, on right. The pupils shown here in 1915 were as follows:

L. to R., Back Row: Mary Kieran, Jim Rolls, Ethel Rolls, Roy Hillman, Anne Monaghan, Tom Dunne, Jim Edwards, Eileen Grogan, Florrie Keddie.

Second Row: Willie Percy, Rene Baird, Cyril Baird, Frank Dunne, Vance Hillman, Percy White, Ethel Sadlier, Jack Keddie, Martha Fry, Lola Pickering, Alice Dunne, Gertie Monaghan.

Third Row: Martha Edwards, Bill Cassels, Mary Monaghan, Chas. Fry, Jessie Fry, Norman Wilkinson, Eunice Hillman, Bert Cassels, Ruby Sadlier, Maud Keddie.

Fourth Row: Jimmy Moss, Toosie Asmus, Jack Edwards, Elsie Assmus, Norm Cassels, Nellie Sadlier, Peter White, Ellie Crowley, Harry Rolls, Dally Harris, Arthur Hallam, Edna Burton, Toni Pickering.

Fifth Row, in front: Jim Keddie, Norm Harris, Irene Madrid, Herb Hallam, Vi Bourke, Jack Bourke, Isobel Rolls, Lily Tilse, Bill Madrid, Arthur Hallam, Audrey Hallam, — Dunne, Charlie Morton.
(Photo by courtesy Lola O'Brien).

Mt. Mulligan township and its coal mine nestling at the foot of the mountain. This photo was taken in 1948, ten years before the town ceased to exist. It had a life of fifty years.

—Author

Horse teams at the surface workings at Mt. Mulligan coal mine in August, 1913.

Harris Street, Mt. Mulligan, in 1921.

This photo shows the mighty buttress at the foot of Mt. Mulligan, and the King Cole Mine which closed in 1957 because of movement in the escarpement.

—Photo by Mary Wardle by courtesy Peter Bell.

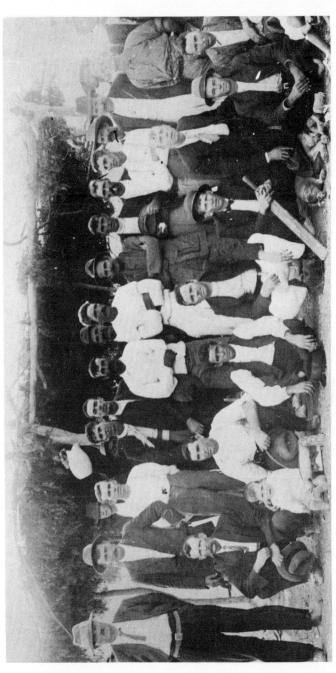

MT. MULLIGAN CRICKET CLUB, 1920

Back row, l to r.: Owen Jolly, unknown, unknown, Ron Grainer, Tom Clarke(?), unknown, unknown, Aubrey Plunkett, Jim Harris, unknown, unknown, Frank Grainer, Mark Harris, Jack Harris, Arthur Griffith. Front row, l. to r.: Tom Evans, underground manager, State Coal Mine, child unknown, unknown, Archie Tudehope, Frank Richards, Bill Stephenson, Henry Harrison. Other two unknown.

—Photo by Doris Smith, by courtesy Peter Bell.

MT. MULLIGAN SCHOOL, 1930.

—J. McColm, photo.

(414)

Older pupils, Mt. Mulligan school, 21 August 1921. Most of them lost their fathers in the mine explosion a month later when 75 men were killed. Far back row, l. to r.: Jim McColm, Sam Casloff, Charlie Archer, John Canoplia, Ken Hourston, Ray Drier. Second row, l. to r.: Neil Smith, Fred Royal, Chris Barry, Joan Hourston, Beatrice Crowley, Mavis Smithson, unknown, Lil Harris, Nellie Hourston (in hat). Third row: Nellie Harris, Tina Casloff, Nura Canoplia, Ida McCormack, Sybil Crowley, unknown, Marg. McColm. In fron, sitting: —Murray, Herbert Smithson, —Leary, Alf Murray, —Barry, Roy Drier.

—Photo by Jim McColm, courtesy Peter Bell.

Traction engines were used to haul logs and sawn timber from the "Atherton Scrub" to Mareeba railhead in 1896-1903. This photo was, however, taken at Ravenshoe in 1917.
—*Photo by courtesy Herberton Shire Council.*

The Etheridge Railway damaged in the big flood in the Einasleigh River early in 1927. This photo was taken eight months later, no repairs having been made by then.

1929
Ravenshoe, the centre of a rich dairying and timber getting district

1. *Pupils at the Ravenshoe School.*
2. *The Main Street.*
3. *Timber Hauling Team at the Ramp.*

(417)

Atherton from the air, 1928.

Cedar Log, Atherton Tableland.

(418)

Man against nature. The task that faced the early settlers on the Tablelands of clearing the jungle, with giant trees like this, was a superhuman one with the means then available. No chainsaws or bulldozers then. This photo was taken in 1908 in the Malanda area.
—A. Atkinson.

1926 — TOWNSHIP OF TUMOULIN, N.Q.

Tableland Tin Company's dredge at Mt. Garnet, at work today.
—State Public Relations photo.

(420)

When mechanised transport began to oust the bullock teams. A Leyland "steam wagon" with a fine kauri log, hauling from Bridle Creek to Mareeba for Lawson & Son's mill in 1925.

Before machines: Planting out tobacco by hand, Mareeba District, twenty-five years ago.

A tobacco crop in the early 'thirties on J. J. Meehan's farm, Atherton Road, showing sharefarmer, H. Mittlehauser, Mr. Meehan (who was then President of the Nth. Qld. Tobacco Growers' Association), and his son, Joe.

The key to the Mareeba-Dimbulah Irrigation Scheme. Tinaroo Dam on the Barron River near Kairi, and magnificent Lake Tinaroo.

—Qld. Govt. Tourist Bureau, photo.

Tinaroo water gravitates through approximately 200 miles of concrete channels and pipes to irrigate the dry lands around Mareeba and Dimbulah, a thousand feet below Tinaroo Dam.
—State Public Relations photo.

*Today, water means wealth. A tobacco crop being irrigated
in the Mareeba district.*

—State Public Relations photo.

Byrnes Street, Mareeba, early in 1940. Looking South.—Author

*Byrnes Street, Mareeba, looking south. The weeping figtrees
in the centre had been severely pruned.*

Cairns Centenary Comtee photo.

The whole length of Main Street, Atherton, is a beautiful display of flowers and palms. Something like 5000 trees were planted in Atherton in 1975 by the Shire Council and private citizens. . The town has won a "Tidy Towns" competition three years in succession.

—Qld. Govt. Tourist Bureau, photo.